Ramsay MacDonald (1977)

Parliament for Europe (1979)

European Elections and British Politics (with David Butler, 1981)

John P. Mackintosh on Parliament and Social Democracy (ed., 1982)

The Unprincipled Society: New Demands and Old Politics (1988)

The Progressive Dilemma: From Lloyd George to Kinnock (1991)

*Towards Greater Europe? A Continent without an
Iron Curtain* (ed. with Colin Crouch, 1992)

*Ethics and Markets: Co-operation and Competition within
Capitalist Economies* (ed. with Colin Crouch, 1993)

The Ideas That Shaped Post-War Britain
(ed. with Anthony Seldon, 1996)

The New Reckoning: Capitalism, States and Citizens (1997)

Religion and Democracy (ed. with Ronald L. Nettler, 2000)

Decline of the Public: The Hollowing-out of Citizenship (2004)

Britain Since 1918: The Strange Career of British Democracy (2008)

The End of the West: The Once and Future Europe (2011)

DAVID MARQUAND

Mammon's Kingdom

An Essay on Britain, Now

ALLEN LANE
an imprint of
PENGUIN BOOKS

ALLEN LANE

Published by the Penguin Group
Penguin Books Ltd, 80 Strand, London WC2R ORL, England
Penguin Group (USA) Inc., 375 Hudson Street, New York, New York 10014, USA
Penguin Group (Canada), 90 Eglinton Avenue East, Suite 700, Toronto, Ontario, Canada M4P 2Y3
(a division of Pearson Penguin Canada Inc.)
Penguin Ireland, 25 St Stephen's Green, Dublin 2, Ireland (a division of Penguin Books Ltd)
Penguin Group (Australia), 707 Collins Street, Melbourne, Victoria 3008, Australia
(a division of Pearson Australia Group Pty Ltd)
Penguin Books India Pvt Ltd, 11 Community Centre, Panchsheel Park, New Delhi – 110 017, India
Penguin Group (NZ), 67 Apollo Drive, Rosedale, Auckland 0632, New Zealand
(a division of Pearson New Zealand Ltd)
Penguin Books (South Africa) (Pty) Ltd, Block D, Rosebank Office Park,
181 Jan Smuts Avenue, Parktown North, Gauteng 2193, South Africa

Penguin Books Ltd, Registered Offices: 80 Strand, London WC2R ORL, England

www.penguin.com

First published 2014
001

Copyright © David Marquand, 2014

The moral right of the author has been asserted

Set in 10.5/14pt Sabon LT Std
Typeset by Jouve (UK), Milton Keynes
Printed in Great Britain by Clays Ltd, St Ives plc

A CIP catalogue record for this book is available from the British Library

ISBN: 978-1-846-14672-5

www.greenpenguin.co.uk

To the memory of
my great-grandfather, Ebenezer Rees (1848–1908),
and my father, Hilary Marquand (1901–1972).

Contenders for justice in an unequal society.

Choose equality and flee greed.

Menander, quoted by
Matthew Arnold in *Equality*

Contents

1 Introduction   1

2 Hedonism Trumps Honour   19

3 Amnesia Conquers History   59

4 The Market State Invades the Public Realm   91

5 From Fate to Choice – and Back Again   124

6 Charismatic Populism Smothers
  Democratic Debate   152

7 Who Do We Think We Are?   182

  Acknowledgements   221

  Notes   225

  Index   243

I
Introduction

We have profoundly forgotten everywhere that Cash-payment is not the sole relation of human beings; we think nothing of doubting, that it absolves and liquidates all engagements of man. 'My starving workers?' answers the rich Mill-owner. 'Did I not hire them fairly in the market? Did I not pay them, to the last sixpence, the sum covenanted for? What have I to do with them more?' – Verily Mammon worship is a melancholy creed.
Thomas Carlyle, *Past and Present*, 1843

There is a dark fascination about money and its power to exalt and destroy. The Greek myth of King Midas, the biblical account of the Israelites worshipping the golden calf and tales of the inexhaustible wealth of King Croesus have haunted Western imaginations for millennia. It is not for nothing that *L'Avare* is one of Molière's most famous plays or that Shylock is one of Shakespeare's most haunting characters. Melmotte, the grotesque and sinister anti-hero of Trollope's biting novel about financial skulduggery, *The Way We Live Now*, comes alive far more vividly than do most of his creator's country clergymen and Westminster politicians. The pettifogging meanness of Dickens's Scrooge at the start of *A Christmas Carol* grips the reader far more than his redemption at the end. There is surely something in Freud's notion that adult fascination with money stemmed from childhood fascination with excreta. When Peter Mandelson declared that New Labour was relaxed about people 'getting filthy rich' he struck a familiar chord. 'Filthy lucre' has been a common term since the sixteenth century, and the thought behind it is much older. Rebutting the charge that his tax on urine was disgusting, the Roman Emperor Vespasian replied briskly, 'Pecunia non olet' ('Money doesn't stink').

Vespasian's gruff common sense captured an obvious truth, but missed a larger reality. In itself, money is morally neutral; it doesn't stink, even metaphorically. Money worship is another matter. It has always been malodorous; all too often, it has been destructive as well. To mention only a few random examples, its fruits have included the brutal Atlantic slave trade of early-modern times; the genocide perpetrated in the Belgian Congo in the late nineteenth century; and the underground labour of small children in the coal mines of Industrial Revolution Britain. More recently it powered the American stock market boom of the 1920s that culminated in the crash of 1929 and paved the way for the Great Depression. Today, it is responsible for the endemic corruption that disfigures almost all the successor states of the old Soviet Union, as well as large swathes of Africa, Asia and Latin America. Among other things, it also drives environmentally destructive deforestation in the Amazon rain forest, the over-fishing of krill that threatens to destroy the complex eco-systems around Antarctica and the murky practices that led to the horse-meat scandal across the EU in early 2013.

In recent years, no large Western democracy has been more devoted to money worship than Britain. It helped to spawn the heady boom of the early noughties; it drove the growth of inequality that has been a prime feature of British society for nearly thirty years; and it has survived the bust that began with the run on Northern Rock in 2007. Yet, in all the anguished debates that have followed, the deeper issues involved have rarely been discussed. We have heard a great deal about the follies of the bankers, the failures of the regulators and the blindness of the politicians, but almost nothing about the culture of egoistic hedonism and unreflective utilitarianism by which bankers, regulators and politicians had been formed. The crisis of 2007–8 has been seen as a crisis of the economy, or in some cases of the political economy.[1] But hardly anyone has pointed out that it was also a crisis of the *moral* economy: of the complex nexus of values, teachings, implicit assumptions and tacit understandings that tells economic agents how they ought to behave. The underlying moral and psychological forces that fostered Mammon worship have not been confronted, much less overcome.

2

In this book I try to redress the balance. An overarching theme is the strange story of the 'moral economy' and its current crisis. The term was coined by E. P. Thompson, the path-breaking historian of the 'making' of the English working class in the late eighteenth and early nineteenth centuries.[2] His usage was intellectually compelling, but curiously restrictive. The repeated bread riots of this period, he argued, reflected a venerable 'moral economy' which held that it was immoral to force up prices 'by profiteering upon the necessities of the people', and insisted that prices '*ought*, in times of dearth, to be regulated'.[3] For Thompson the 'moral economy' was, by definition, the ideological property of the crowd; the notion that the farmers and millers whom the crowd targeted might have appealed to a different moral economy seemed to him absurd.

I range more widely. I shall suggest that it is perfectly possible for different (and rival) moral economies to co-exist in the same society at the same time; that such a rivalrous co-existence was one of the hallmarks of the society that Thompson described; and that a struggle between different moral economies has been a leitmotiv of British history for more than two centuries. I believe that Britain has seen at least four moral economies in the last 200 years: that of Thompson's crowd; a laissez-faire rival that gradually displaced the first; a solidaristic, partly social-democratic and partly 'Middle Way' conservative[4] alternative that followed the second; and in our time another laissez-faire variety, which George Soros and Joseph Stiglitz have both termed 'market fundamentalist'.[5] Just as the moral economy that Thompson described legitimized the bread riots of the late eighteenth century, the market fundamentalist moral economy of our day legitimized the speculative fever that led to the crash of 2007–8. That is why it is now in crisis.

MAMMON IN BRITAIN

That story is part of a larger one: the curious history of Mammon worship in my own country, Britain. I focus on the changing moral and ideological contexts within which it has waned and waxed, and examine its impact on the public culture and the public realm. Some may think this a parochial focus, but I make no apology for it. This is where I was born, where I live and where I shall some day die. There are many black pages in our history, but we also have a lot to be proud of. I shall argue that many of the things in which we can legitimately take pride are now in danger.

George Orwell once wrote that 'England', by which he meant Britain, was 'a family with the wrong members in control'.[6] That was an apt description in 1941 when he coined it. Despite the unprecedented range of social, economic and demographic changes which have made Britain a multi-ethnic and multi-cultural society, it is still reasonably apt today. Like most families, we have had lots of ups and downs in our long history. The 'Glorious Revolution' of 1688–9 – which the American historian Steve Pincus aptly calls the 'first modern revolution'[7] – initiated a remarkable 'up' that included the peaceful union of the Scottish and English parliaments, the philosophy of David Hume, the economics and moral philosophy of Adam Smith, the history of Edward Gibbon and (despite the brutality of the criminal code) the establishment of equality before the law. The early nineteenth century saw a 'down', when Parliament passed a series of repressive statutes, some designed to crush the British supporters of the French Revolution, and some to force the straitjacket of a peculiarly rigid version of laissez-faire economic theory onto an old society formed in a quite different mould; Carlyle's scorn for Mammon worship came towards the end of that period. The Second World War and its immediate aftermath saw another 'up', culminating in the managed economy and welfare state instantiated under the Attlee Government. Now we are in the midst of a prolonged and bitter 'down'. We have no hope of escaping from it unless we understand how and why we got into it; and to do so we must first probe the psychology of money worship through the ages. That is easier said than done. There is a mystery about money as well as a fascination. It is fungible, protean, evanescent and indefinable, as hard to pin down as mercury sliding along a polished surface. To mention only a few examples, cowrie shells, whales' teeth, cigarettes and nylon stockings have all done duty as currency at one time or another.

Today, unimaginable quantities of money can speed invisibly across the globe in the form of electronic pulses. The Conservative Government of the 1980s found that there were so many definitions of money that control of the money supply – its flagship policy – was unfeasible. The journalist and author James Buchan has called money 'frozen desire'; the moral philosopher Michael Walzer termed it 'the universal pander'; for Dostoevsky it was 'coined liberty'; for Karl Marx currencies were 'cabbalistic signs'.

Perhaps because of its mystery, fascination with money extends to the doings and sayings of its possessors. Around a hundred years ago, the angular, maverick American economist Thorstein Veblen offered one of the most subversive theories in the history of economic thought to explain why. He called it the 'theory of the leisure class'. With joyous irony he subverted one of the most frequent tropes of free-market rhetoric: the myth of the abstinent rich, gaining their wealth through self-denial and hard work, and using it as the seed corn of future economic progress. The rich, Veblen held, were not in the least abstinent; their social status and the power they derived from it did not allow them to be. In modern societies 'good repute' depended on 'pecuniary strength'; and 'pecuniary strength' could be demonstrated only by 'leisure and a conspicuous consumption of goods'.[8] Economic behaviour was not rational, as conventional economic theory assumed, and still assumes. It was governed by bizarre rituals of emulation reminiscent (though Veblen did not put it like this) of the mating displays of peacocks. Veblen was probably thinking of the vulgarity and extravagance of the new rich in America's Gilded Age, but there is no better guide to the celebrity culture of contemporary Britain. Like their American predecessors a century ago, today's 'celebs' are Mammon's most glittering acolytes and Mammon worship's most successful missionaries. We can't all be David Beckham or Kate Moss, but we can – and mostly do – try to consume at least as conspicuously as our peers.

With fascination and mystery goes lust. Economic history is studded with bubbles and bursts, scams and scamps, fraudsters and defrauded. During the tulip bubble in the seventeenth-century Netherlands the price of a single bulb soared to more than the annual income of a skilled craftsman before collapsing. In the South Sea Bubble in eighteenth-century England, the price of South Sea Company stock rose tenfold in a single year before crashing back to its original level; after the crash, revelations of fraud among the directors provoked calls for them to be tied up in sacks and dumped in the Thames. Unlike the tulip and South Sea bubbles, the wild railway boom of the 1840s left a tangible legacy in the shape of (often bizarrely located) railway lines, but there was more than a touch of the South Sea Bubble about it; the inevitable bust came when the accounts of the notorious 'Railway King', George Hudson, turned out to be fraudulent.

A more engaging conman was 'Baron Grant', originally Abraham Gottheimer, born in Dublin in 1831, the son of a Jewish pedlar. He changed his name to Grant by deed poll, was ennobled by the King of Italy, entered Parliament as Liberal MP for Kidderminster, published his own newspaper, promoted railway and mining companies all over Europe, and gifted what is now Leicester Square to the Metropolitan Board of Works, before being unseated for bribery. He survived his ejection, but nemesis came when a Utah silver mining company he had promoted turned out to have no silver in its mines. He died in poverty and obscurity in 1899. Thirty years later, the company promoter Clarence Hatry was sentenced to penal servitude for fraud after his financial empire collapsed. In our own day, the egregious Robert Maxwell ('the bouncing Czech') was a cross between Grant and Hudson. He too bluffed his way into Parliament in his great days, but ended his career by plundering the pension funds of his companies to stave off bankruptcy and died at sea in mysterious circumstances.

If Mammon worship has a long history, so have anathemas against it. When Moses returned from his sojourn with God on Mount Sinai and discovered the golden calf, he ground it into a powder, mixed it with water and forced the Israelites to drink it. In one of the most resonant passages in the Christian New Testament, the evangelist Matthew has Christ proclaiming the immortal message, 'No man can serve two masters ... Ye cannot serve God and mammon'. Aristotle condemned usury as unnatural. Christian theologians in medieval times saw avarice as one of the seven deadly sins and forbade usury. The Islamic tradition still prohibits *riba* – lending money at interest and acquiring it in unjust ways. Dante consigned the avaricious to the fourth circle of hell (he was particularly hard on avaricious church-men) and usurers to the seventh. Echoing Aristotle, Martin Luther held that usurers were acting against nature, and therefore guilty of a mortal sin. In John Bunyan's *Pilgrim's Progress*, 'the treasures and riches of the world' displayed in Vanity Fair bring perdition. In Milton's *Paradise Lost*, Mammon is the 'least erected spirit' to follow Lucifer to hell, and also the most squalid. Even in heaven:

> his looks and thoughts
> Were always downward bent, admiring more
> The riches of heaven's pavement, trodden gold,
> Than aught divine or holy else enjoyed
> In vision beatific: by him first
> Men also, and by his suggestion taught,
> Ransacked the centre, and with impious hands
> Rifled the bowels of their mother earth.

We should not exaggerate the impact of such anathemas. If Mammon had had no worshippers no one would have bothered to condemn them. There has never been a greedless society, and it is hard to believe that there ever will be. As visitors to the old Soviet Union soon discovered, greed and corruption were as common under Communism as under capitalism; the kleptocratic oligarchs who pillaged the Russian state and people after Communism fell were Brezhnev's children, even if not Stalin's. But there are degrees of greed; and its acceptability varies over space and time. In some cultures – and some periods of history – it is contained. But the dikes holding it back are easily breached, and in other cultures and times it carries all before it. Trollope's Melmotte was not a solitary rotten apple. He was a monetary Colossus whose operations extended far beyond the frontiers of his adopted country, and who bent his multifarious hangers-on to his will. The fraudulent financier 'Mr Merdle' in Dickens's *Little Dorrit* had a similar retinue of upper-class sycophants; when he could no longer conceal his frauds and committed suicide, ruin spread far and wide through fashionable London. There have been plenty of Melmottes and Merdles in twenty-first-century Britain – and plenty of hangers-on and sycophants as well.

FRED THE SHRED

The rise and fall of the Royal Bank of Scotland is a textbook case in point. The story is all too familiar now, but it throws a harsh beam of light onto Britain's current predicament, and therefore deserves a close look. RBS received a royal charter in 1727, and for more than 250 years it was a 'modest and careful' regional bank.[9] At the end of the last century, however, it suffered a collective rush of blood to the head. In 1999 its rough, tough CEO, George Mathewson, opened a bidding war against the Bank of Scotland for NatWest, then three times RBS's size. In 2000, he won. RBS acquired NatWest for £20bn, becoming the second-largest bank in the United Kingdom. Shortly afterwards, Mathewson stepped down as CEO, to be succeeded by his deputy, 'Fred the Shred' Goodwin.[10] In Goodwin, the RBS board found a financial Rottweiler. He was ruthless, driven, domineering, ferociously ambitious and increasingly prone to megalomania. The scene was set for a saga of greed, self-deception, braggadocio and hubris worthy of Shakespeare.

At first, Goodwin was astonishingly successful. In his first four years as CEO, RBS gobbled up more than twenty businesses, ranging from the Churchill Insurance Group to the Irish bank First Active. Under Goodwin, RBS earnings per share soared from a little more than 50 pence in 2000 to well over 200 pence in 2007. Its assets grew by an average of more than 40 per cent a year. Its share price rose from £2.70 when Goodwin became CEO in 2000 to £5.78 in April 2007. Before it acquired NatWest RBS had not even figured on the list of the world's top twenty banks by market capitalization; in 2007 it ranked ninth. By the summer of 2008 its assets totalled more than Britain's GDP.[11]

Yet, by then, nemesis was haunting its lavish new headquarters on the outskirts of Edinburgh. One reason was that, in a rash gamble in April 2007, RBS had put together a transnational consortium to carry out a hostile takeover of the giant Dutch bank, ABN AMRO. The consortium procured the biggest cross-jurisdictional acquisition in history, but though the bid succeeded, the gamble failed. ABN AMRO was loaded with toxic assets that the consortium's lackadaisical due diligence had failed to uncover; RBS made its decision on the basis of 'two lever arch folders and a CD'.[12] When the global financial crisis brought their toxicity into the open, these assets helped to bring RBS down. However, the ABN AMRO deal was merely the most egregious symptom of a managerial culture of aggressive expansion and reckless acquisition that had fostered risky lending, low capitalization and swollen leverage (the ratio of borrowing to capital) throughout Goodwin's reign. During the boom that culture had propelled RBS into the stratosphere of global finance; during the bust its consequences were disastrous.

Like wolves savaging a wounded bear, market sentiment turned against RBS with devastating force. On 7 October 2008, the Chancellor of the Exchequer, Alistair Darling, had to slip out of a meeting of European finance minsters in Luxembourg to take an urgent call. He was told that the price of shares in the monster Royal Bank of Scotland had collapsed. A few minutes later he had a second call: dealing in RBS shares had been suspended. It was the biggest bank failure in British history. To stave off liquidation, the Government pumped £20bn of public money into RBS, effectively nationalizing it. Eventually, that was followed by a further £25.5bn. In addition to the direct cost to British taxpayers the ripple effects of the failure imposed incalculable indirect costs on the rest of the financial sector and in doing so helped to deepen the worst depression since the 1930s. What Mammon had given, Mammon took away.

RBS was not the sole author of the saga. Three years after the denouement the Financial Services Authority, the body charged with bank regulation at the material time, published a long and detailed report on the affair. (My account here is largely based on it.) As well as recounting the follies of Goodwin and the RBS board, and anatomizing the culture that spawned them, the FSA report contained a damning account of the Authority's own regulatory failures and an equally damning – if only partial – picture of the ideological and political environment in which it operated. *Mea culpa* after *mea culpa* stud its pages. It confessed to 'inadequate supervision', to neglecting 'core prudential issues' and to underestimating the complexity and vulnerability of the banking system as a whole.

Peeping between the lines of these confessions were guarded hints of a more disturbing theme: continual pressure from the Government to blunt the edge of financial regulation in the interests of the international competitiveness of British financial services. Thus, the then Chairman of the FSA found it necessary to write to Tony Blair in June 2005, to assure him that the FSA's regulation of the largest British banks was far less strict than that 'applied by US regulators to banks of equivalent size'. For the Treasury Economic Secretary, Ed Balls, in 2007, the FSA was a world leader whose laid-back regulatory philosophy could 'only be good for the competitiveness of the UK financial sector'. For the Chancellor, Gordon Brown, in May 2005 Britain offered the financial sector 'no inspection without justification, no form filling without justification and no information requirements without justification. Not just a light touch but a limited touch.'[13] Buttressing, and even egging on, the Mammon worshippers in hedge funds, pension funds, insurance companies, investment banks and private equity partnerships was a mighty congregation of Mammon worshippers in Downing Street, Whitehall and Westminster.

FINANCE AND THE STATE

To understand why, we need to dig deeper than the authors of the FSA report had time to do. Britain's financial sector has been a world leader since the eighteenth century, in part because of its close links with the state. Thanks to the creation of the Bank of England in 1694 and the contemporaneous invention of the National Debt, first the English and then the British state could mobilize credit on a scale none of its Continental rivals could emulate. That helped to make it one of the two most successful imperial predators in Europe, not least by financing allies on the European mainland. (The other successful predator was Russia, but Russian predation was enabled by land and population, not by finance.) A further result was a marriage of convenience – and eventually of affection – between the political elite that managed the state and the City magnates who headed the financial sector. A subtle symbiosis between state power and financial power made London the lynch-pin of the first truly global market in history as well as the capital of the greatest empire the world had ever seen. For Sir John Graham, First Lord of the Admiralty during the Crimean War, Britain was the world's 'great emporium'; for Lord Rosebery, Liberal Prime Minister from 1894 to 1895, she was 'the strong box and the safe of Europe'. The end result was a political economy in which her dynamic and competitive London-based financial services had more political clout than any other economic sector, including financial services in the provinces.[14]

The fundamental logic of that political economy – a logic of state-supported financial-sector primacy – survived long after the circumstances which had given birth to it disappeared. One classic example came in 1925. Winston Churchill, then Chancellor of the Exchequer, came under heavy pressure from the Bank of England, the official Treasury and the financial-services sector to return to the gold standard at the pre-war parity. He put up a stubborn resistance to these pressures, famously writing that he wanted to see 'Finance less proud and Industry more content',[15] but lost the battle. Britain duly returned to the gold standard and stayed on it, to the great detriment of the real economy, until she was forced off in 1931. A similar example was the Wilson Government's refusal to devalue the pound in 1966, though this time the inevitable forced devaluation came only a year later.

Against this background the contorted story of RBS recklessness and FSA passivity falls into place. The Thatcher Government's 'Big Bang' of 1986, effectively deregulating the City, and the Blair–Brown regime's fierce solicitude for it, were yet more examples of the same logic. Deregulation opened the City up to unprecedented influxes of foreign capital and fostered further financial-services growth. New Labour followed suit, not just with the 'limited touch' regulation hymned by Gordon Brown, but with negligible taxes: in 2006 fifty-four UK-based billionaires, with a combined fortune of £126bn, paid a total of only £14.7m in income tax.[16]

Tenderness to the rich and obsequiousness to the City spawned a ballooning and rootless financial sector, detached from nation and place. Following the Big Bang, American investment banks such as Goldman Sachs, Morgan Stanley and Merrill Lynch, the Japanese bank Nomura and German banks such as Dresdner Bank and Deutsche

Bank became major players in London; as Philip Augar puts it, the 'power breakfast and the sandwich at the desk replaced the port and cigars'.[17] Except geographically, the City was no longer British; like Heathrow airport, it was a global hub. But its role as a financial centre was enhanced. In no other large economy were financial services more exposed to the global crisis of 2007–9. By 2008 they accounted for approximately 9 per cent of Britain's GDP;[18] the British trade surplus in financial services was the largest in the world.[19] The London Metal Market was the world's chief market for non-ferrous metals; the daily turnover in London's derivatives market* totalled $2.105tn, more than twice the American figure.[20] On the eve of its collapse, RBS ran a trading desk of more than £500bn of derivatives, approximately one third of the nation's GDP.

Wild exuberance went hand in hand with growing vulnerability. Northern Rock, a former provincial building society which had become a commercial bank in 1997, followed a trajectory reminiscent of RBS's. In its days as a building society, owned by its depositors, it had lent out mortgages backed by deposits. As a bank it adopted a wildly imprudent lending strategy, with some mortgages six times the mortgagee's annual income; its boss, Adam Applegarth – a mini-Fred Goodwin – joined the ranks of the super-rich while its share price soared. Appropriately, its collapse in 2007 was the first British intim-

---

* A derivative is a financial instrument whose value is derived from other assets, such as stocks, bonds, currency exchange rates, gold and real estate or from other financial instruments. There are three basic classes of derivative: futures (agreements to buy an asset at a set future date at a fixed price); options (the right but not the obligation to buy or sell an asset in the future at an agreed price); and swaps (agreements to exchange foreign currencies or interest payments at agreed prices). These basic forms have been used to trade commodities for centuries, and financial assets for decades, but in the last quarter of the twentieth century derivative trading became much more complex and much more risky. So-called 'over-the-counter' (OTC) derivatives, privately negotiated between buyers and sellers, became increasingly common; by the early twenty-first century they accounted for 85 per cent of derivative trading. Many of these OTC derivatives blended different assets into interconnected and interdependent securities, and were characterized as complex or 'exotic'. OTC derivatives were effectively unregulated and a magnet for speculators. See Philip Augar, *The Greed Merchants: How the Investment Banks Played the Free Market Game*, Penguin Books, London, 2006, pp. 77–9; and *The Financial Times Lexicon*, http://lexicon.ft.com/Term?term=derivatives.

ation of the crisis to come. At the height of the boom, British bank loans totalled more than five times national output, while the British financial sector was one of the most highly leveraged in the world, more so than its American counterpart. Not just in RBS and Northern Rock, but right across the sector, ever-growing debts were the launching pad for ever-more risky bets. While the boom lasted it seemed the financial equivalent of perpetual motion. After the crash vast sums of public money were poured into banks threatened with failure. The United Kingdom spent almost as much on bank bailouts as did the United States; its GDP shrank by 6 per cent as against the American figure of 4 per cent.

The strangest feature of the crash is not that it finally arrived, but that so few people saw it coming. (One who did was Vince Cable; another was the American economist Nouriel Roubini.) In an authoritative study, the economists Carmen M. Reinhart and Kenneth S. Rogoff show that, since 1800, the United Kingdom has gone through a banking crisis once every sixteen years.[21] Of course, memories are short and wishful thinking endemic, but that truism is not an adequate explanation. After the crash, the left blamed the greed and folly of 'the bankers', while the right blamed the profligacy of the state. David Cameron's deadly post-election soundbite, 'people understand that the debt crisis is the legacy of the last government', became an endlessly repeated Coalition mantra. In 2009, the economic commentator Will Hutton denounced the bankers for 'betting our cash for personal gain', while Vince Cable, then still in opposition, compared Britain's 'financial aristocracy' to Marie Antoinette.[22]

There is truth in both these stories. As we have just seen, 'the bankers' *were* foolish and greedy; and under New Labour the state was certainly extravagant, even if not profligate. In its first term, New Labour stuck to the 'eye-wateringly' tight spending plans set out by the previous Conservative Government. Treasury meanness then gave way to munificence, increasingly financed by borrowing. In 2000 public spending accounted for 34.5 per cent of GDP. By 2007 the figure was 41 per cent. In 2007, the structural deficit in the public finances (in other words the deficit that remained even when the economy was fully employed) was 3.1 per cent of national income, the second largest in the G7.

Yet the blame games miss the point. The bankers and New Labour ministers were not aliens, descending on planet Britain from outer space. They were part of a syndrome that infected the entire society. House owners who gambled on ever-rising house prices and took out mortgages they could not afford, credit card holders who borrowed more than they could realistically expect to pay back, voters who thought they were entitled to ever-rising material living standards and political leaders who tried to satisfy them with borrowed money were part of it too. The level of private debt was more exorbitant than in any other large economy in Europe, while the associated boom in house prices was more feverish. The growth of private debt far outstripped that of government debt. Total private sector debt (including financial companies as well as households and non-financial companies) increased from 250 per cent of GDP in 2000 to 400 per cent in 2007. Total personal debt stood at £650bn in 2000; by 2007 it totalled almost £1.4tn. From 1996 to 2006, house prices rose by 152 per cent, a higher figure than in any Eurozone country apart from Ireland.[23]

Another sign of the times was that London became a haunt of choice for sleazy Russian oligarchs. The extraordinary 2012 legal battle between Boris Berezovsky and Roman Abramovich over the former's allegation that the latter had cheated him of £3bn was one result; the Litvinenko murder in 2006 was another. Less lurid, but more pervasive, was the obsession with effortless monetary gain that permeated popular television programmes and the tabloid press. Pre-crisis Britain was a merry-go-round of irresponsible lending, careless borrowing and debt-fuelled consumption. As long as the merry-go-round was whirling, no one wanted to jump off, and hardly anyone warned that it could not go on whirling for ever. Like Cassandra, the few who did were ignored or laughed out of court. Perhaps that was inevitable. When even Gordon Brown, possessor of a first-class history degree from Edinburgh University, convinced himself that there would be 'no return to boom and bust',[24] it was not surprising that lesser folk, dazzled by fools' gold, followed suit.

POST-CRISIS BRITAIN

The sequel is more surprising. At first sight, post-crisis Britain is a very different place from boom-time Britain. Austerity has been the order of the day. When this book went to press, the United Kingdom's economy was around 3 per cent smaller than in 2008. Asset prices had risen, to the great benefit of the rich, but real wages had fallen by 7.5 per cent. Despite signs of an economic upturn in late 2013, GDP growth was feeble. Unemployment and youth unemployment in particular were still substantially higher than they had been before the boom broke. Both main parties were committed to eliminating the deficit in the public finances in due course; they differed over the timing, not the principle. Big cuts in public spending had already been made and more were in prospect. House prices were rising, but the increase was heavily concentrated in London and the South-East. Household names such as Woolworths, Barratts, and Habitat had disappeared from the high street.

A closer look reveals a more complex picture. The crisis of the market fundamentalist moral economy has not been resolved and no potential successor is in sight. Mammon still has plenty of worshippers, by no means all of them in his City temples. One significant indicator is the fate of consumer debt, an outstanding feature of the pre-crisis merry-go-round. At the end of July 2013 outstanding personal debt stood at £1.426tn, up from £1.421tn since July 2012. Outstanding unsecured credit lending stood at £158.3bn, compared with £157.3bn twelve months before. The Office for Budget Responsibility forecasts that average household debt will reach £73,324 in the first quarter of 2018, up from £54,110 in July 2013.[25]

In a very different way, the riots and outbreaks of looting that erupted in a number of big cities in early August 2011 tell essentially the same story. They were sparked by a protest march in Tottenham following the death of Mark Duggan, a young black man whom the police had shot dead two days before. As the disturbances spread, however, the original spark was forgotten. Shocking images of arson, violence, robbery and looting filled the nation's television screens; by early September police forces across the country had arrested almost 4,000 people, the vast majority of them young males. (Whites slightly outnumbered blacks.) It was not so easy to tell what the riots meant. Some saw them as mindless violence, others as an inarticulate protest against an unjust social order. However, the most persuasive interpretation, proposed by the criminologist David Moxon, is more subtle. The rioters' targets, he points out, were not remote 'citadels of power and authority', but property and people in their own neighbourhoods. So far from wishing to tear down the existing social order, they were signalling their membership of the consumer culture that embraces virtually the entire society. Their grievance was that they were too low down in the consumerist pecking order. They worshipped Mammon as fervently as did indebted householders or highly rewarded bankers; they only sought to get closer to the front of the congregation.[26]

Higher up the social scale, David Cameron is as zealous in defence of the financial sector as was Gordon Brown. In December 2011 he imposed what he miscalled a 'veto' on a proposed EU fiscal agreement, marginalizing Britain from the rest of the Union, to protect the City from potentially intrusive EU regulation. Since then he has threatened to veto any EU move towards a financial transactions or 'Tobin' tax designed to mitigate exchange rate volatility and impede currency speculation. Meanwhile the British Government had filed a complaint at the European Court of Justice designed to stymie an EU attempt to cap bankers' bonuses. As all this implies, financial skulduggery is as widespread as it was before the crash. To mention only a few examples, in the course of 2012 HSBC paid the relevant American authorities $1.9bn to settle a case against it for money laundering; the UK-based Standard Chartered Bank was fined $300m for sanctions busting; and Boots moved its headquarters from Nottingham to a Swiss tax haven, cutting its tax liability by more than £500m. In September 2013 Barclays, RBS and UBS of Switzerland were reported to have paid a combined fine of £2.5bn for their role in rigging the interbank lending rate known as Libor. Meanwhile, the financial sector's 'masters of the universe', as Tom Wolfe called them in his novel *Bonfire of the Vanities*, have fought like tigers to defend their lavish remuneration packages.

A WAKE-UP CALL

In the mid-nineteenth century, Dickens and Trollope painted mordant pictures of the moral corruption that comes when wealth is equated with worth and greed is thought to be good. It is time to learn the lesson of their depictions anew. In the rest of this book I try to encourage and deepen the learning process. But this is not a programme for government, still less a manifesto. It is meant to be a wake-up call to a society sleepwalking towards a seedy barbarism. I argue that our present way of life is unsustainable environmentally, emotionally and morally; that it denies the human need for continuity, dignity and meaning; that the conception of individual freedom that legitimizes it is fundamentally flawed; and that the understanding of modernity that its apologists pray in aid is both banal and misleading.

In Chapter 2, I explore the origins of contemporary Mammon worship, trace the changes in the moral economy that have fostered it, and describe the evolving intellectual and cultural environment within which these changes have taken place. In Chapter 3 I describe the social amnesia that accompanies present-day Mammon worship and dissect the contradictions in the doctrine that legitimizes it. In Chapter 4 I trace the attrition of the public realm which I see as its most damaging consequence. After turning to the thirty-year-old growth of inequality and its cruel social consequences in Chapter 5, I argue in Chapter 6 that they are reflected in a profound crisis of democratic politics. In the last chapter, I argue that it is time for a 'revolution of sentiment' to replace the moral economy which is now in crisis and point the way to a new and better one. Such a revolution, I shall suggest, should transcend the conventional dividing lines of party and creed and draw on the most resonant traditions of our political culture, from Burkean conservatism to ethical socialism. But I do not believe that the revolution should stop at politics. I argue that it should also embrace the religious traditions which are the bedrock of resistance to the imperialism of money and draw on the idealism manifested in a growing variety of protest movements and campaigning groups. I shall end by outlining the lineaments of a new public philosophy, based on the values of stewardship, democratic dialogue, republican self-respect, personal growth and freedom from humiliation. Reverberating in the background throughout is the Athenian dramatist Menander's cry: 'Choose equality and flee greed.'

Five antinomies structure my argument: Honour versus Hedonism; History versus Amnesia; the Public Realm versus the Market State; Fate versus Choice; Open Debate versus Charismatic Populism. In the next chapter I examine the first.

2

Hedonism Trumps Honour

[T]he ideas of economists and political philosophers, both when they are right and when they are wrong, are more power-ful than is commonly understood. Indeed, the world is ruled by little else. Practical men, who believe themselves to be quite exempt from any intellectual influences, are usually the slaves of some defunct economist. Madmen in authority, who hear voices in the air, are distilling their frenzy from some academic scribbler of a few years back ... [S]oon or late, it is ideas, not vested interests, which are dangerous for good or evil.
J. M. Keynes, *The General Theory of Employment, Interest and Money*, 1936

We can return to the beasts. But if we wish to remain human, then there is only one way, the way into the open society. We must go on into the unknown, the uncertain and insecure, using what reason we may have to plan for both security and freedom.
Karl Popper, *The Open Society and Its Enemies*, 1945

Like the opening pages of a murder story, the introduction to this book presented a mystery: granted that the boom of the noughties engulfed the entire developed world, why was it more frenetic in Britain than in any other large economy? Why were British-based financial services more exposed to the eventual crisis than those of continental Europe and the United States? Why did the solidaristic moral economy of the mid-twentieth century give way to its market fundamentalist successor? Why did Mammon worship become so fervent and so widespread, and why is it still in rude health?

There is no single answer. The IT revolution; globalization; changes in the occupational and class structures; the decline of manufacturing and the rise of services all played clamant parts in the drama. Credit-card debt would not have soared if stores of all kinds had not been able to install computerized tills. Without the computing power available to ordinary consumers, as well as to bankers, hedge fund managers, private equity firms and the like, boom-time Britain would not have been able to float on the sea of debt that swept it towards the bust. The build-up of toxic assets that ruined once-respected banks right across the developed world and spawned the credit crunch would not have been possible before globalization got into its stride in the 1990s. The technological and economic changes which have transformed Britain from an industrial into a post-industrial society, where middle-class occupations outnumber working-class ones, helped to drive the upsurge of private debt and the booming house prices that were the stigmata of British society in the noughties.

But technological and economic changes do not take place in a cultural or intellectual vacuum. They are mediated by values, beliefs and myths; their impact on behaviour owes at least as much to ideas as to impersonal social forces: Keynes was exaggerating when he said that the world is ruled by 'little else' other than ideas, but he was right that self-styled 'practical men' are often slaves to the ideas of long-dead thinkers. Focussing solely on 'hard', measurable changes at the expense of the impalpable and qualitative banalizes a rich and complex story. The crash of 2008 was the civilian equivalent of defeat in war, the boom of the noughties the equivalent of the vainglorious assumptions and wrong-headed military doctrines that can doom armies to disaster before they fire a shot. Just as differences in matériel are rarely the sole cause of military defeat, the changes mentioned in the last paragraph do not, in themselves, explain the catastrophe of 2008 or the orgiastic splurge of borrowing and spending that preceded it. Software, not hardware, holds the key to the tragedy.

I shall try to show that the chief culprit is a profound cultural shift which has been a leitmotiv of British history for more than forty years. One manifestation is the downfall of three redoubtable elites that I shall call the 'clerisy', the 'professional service elite' and the 'working-class elite'. Another is the erosion of the partly liberal and partly collectivist public doctrine of mid-twentieth century Britain which these elites had hammered out. A third is the mutation of the moral economy that accompanied its erosion. To understand how and why the elites fell I begin this chapter by describing the society and culture that nurtured them and that they helped to shape. I then turn to the social and economic crises that tore gaping holes in their public doctrine at the start of the last quarter of the twentieth century and examine the currents of thought and feeling that procured the public doctrine that guides policy makers today.

EXPOSED NERVE

I begin my story by examining the high-minded, self-confident, yet often tormented clerisy, the exposed nerve of a society in the throes of disorientating and often painful change. Though the clerisy survived until the mid-point of the last century, it reached its apogee in the Victorian Age, when a hunt was on for new ideas to make sense of a new social world. The clerisy was not a representative cross-section of the society around it: highly educated intellectuals are, by definition, exceptional. In Zygmunt Bauman's language, its members were 'interpreters' not 'legislators'.[1] They held up a mirror to their society, and hoped to change it by doing so. They were not a school; they disagreed with each other, sometimes violently. But most of them marched in broadly the same direction; and so did the society to which they spoke.

A. V. (Albert Venn) Dicey, Vinerian Professor of Law at Oxford from 1882 to 1909, defined the direction in a seminal study of the relationship between ideas, opinion and public policy in the nineteenth century.[2] In the second half of the nineteenth century, he argued, Britain had experienced a slow, but profound transition from 'individualism' to 'collectivism'. He cited a range of statutes to prove his point: acts limiting hours of work; acts to prevent the adulteration of food and regulate the sale of drugs; acts establishing free and compulsory elementary education; an act obliging employers to insure their employees against the risks entailed by their employment; acts enjoining local authorities to close or demolish unhealthy dwelling-houses; and an act empowering local authorities to acquire land for allotments. The suggestion that collectivism was replacing individualism was not original. In 1887, William Harcourt, Gladstone's Chancellor of the Exchequer, famously declared, 'We are all socialists now.'[3] (In those days collectivism and socialism were often seen as the same thing.) By the beginning of the twentieth century the triumph of collectivism was almost a commonplace.[4] But Dicey was not content to show that collectivism was on the march. His central thesis was that collectivist practice stemmed from collectivist opinions; and he showed that thinkers and writers – in effect, a clerisy – played a decisive role in shaping the opinions that eventually translated into collectivist policies.

Who were the clerisy? The choice of examples is bound to be arbitrary. The fiction of novelists such as Dickens, Mrs Gaskell and George Eliot did as much to shape the mood of their age as the writings and speeches of historians, philosophers, economists and theologians. (Dicey paid a lot of attention to Dickens.) But I am concerned with overt argument, not with the slow workings of imaginative literature in the minds of its readers. For my purposes, the most notable examples of the Victorian clerisy are Thomas Carlyle, doom-laden prophet of heroic leadership; John Stuart Mill, administrator, economist, philosopher and feminist; Cardinal Manning, austere Catholic convert, champion of the poor and unemployed and hammer of employer exploitation; John Ruskin, art critic turned social critic; and Matthew Arnold, bane of middle-class philistinism and proponent of a strong state. All five figured in Dicey's account, Mill at great length.

They were very different. Carlyle was born in Ecclefechan in Dumfriesshire to poor and forbiddingly pious Presbyterian parents, but by dint of heroic efforts became one of the most famous historians of the time. He savaged popular government and the inhumanity of Victorian capitalism with equal passion. In a frenzied attack on the 1867 Reform Act, which he rightly saw as a stepping stone to democracy, he wrote that the guiding principle of the new order would be '"the equality of men", any man equal to any other; Quashee Nigger to Socrates or Shakespeare; Judas Iscariot to Jesus Christ'.[5] Yet he was equally appalled by laissez-faire capitalism. Laissez-faire was 'Do-nothingism', the source of the terrible, 'unendurable conviction' of the working class 'that their lot in this world is not founded on right'.[6] These apparently divergent attitudes formed a seamless web: democracy would be a disaster for the working class as well for everyone else; only strong men could save them from laissez-faire.

In stark contrast, John Stuart Mill, son of the utilitarian thinker James Mill, was born into the radical equivalent of the purple. We shall meet him again in the last chapter of this book. What matters for the moment is that his opinions changed radically as he grew older. Dicey thought him 'a teacher created for, and assured of a welcome in, an age of transition'; the changes in Mill's convictions, he added, both symbolized and helped to cause the advance of collectivism in the last third of the century.[7] Despite writing a bestseller championing the laissez-faire political economy that Carlyle loathed, Mill ended his life as a proponent of a form of market socialism. In a tantalizing fragment, 'Chapters on Socialism', he conceded the central socialist charge against capitalism: that 'force of poverty' enslaved the great majority. He rejected state socialism, but favoured worker co-operatives and subverted the conventional laissez-faire view that property rights were sacrosanct. Property was not 'identical throughout history'. Its rights could perfectly well be modified for the sake of the public good. The abolition of serfdom in Russia and of slavery in the United States were cases in point. Mill died before completing the argument, but the central message is clear: property should become society's servant instead of its master.

Manning was born into a wealthy family and proceeded from Harrow School to Balliol College, Oxford. After ordination as an Anglican priest, he plunged into the complex religious battles that convulsed the Church of England in the early nineteenth century. After much inner struggle, he converted to Catholicism; he ended his career as Cardinal Archbishop of Westminster. In that role he championed Joseph Arch's Agricultural Labourers' Union and the American Knights of Labor. In the 'great' London dock strike of 1889, as the historian F. M. L. Thompson justly called it,[8] he played a leading part in settling the strike on the dockers' terms. Soon afterwards, he helped to inspire Pope Leo XIII's famous encyclical *De Rerum Novarum*.

The encyclical insisted that the prime purpose of the state was to secure the common good and that workers were entitled to a living wage; long after Manning's death it became a fundamental text for twentieth-century Christian Democrats. The crowds that lined the streets as Manning's funeral cortège passed by in 1892 had had no precedent since the death of the Duke of Wellington.

Ruskin was the only son of a successful wine merchant and a devoutly Evangelical mother. He made his name as an architectural historian and critic of painting, but his role as a prime exemplar of the Victorian clerisy owes more to his blistering critique of the fundamental assumptions of classical political economy. The social value of wealth, he insisted, depended 'on the moral sign attached to it'. Wealth earned by 'faithful industries, progressive energies and productive ingenuities' was one thing, wealth that signified 'mortal luxury, merciless tyranny, ruinous chicane' was quite another. The notion that the sole purpose of economic activity was to accumulate wealth was the 'most insolently futile of all that ever beguiled men'.[9] Ruskin College, Oxford – alma mater of trade union leaders as varied as Arthur Jenkins, Roy Jenkins's father, and George Woodcock, General Secretary of the TUC from 1960 to 1969 – is named for him. So is the Ruskin School of Drawing and Fine Art, also based in Oxford.

Matthew Arnold was the son of Thomas Arnold, the legendary headmaster of Rugby. Like Mill, he saw himself as a Liberal (albeit a 'Liberal of the future'), but they were on opposing sides in a debate which has rumbled on for a century and a half. For Mill, the state was at best a suspect ally, and at worst an enemy. For Arnold, the most serious weakness in Britain's public culture was precisely that she lacked the notion 'of *the State* – the nation in its collective and corporate character, entrusted with stringent powers for the general advantage'.[10]

Common themes cut across these differences. My quintet were all public moralists.[11] They struggled tirelessly to find answers to what Carlyle called 'The Condition of England Question'. They saw themselves as custodians of the public conscience, tutors to the nation. They were driven by a ferocious work ethic, no doubt sharpened by deep psychic needs as well as by an essentially religious sensibility. For all of them the condition of England fell far short of what it ought to have been, intellectually, culturally and above all morally, and they all believed that it was up to them to expose its shortcomings as powerfully as they could.

They were unashamedly elitist. Carlyle's mixture of pity and contempt for the masses was peculiar to him, but even Mill declared publicly that the working class were 'habitual liars', while Arnold chastised the 'populace' for its propensity for 'bawling, hustling and smashing'.[12] With the partial exception of the later Mill, there were no socialists in the quintet, but for all of them the buccaneering, masterless capitalism of the day – the capitalism of the fictional Melmotte and Merdle and the real East and West India Docks Company – was morally disgraceful as well as emotionally repugnant. Like Mill, they all loathed the 'trampling, crushing, elbowing and treading on each other's heels' that industrial progress had bred.[13] They were for the exploited against the exploiters, for an ethic of civic virtue against the narrow, self-satisfied egoism that seemed to them to dominate the public culture. Matthew Arnold spoke for all of them when he championed 'sweetness and light' against a debased and debasing materialism. Their values were pre-capitalist, even aristocratic. Words like 'noble', 'honour' and 'duty' rolled off their pens. Yet they blazed the trail to the solidaristic moral economy of the mid-twentieth century, and their ghosts presided over the triumphant public realm of that era.

The half century following Ruskin's death in 1900 saw profound changes in the social and political environment which the Victorian clerisy had taken for granted. The belated arrival of a democratic suffrage in Britain, two world wars, the deepest crisis in the history of capitalism, a dramatic, though uneven increase in the size and role of the state, the Bolshevik revolution in Russia and the Nazi revolution in Germany undermined the certitudes of the Victorian age – including the oppositional certitudes described above. (Einstein's theory of relativity and Heisenberg's uncertainty principle may have had a similar effect.)

'The only golden rule is that there are no golden rules,' wrote the brilliant, but wayward gadfly George Bernard Shaw in the 'Revolutionist's Handbook' appended to *Man and Superman*. The mood epitomized in his aphorism was the sea in which the twentieth-century clerisy swam. The result was a cacophony of discordant voices. A few examples will illustrate the point. T. S. Eliot, a revolutionary in poetry, but a reactionary in politics, declared that modern society was 'worm-eaten with liberalism' and that Britain was making ready 'the ground upon which the barbarian nomads of the future will encamp in their mechanised caravans'.[14] At the opposite end of the ideological spectrum, two Christian socialists – the economic historian R. H. Tawney and William Temple, Archbishop of York from 1929 to 1942 and of Canterbury from 1942 to 1944 – rooted their political beliefs in their religious faith. For Tawney, what mattered about human beings was 'not the nature they share with other animals, but their humanity which, in virtue of the incarnation, they share with God';[15] for his part Temple declared that if laissez-faire economics were true, then 'Christ was wrong'.[16]

Tawney and Temple stuck to their guns; others were as wayward as Shaw. As a young man, the philosopher Bertrand Russell had a strong mystical streak and spent long hours discussing religion with his lover Lady Ottoline Morrell; after their affair ended he became violently hostile to religion and particularly to Christianity. Political change-lings were equally common. Harold Laski started as a liberal pluralist before the First World War and became a maverick Marxist before the Second. Sidney and Beatrice Webb, sometime pioneers of gradualist Fabian socialism, were bowled over by a visit to Stalin's Soviet Union in the early 1930s, and returned to praise it as a 'new civilisation'. Before the First World War the endlessly fertile G. D. H. Cole offered a participative alternative to state socialism, which he called 'Guild Socialism'. Loosely federated 'National Guilds' of workers by hand and brain would run the nation's industries. Between the wars, he forsook industrial self-government for state planning, then the talis-man of the left; he returned to his participative, anti-state enthusiasms in the dying days of the post-war Attlee Government.

No latter-day Dicey has measured the twentieth-century clerisy's impact on public policy, but there is no doubt that it was much closer to public politics than its nineteenth-century predecessor had been. Shaw was a vestryman in St Pancras as a young man. Sidney Webb was a leading figure in the London County Council before 1914, and held Cabinet office in 1924 and from 1929 to 1931. A. D. Lindsay,

Master of Balliol College, Oxford, from 1924 to 1949 stood unsuccessfully as an anti-appeasement candidate in the Oxford by-election of 1938. Harold Laski served for twelve years on Labour's National Executive, and became party chairman in 1945. Bertrand Russell was a leading pacifist campaigner during the First World War, served a prison sentence for his pains and twice stood for Parliament as Labour candidate for Chelsea.

Like their nineteenth-century predecessors, the members of the twentieth-century clerisy were public moralists first and foremost. They too wrestled endlessly with Carlyle's 'Condition of England Question'; they too disdained the mean-minded materialism that seemed to them inseparable from capitalism. Many of them added a new theme to that repertoire: the nature, scope and potentialities of democracy. Was it compatible with capitalism, as Tawney and Laski wondered? Was Tawney right in thinking that, unless it embraced the culture as well as the polity, it was an empty façade? Did it embrace the workplace, as Cole thought in his Guild Socialist incarnation? Did it merely mean the right to put a cross on a ballot paper once every few years, as the British doctrine of absolute parliamentary sovereignty presupposed? Or did it mean discussion and debate in small groups before the votes were cast, as Lindsay held?[17] These questions are at least as pressing today as they were when the twentieth-century clerisy grappled with them; current debates on the use of the popular referendum are an example. As we shall see in the final chapters of this book, the Nobel Prize-winner Amartya Sen has argued forcefully that the essence of democracy lies in 'public reasoning'.[18] Echoes of Lindsay are hard to miss.

Many of these preoccupations came together in the most unlikely member of the twentieth-century clerisy – the self-described 'lower-upper-middle-class' old Etonian[19] and sometime Assistant Superintendent in the Imperial Indian Police Eric Blair, better known as George Orwell. Since his death, he has become a secular saint for the *bien pensant* intelligentsia. There is an Orwell Prize and a George Orwell Award for Distinguished Contribution to Honesty and Clarity in Public Language. Some of Orwell's coinages in *Ninety Eighty-Four* – 'Big Brother', 'Newspeak' and 'Doublethink' – have entered the language. The trouble is that the worshippers who throng his shrine obscure the ambiguities in his legacy, like varnish coating an Old Master. We know what he was against. It is not so clear what he was for.

He was a tough-minded social patriot; and the toughness some-times verged on the Blimpish. Tender-minded middle-class socialists filled him with horror. The mere words 'Socialism' and 'Communism', he wrote in the famous peroration to *The Road to Wigan Pier*, 'draw towards them with magnetic force every fruit-juice drinker, nudist, sandal-wearer, sex maniac, Quaker, "Nature Cure" quack, pacifist and feminist in England'.[20] But Orwell the curmudgeonly Blimp was eclipsed by Orwell the hammer of capitalism and the ruling class. The war, he argued in his stirring 1941 polemic, *The Lion and the Unicorn*, had proved once and for all that capitalism had failed. As for the ruling classes, they were 'simply parasites, less useful to society than his fleas are to a dog'.[21] There was no hope of winning the war while they were in control. The choice was between defeat and a socialist revolution, achieved by a 'real push from below'.

The push would not come from the Labour Party, or from the working class. They would rally to the revolution, but its directing brains would come from 'the new intermediate class of skilled work-ers, technical experts, airmen, scientists and architects, the people who feel at home in the radio and ferro-concrete age'. It would be a very English revolution, with an extraordinary capacity to assimilate England's past that might lead foreign observers to wonder if the revolution were real.

> But all the same, it will have done the essential thing. It will have national-ized industry, scaled down incomes, set up a classless educational system. Its real nature will be apparent from the hatred which the surviving rich men of the world will feel for it . . . It will fight in such a way that even if it is beaten its memory will be dangerous to the victor, as the memory of the French Revolution was dangerous to Metternich's Europe.[22]

Orwell's dream of a revolutionary war did not come true, but Churchill's wartime coalition brought in a form of state-directed war socialism that amounted to a revolution of sorts. A command econ-omy replaced the market economy of peacetime; the distribution of post-tax incomes was more egalitarian than anything seen in Britain before or since. Orwell's intermediate class did not lead this revolution, but as NCOs and subalterns in the services and as shop stewards and junior managers in industry they were its shock troops. Orwell's writings helped to inspire the effervescent public culture of wartime, along with the journalism of Michael Foot and Arthur Koestler, the broadcasts of J. B. Priestley, the lectures to the troops organized by the Army Bureau of Current Affairs (ABCA), the factory concerts run by ENSA (Entertainments National Service Association), the stream of hard-hitting left-wing booklets published by Victor Gollancz and the rambustious radicalism of the *Daily Mirror*.

Between the wars, the clerisy had swum against the tide. During the Second World War, it came into its own. In doing so, it reflected – and at the same time nurtured – an intellectual revolution. For the first time in British history private ownership and the free market were on the defensive, while the language of the public interest became common currency. *The Times* summed up the new mood. 'If we speak of democracy', it proclaimed, 'we do not mean a democracy which maintains the right to vote but forgets the right to work and the right to live. If we speak of freedom, we do not mean a rugged individualism which excludes social organization and economic planning. If we speak of equality, we do not mean a political equality nullified by social and economic privilege.'[23]

PUBLIC SERVANTS, CONVENTIONAL AND UNCONVENTIONAL

Paralleling the clerisy was the professional service elite. Its members manned the upper reaches of the great departments of state, dominated the ruling bodies of the self-governing professions and headed the leading Oxbridge and London colleges. The cast list is enormous. I shall pick out a few examples to illustrate it. The first is Lord (Tom) Denning. He was the son of a country draper in Hampshire, a scholarship boy at Andover Grammar School, a Demy (i.e. Scholar) of Magdalen College, Oxford, Lord Chief Justice for eleven years, Master of the Rolls for twenty, author of a hilarious official report on the Profumo Affair in 1963 and a radical legal modernizer who believed that a judge's duty is to do justice, and not merely to apply the law.

Edward Bridges, eventually Lord Bridges, was more conventional, though he once shocked a Treasury messenger who noticed that there were holes in his socks. He won an MC during the First World War, and served as an inspirational Cabinet Secretary during the Second; in the early post-war years he was Head of the Civil Service and Permanent Secretary to the Treasury. He personified the austere virtues of the generalist civil service, trained to think beyond the tramlines of any particular government department and to tell truth to power – virtues which a later generation of politicians and officials were distressingly apt to forget. Two Directors General of the BBC, Lord (John) Reith, the first, and Sir William Haley, the third, have high places on the cast list: they helped to make the Corporation one of the most potent cultural institutions in the land, and to imbue it with an ethic of public service and enlightenment to which it has remained substantially true, despite political interference, commercial pressures and a top-heavy bureaucracy, for more than eighty years.

'Inners and outers', circulating between the academy and Whitehall, helped to give the professional service elite its special flavour. One of these was Oliver, eventually Lord, Franks, Glasgow professor of moral philosophy in the 1930s, Permanent Secretary of the Ministry of Supply during the later stages of the war, Ambassador to Washington from 1948 to 1952, Provost of Queen's College, Oxford, and later of Worcester College and perhaps the most accomplished mandarin of the age. He was not just present at the creation of the post-war world order; he was one of the creators. He co-ordinated the European response to the American offer of Marshall Aid and worked closely with the American Secretary of State, Dean Acheson, to create the North Atlantic Alliance.

The most famous inner and outer was William Beveridge, messianic Director of the London School of Economics after the First World War and author of the Beveridge Report, one of the most resonant state papers of the century, during the Second. The Report proposed a single, comprehensive, cradle-to-the-grave system of social insurance, buttressed by family allowances, full employment and a free health service, designed to overcome the 'five giants' of 'Want, Ignorance, Idleness, Squalor and Disease'. Insurance benefits were to be entitlements, earned by past contributions and paid as of right, not doles funded by general taxation. 'A revolutionary moment in the world's history', Beveridge declared in an unconscious echo of Orwell, 'is a time for revolutions, not for patching.'

Eric Roll, later Lord Roll, started unconventionally but ended conventionally. He was born near Czernowitz, then part of the Hapsburg empire, today in Ukraine. He studied economics at Birmingham University, became a protégé of Keynes, and taught at the universities of Hull and Austin, Texas, before taking the well-trodden road from academic economics to the mandarinate. Thanks partly to his knowledge of languages (he spoke seven and could lip-read in both French and German) he became one of his adopted country's most accomplished multi-national negotiators. But after an unhappy spell as Permanent Secretary of the ill-fated Department of Economic Affairs in the mid-1960s, he left the civil service for a third career as a merchant banker. Throughout, he remained a Keynesian in economics and a passionate supporter of European integration in politics. Like Franks, though at a less exalted level, he was one of the midwives of the post-war economic order, but what he did matters less than what he was: living proof of the professional service elite's remarkable capacity to absorb and shape talented outsiders, a prime source of its power and longevity.

Three very different younger public servants also figure in my cast list: Ian (Lord) Bancroft, Head of the Civil Service from 1977 to 1981 when Margaret Thatcher summarily abolished the Civil Service Department; Sir Michael Palliser, unyielding supporter of British entry into the European Community and eventual head of the Foreign Office; and Sir Leo Pliatzky, child of the Salford slums who rose to be head of the Department of Trade. All three served in the armed forces during the Second World War: Bancroft in the Rifle Brigade, Palliser in the Coldstream Guards and Pliatzky in the REME. All three saw action; and all three were profoundly affected by their wartime experiences. Like many of their generation they came home determined to do what they could to make their country and the world better places. They became public servants in that spirit. They were inspirational figures for younger people fortunate enough to know them.[24] Their commitment to the values of disinterested public service and their sometimes inconvenient insistence on telling ministers what they did

31

not wish to hear shone through till retirement. (Pliatzky's run-ins with Denis Healey when the latter was Chancellor of the Exchequer were famous; Bancroft's unwillingness to kow-tow to Margaret Thatcher at the start of her prime ministership earned him the sack.)

Civil servants like these were servants of the Crown; and as Sir Robert Armstrong, then Cabinet Secretary, put it in 1985, 'the Crown in this context means and is represented by the Government of the day'.[25] But service to the Government as the Crown's representative did not mean self-abasement before it. The civil service of Bridges and his fellow public servants was the product of the reform of public administration that followed the 1854 Northcote–Trevelyan Report on the organization of the civil service. The report argued that the existing civil service, recruited by patronage, should be replaced by one recruited on merit, proved in examinations. This patronage-free service should consist of officials, formed by a broad education in the humanities, and with 'sufficient independence, character, ability, and experience to be able to advise, assist, and, to some extent, influence, those who are from time to time set over them'.[26]

The new, post-Northcote–Trevelyan civil service became one of the most prestigious professions in the land, on a par with the great professions of law, medicine, the armed forces and the Church. It was the memory, the hard disk, of the state: a check on the incorrigible short-termism of elected persons. Its political masters were transients; the civil service went on for ever. Perhaps because of this, secrecy was in its blood; so was a certain wary scepticism. Keynes, who served in the Treasury as a temporary official during the First World War, captured that mentality in a limpid phrase: 'very clever, very dry and in a certain sense very cynical'.[27] In the last third of the twentieth century, as debate over Britain's decline from the high point of 1945 gathered pace, the civil service became a favourite whipping boy, particularly among unsuccessful former ministers who had mistaken disinterested advice for obstruction.[28] But at mid-century its prestige and authority were undaunted.

At the very peak of the professional service elite stood John Maynard Keynes, who was also a glittering ornament of the clerisy. There was a magic about him, which makes his genius extraordinarily hard to grasp. As a young man he was incontinently homosexual, but he spent the last twenty-one years of his life happily married to the love of his life, the Russian ballerina Lydia Lopokova. He had a magical prose style, a luminous intellect, unshakable self-belief and captivating charm. He spent his adult life at the heart of the establishment, but no one did more to overturn the economic assumptions that most of its members took for granted.

Yet the revolution in economic thought that he and his disciples believed he had made[29] was not as revolutionary as they imagined. His great insight was that, contrary to what he called the 'classical theory', market economies were inherently prone to depressions and unemployment, and that when these occurred public investment would be needed to increase demand and take up the slack – in other words that the state would have to play a crucially important economic role that it had never played before. Unfortunately, Keynes did not explore the implications of this insight for democratic politics or for the *nature*, as opposed to the role, of the state. The Keynesian state would be the familiar old state, run in the familiar old way, by the familiar old people, among whom the mature Keynes held a high place. Equally, he did not foresee that, when the state became the visible guarantor of the level of employment and the growth of the economy, instead of a remote presence in the background, economic policy would become a political football, in a sense which had never been true before. Willy-nilly, the aloof state of the past – the state under which Keynes had grown up – would have to mobilize public consent for its policies; the tried and tested mechanisms of parliamentary accountability would no longer win them acceptance. It would be wrong to carp. Keynesian theory had a thirty-year run for its money; Keynesian practice helped to underpin unprecedented abundance for a generation. When Keynes died, Keynesian economic management was barely in its infancy. The tragedy was that after his death his successors failed to fill the gaps he had left in his system.

SOCIAL PATRIOTS

The clerisy and the professional service elite were not all saints, or even saintly. T. S. Eliot was an anti-Semite, an arrant snob and an oleaginous social climber. Reith was a shameless careerist, forever complaining about his salary and always on the lookout for better jobs. At different times he thought himself ideally fitted to be Viceroy of India, Secretary-General of the United Nations, Ambassador to Washington and, somewhat anti-climactically, Chairman of the National Coal Board. Orwell snitched to the Foreign Office on writers and entertainers he believed, often on scant evidence, to be undercover Communists or fellow travellers. Beveridge was a relentless and dictatorial self-promoter with a remarkable talent for making enemies.

Saintly or not, however, both the clerisy and the professional service elite took it for granted that it was up to them to lead their country in the right direction. Both had internalized an ethic of honour, patriotism and civic duty. Being human, they did not always live up to it, but they knew that they were morally bound to put the public interest ahead of private interests, including their own. When they fell from grace, as inevitably they sometimes did, we can be fairly sure that they felt at least a twinge of guilt.

The same was true of the equally self-confident, patriotic and public-spirited working-class elite represented by such granite figures as Ernest Bevin, Aneurin Bevan and Arthur Horner, as well as by lesser ones, such as Walter Citrine, long-serving General Secretary of the TUC and the Durham miners' leader, Sam Watson. The first three deserve particular attention. As he well knew (and never tired of saying), Bevin was a 'turn-up in a million': Foreign Secretary in the post-war Attlee Government, the greatest leader the British working-class movement has ever had, and a unique combination of creative imagination, sober common sense, earthy eloquence, occasional ruthlessness, an elephantine memory and rock-like loyalty to those who earned his trust. He had had virtually no formal education, but he had learned more from what he called the 'hedgerows of experience' than most university graduates learned from their studies. He was proud of his country and proud of his class: 'the last great class', as he told a union conference, 'to march onward, to rise to power and equity'. He was the master builder of Britain's most formidable trade union behemoth, the Transport and General Workers' Union; and as Minister of Labour during the Second World War he was the chief architect of a subtle form of industrial partnership that transformed the trade unions from suppliants for ministerial favour into an estate of the realm.

Bevan and Horner both hailed from that cradle of political talent, the South Wales coalfield, but they took different paths to prominence. At thirty-one Bevan was elected to Parliament for the mining constituency of Ebbw Vale. Along with Stafford Cripps, later the Attlee Government's iron chancellor, he was briefly expelled from the Labour Party in the late 1930s for advocating a popular front. In 1945, still under fifty, he was given Cabinet office as Minister of Health. As such he masterminded the creation of the National Health Service, the most far-reaching extension of social citizenship in British history. To his enemies on the right of the Labour Party, Bevan was a megalomaniac and disruptive prima donna. To his admirers on the left he was a socialist Sir Galahad, doing battle for the eternal verities against opportunists and lickspittles. In reality he was neither. He set out his subtle, tenaciously held but slightly wistful credo in the final pages of his flawed masterpiece, *In Place of Fear*. Democratic socialism, he wrote, was 'cool in temper'. It eschewed 'absolute prescriptions and final decisions'. Not for it,

> the thrill of the abandonment of private judgement which is the allure
> of modern Soviet Communism and of Fascism, its running mate. Nor
> can it escape the burden of social choice so attractively suggested by
> those who believe in *laissez-faire* principles and in the automatism of
> the price system . . .
> . . . Its chief enemy is vacillation, for it must achieve passion in action
> in pursuit of qualified judgements.[30]

'Passion in action in pursuit of qualified judgements': that was the essence of the social-democratic ethos in its prime, in Roosevelt's America, Léon Blum's France and Tage Erlander's Sweden as much as in Attlee's Britain.

At first sight, Horner seems an odd partner for Bevin and Bevan. They were social democrats; he was a foundation member of the Communist Party of Great Britain (CPGB) and never left it. But he refused to toe the party line through all its bewildering vagaries. He defied the disastrous 'class-against-class' Comintern line that pitted Communists against social democrats in the late twenties and early thirties, to the great benefit of the Nazi party; and he had no truck with the CPGB's opposition to war with Germany in the first two years of the Second World War when Stalin and Hitler were at peace with each other. (On the contrary, he worked with the Government to prepare armed resistance in the event of a German invasion.)

As that implies, he too was a social patriot, albeit of his own special kind. He was the chief architect of the National Union of Mineworkers that replaced the unwieldy Miners' Federation of Great Britain in 1945, and was elected its General Secretary in 1946. At a time when coal was king – when around 600,000 miners produced more than 200 million tons of coal a year – this was a pivotal position, not just in Labour politics, but in Britain's grim struggle to avert national bankruptcy. Horner threw himself into the struggle, condemning unofficial strikes, accepting a wage freeze and, above all, helping to shape the enlightened ethos of the National Coal Board that replaced the hated coal owners when the mines were nationalized in 1946. Coal nationalization was a key element in the growth of the public realm during the Attlee years. No one did more to make a success of it than Horner, social democrat in Communist clothing; class warrior turned industrial statesman.

BRITAIN AT MID-CENTURY

All three elites took for granted a society with a common identity and common values incarnated in stable structures – notably Parliament, the Civil Service, the Cabinet, the judiciary, the professions, the monarchy, the churches and, above all, marriage and the family. The last three need a closer look. The forced abdication of the louche, Germanophile Edward VIII in 1936 had brought the reassuringly respectable, domesticated George VI to the throne; the latter's speech impediment earned him sympathy and the royal family's exemplary conduct during the Blitz had earned it admiration. The sociologists Edward Shils and Michael Young were over-egging the pudding when they described Elizabeth II's coronation in 1953 as a national 'communion with the sacred',[31] but the myth of a familial monarchy and the myth of Britain and the British Empire as an extended family fed off each other. The churches were part of the family: though church membership at mid-century was a little lower than it had been in

1900, nearly 70 per cent of the population believed that Jesus was the son of God while nearly 90 per cent of infants were baptized. As for marriage and the family, only 2 per cent of the marriages of 1926 ended in divorce after twenty years, only 6 per cent of the marriages of 1936 and only 7 per cent of the marriages of 1951.[32]

Big private-sector employers such as ICI, GEC, Courtaulds, Morris Motors, the steel giant Richard Thomas and Baldwins and the famous ship-building firm Harland and Wolff seemed equally stable. They had little in common with the risk-haunted, insecure, exploitative owner-managed undertakings of early industrial capitalism. Big private firms were run by salaried professional managers, most of them eager to play their parts, alongside government and the unions, in the industrial power-sharing arrangements that post-war Britain inherited from the wartime coalition. Flanking them were mass trade unions, notably Horner's NUM with 600,000 members, Bevin's TGWU with 1,200,000, the General and Municipal Workers' Union (GMWU) with nearly 800,000 and the Amalgamated Engineering Union (AEU) with more than 700,000. The two major political parties were mass organizations too: the Conservative Party had nearly three million members in 1951 and the Labour Party nearly 900,000.

The equally stable, but publicly owned BBC enjoyed an apotheosis in the wartime and post-war years. The defiantly highbrow Third Programme, robust ancestor of today's punier Radio Three, was launched in 1946; not just classical music and contemporary jazz, but talks by public intellectuals such as Bertrand Russell, Isaiah Berlin and the astro-physicist Fred Hoyle, were staple fare. Highbrows, middlebrows and lowbrows came together during the weekly broadcasts of *ITMA* (*It's That Man Again*), starring the immortal Tommy Handley. Listening to *ITMA* was a nation-wide, classless rite from 1939 to Handley's death ten years later. Catchphrases like the melancholic Mona Lott's 'It's being so cheerful as keeps me going', Colonel Chinstrap's 'I don't mind if I do' or Mrs Mopp's (the office charlady) 'Can I do you now, sir?' were part of the language. In those old enough to remember them, they still evoke a lost age of shared austerity and hope.

The Post Office, publicly owned and publicly accountable through its ministerial head, the Postmaster General, was a universal presence, a ubiquitous link between the citizen and the state. Pensions were collected from post offices; red Post Office pillar boxes were every-where; small savings were deposited in post offices; the Post Office ran the telephone service. In 1946, it employed 350,000 people.[33] The Co-operative Movement, a vast congeries of self-governing local soci-eties owned by their members, was almost as ubiquitous, at any rate in working-class districts: in these, as the catchphrase had it, there was a 'co-op store on nearly every corner'.[34] The movement embodied a tradition of mutualism and self-help older and more deeply rooted than that of state socialism, but it too offered a collectivist alternative to private ownership and profit-seeking private enterprise. Under the post-war Labour Government, these were joined by a range of nation-alized industries, including railways, electricity, gas and civil aviation as well as coal – all charged, in a ringing phrase of the nationalization supremo Herbert Morrison, to act as 'high custodians of the public interest'.[35]

The highest custodian of all was the National Health Service. As the social policy thinker Richard Titmuss wrote, it was the product of the 'most unsordid act of British social policy in the twentieth cen-tury'.[36] It revolutionized the social meaning of health care. Under the 1911 National Insurance Act, most working-class male breadwinners were compulsorily insured against sickness. Bevan's Act went much further. Health care ceased to be a commodity. It became a public good, fenced off from market forces and available to all who needed it irrespective of their means: an island of solidarity where strangers were bound together by common needs and equal treatment, and where the cash nexus had been abolished. The nationalizations that Morrison lauded had counterparts all over Western Europe. The National Health Service was unique. It was also uniquely popular: as an American observer put it, 'almost part of the constitution'.[37]

We should not idealize the society that nurtured these structures. It was constricting, often unfair and sometimes cruel. A nasty, furtive vein of anti-Semitism still lingered below the surface of polite society, and above the surface lower down the social scale. Open colour preju-dice was rife. Capital punishment was in force. In the terrible words of a judge pronouncing the death sentence, innocent people were sometimes hanged by the neck until they were dead. A particularly shocking example was the execution of Derek Bentley in 1956. Bentley was found guilty of murder after a blatantly unfair trial in which the vindictive and sadistic Lord Chief Justice, Lord Goddard, misdirected the jury. (According to his valet Goddard experienced orgasm when he pronounced death sentences.)[38]

Abortion and homosexuality were illegal. For obvious reasons, no one knew how many pregnancies were terminated illegally, but estimates varied between 40,000 and 200,000 a year. Prosecutions for 'gross indecency' had risen from around 300 a year before the war to around 750 in 1951. A particularly poignant case was that of Alan Turing, one of the world's paramount pioneers of computer science. He deserved the lion's share of the credit for breaking the German naval cipher during the Battle of the Atlantic and had been awarded an OBE. He was elected a Fellow of the Royal Society in 1951 at the age of thirty-nine. A year after his election, he was found guilty of gross indecency. He chose to be chemically castrated (in other words injected with female hormones) in preference to imprisonment; after two tormented years of close surveillance as a security risk he committed suicide in 1954. An official apology fifty-five years later only underlined the malevolence of his treatment at the hands of the country he had served so well.

There was little social mobility. Few working-class children stayed at school beyond fifteen, from 1947 the school-leaving age; only a trickle went to university. Public-school and Oxbridge alumni dominated the professional service elite, though some of its members had been to grammar schools and other universities. All three elites were overwhelmingly male. Margaret Bondfield, the first woman to chair the Trades Union Congress and the first woman Cabinet minister, reached the fringes of the working-class elite, but she never penetrated to its heart. Virginia Woolf, prolific essayist as well as novelist, and the pacifist and feminist campaigner Vera Brittain were both illustrious members of the clerisy, but few, if any, other women could say the same.

A handful of exceptionally able, courageous and self-denying women reached the heights of the public service elite. A few examples give the flavour. One of the most remarkable was Barbara (eventually Baroness) Wootton, economist, socialist, humanist, author, inveterate crosser of academic boundaries and a member of four Royal Commissions during her long and extraordinarily active life. Dame Janet Vaughan, haematologist, radiobiologist and Principal of Somerville College, Oxford, for twenty-two years was another socialist. At the age of eighty she was elected a Fellow of the Royal Society, a distinction that many thought she should have had long before. Dame Margery Perham, a formidable, not to say awe-inspiring fellow of Nuffield College, Oxford, in her later years, started as an academic historian, but 'fell in love with Africa' during a visit to Somaliland, where she hunted big game and rode on patrol with the camel corps. She became one of Britain's most eminent Africanists and a close friend of Lord Lugard, champion of indirect rule in the colonies, whose biography she wrote in two substantial volumes.

In the same category was Dame Evelyn Sharp, who rose to be Permanent Secretary at the Ministry of Housing and Local Government and Whitehall's first woman Permanent Secretary. She had several clashes with her most obstreperous minister, Richard Crossman, but they had a wary respect for each other. A vignette in his diary conveys a sense of the emotional armour that a gifted woman of her generation had to wear to make her way in a man's world.

> She is a biggish woman, about five feet ten inches, with tremendous blue eyes which look right through you, a pale, unmade-up face, uncoloured lips. She is dressed as middle- or upper-class professional women do dress, quite expensively but rather uglily . . . She is rather like Beatrice Webb in her attitude to life, to the Left in the sense of wanting improvement and social justice quite passionately and yet a tremendous patrician and utterly contemptuous and arrogant, regarding local authorities as children which [sic] she has to examine and rebuke for their failures.[39]

Women like these were portents of things to come, but in the early post-war years they were too few to shake male dominance.

KEYNESIAN SOCIAL DEMOCRACY TRIUMPHANT

For all that, the structures gave people something solid and reassuring to hold on to in a harsh world. They strengthened communities, generated loyalties and promoted public trust. They told people who they were and where they belonged, and fostered the values that underpin a civic culture. Like communal rituals ranging from the monarch's Christmas Day broadcasts to the Durham Miners' Galas, from church weddings to the parades of Pearly Kings and Queens, from Whit walks in northern cities to the last night at the Proms, and from the two minutes' silence on Remembrance Day to the Cup Final, they provided a link between the past, present and future: a framework within which individuals of all classes could find meaning, dignity and pride, essential prerequisites of a good life.

They were also the guardian angels of the social and cultural settlement foreshadowed in the darkest years of the Second World War and hammered out after 1945. The state had responded to the shared dangers of wartime by sharing resources on a scale that would have been unthinkable before 1939. Wartime sharing – and, not least, the language of sharing – was carried over into peace. 'Fair shares' became an uncontested trope of public rhetoric. There were plenty of arguments about its practical implications, but hardly anyone disputed the principle. Conservatives, liberals and socialists all agreed that Britain should be a fair society; and that public policy should be directed to that end. The 1944 Education Act making state-funded secondary education free was the brainchild of the Conservative minister R. A. Butler. The laissez-faire picture of the state as a potentially oppressive martinet that should not be allowed to intrude on the lives of its citizens had dissolved in the landing craft pouring troops onto the Normandy beaches, in the munitions factories and blitzed cities of the Home Front, and in the planning for peace that gave the general public reason to hope for better times once the war was over. On the political right as well as on the left Matthew Arnold's alternative vision of the state as 'the nation in its collective and corporate character' held the field.

During the war the Arnoldian state had used its powers with astonishing skill and success. It had rationed food and clothing, evacuated children, conscripted women, controlled industries, fixed prices and profit margins, and achieved a level of mobilization, both of people and of goods, that no other belligerent state had matched. Precisely where the boundaries of the state should lie in the post-war years was moot, but no one thought it should return to the pre-war status quo. In striking contrast to the mood of the twenties, when many hoped to return to the supposedly halcyon years before 1914, no one in the forties and fifties felt nostalgic about the thirties. The great question was how not to go back.

Keynes and Beveridge, the chief pathfinders to the post-war settlement, gave essentially the same answer: the state would make sure that the bad old days were gone for ever. For more than a generation, it did so. Political debate focussed on how, not on why or whether. Left-of-centre and right-of-centre political leaders gave slightly different answers, but despite occasional grumbles among some of their followers the differences were marginal: irrespective of the political complexion of the government in power, the combined effect of the tax and welfare systems made incomes less unequal; unemployment oscillated between a high of 2.1 per cent and a low of 1.2 per cent – figures that Keynes and his wartime associates would have thought inconceivably low.

Few disputed that there was a public interest distinct from private interests, or that the state was duty-bound to pursue it. Equally, hardly anyone denied that citizenship entailed equal social rights as well as equal legal and political ones, while the notion that society was merely a collection of individuals, pursuing their own interests as they saw fit, had no political resonance. Everyday experience, from waiting your turn in a doctor's surgery to travelling on the London Underground or reading in a public library, told the same story: public goods, held in common by the public at large, were fundamental to a good society. The result, as the social theorist T. H. Marshall wrote, was 'a general enrichment of the concrete substance of civilised life'.[40]

In all this, Britain was not alone. When the British looked across the Channel, and even across the Atlantic, they saw a number of different versions of their own settlement. In Truman's (and later Eisenhower's)

United States the essentials of Roosevelt's New Deal remained in place. In France the *économie concertée*, stemming from a centuries-old tradition of state-led economic development, and in Germany the 'social-market economy', stemming from a symbiosis between German economic liberalism and the Catholic social teaching embodied in the Christian Democratic Party, repeated the same themes in different idioms. What French writers later called the '*trente glorieuses*' were in full swing right across the Western world. From the Pacific coasts of Canada and the United States to the Baltic and the Adriatic capitalism had apparently been tamed. Though there were large Communist parties in France and Italy, capitalism's tamers scorned the Communist alternative which had dazzled many in the 1930s, as did most of their fellow citizens. In essence, though rarely in name, a novel Keynesian social democracy,[41] incarnating Karl Popper's vision of a synthesis between security and freedom, was everywhere triumphant.

HUBRIS – AND NEMESIS

Or was it? At this point, my story takes a new turn. As so often in history, success bred hubris. Nemesis came slowly, but inexorably. The story is convoluted; I shall look only at the broad outlines. In the hands of Keynes's disciples in officialdom and the political class, his supple and indeterminate system became a set of tools for unimaginative social engineers. Breathing down the necks of the engineers were political leaders with their eyes fixed on the next election. Economic growth – something to which Keynes had been indifferent – became a mixture of political talisman and virility symbol. In pursuit of electoral victory political leaders promised growth (code for higher living standards) and full employment. Thus, wage bargainers operated in a sellers' market for labour. Not surprisingly, wage inflation followed. To curb it, governments resorted to wage controls, sometimes voluntary and sometimes statutory. In the end, the controls always broke on the rock of trade union opposition, often inspired by rank-and-file resentment of their leaders as much as by hostility to government policy.

The Wilson Government of 1964–70 left office with its wages policy in tatters. The Heath Government of 1970–74 was forced into a humiliating U-turn by a miners' strike in 1972; in 1974 a second miners' strike led Heath to call a general election on the ticket of 'Who Governs?', which he proceeded to lose. The Callaghan Government of 1976–9 ended its term of office in the wake of a devastating wave of unofficial strikes in the harsh winter of 1978–9 (soon known as the 'winter of discontent'), provoked by swelling rank-and-file indignation with yet another wages policy. Governments of both the main parties sought to reform industrial-relations law, so as to make it more difficult to engage in unofficial strikes. Each attempt ended in retreat, confusion and humiliation.

The travails of the governments of the 1970s reflected a crisis of 'stagflation' (an almost unprecedented combination of high unemployment and high inflation) that struck most developed Western countries in that disaster-prone decade. The proximate cause was the oil price hike that followed the Arab–Israeli war of 1973, but it is clear in retrospect that a crisis of the moral and political economies had been waiting to happen for some time. Keynesian economic management could not cope; the managers floundered from one expedient to another. The estimates on which Treasury policy was based were often wildly out.[42] The entire Keynesian paradigm seemed discredited. In 1976, Callaghan pronounced its requiem. The 'cosy world' in which 'we used to think that you could just spend your way out of a recession to increase employment by cutting taxes and boosting Government spending', he told an astonished Labour Party conference, had gone. That option no longer existed; 'insofar as it ever did it only worked by injecting inflation into the economy'.[43] When his Government staggered to its doom in 1979, the Keynesian social democratic settlement was in tatters.

Industrial militancy was only one feature of an ever-more widespread mood that also encompassed rebellious young people protesting against the Vietnam War; a burgeoning women's liberation movement; rock and roll bands; civil-rights campaigners protesting against anti-Catholic discrimination in Northern Ireland; growing nationalist sentiment in Wales and Scotland; and the first stirrings of the Green movement. An emblematic product of this mentality was Germaine Greer's *The Female Eunuch*, a plangent appeal to 'castrated womanhood' to emancipate itself.[44] Another was E. F. Schumacher's

Small is Beautiful,[45] arguing for an economics focussed on human needs instead of on GDP growth. In a haunting phrase, Samuel H. Beer, Harvard Professor of Government, diagnosed a 'romantic revolt' whose themes – the heart before the head; spontaneity before calculation – echoed those of Blake, Wordsworth, Shelley and Goethe.[46]

Romantic or not, revolt was omnipresent. It was not political in any conventional sense. It cut across the dividing lines of ideology; it had nothing to do with parties, or elections or governments. Unlike the crisis of stagflation and the industrial militancy associated with it, it did not pose an overt threat to the Keynesian social-democratic settlement. What it did was to challenge the structures of mid-twentieth-century Britain at their heart. It was a revolt against structure, against conformity, against identities imposed from outside instead of growing authentically within. It was also a revolt against the old elites which personified and presided over the old structures.

HAYEK'S WISTFUL UTOPIA

In the early post-war years, the old elites had walked tall. They thought they deserved well of their country, and on the whole their country had agreed. As the sad and conflicted decade from the late sixties to the late seventies wore on, they could feel the ground shifting beneath their feet, but they did not know how to respond. They were baffled by the crisis of stagflation, and, if anything, more baffled by Beer's romantic revolt. Little by little, they lost their self-belief and with it their authority. Two very different, but parallel streams of doctrine and emotion – one looking to an imaginary past for inspiration and the other to a nebulous future – gradually overwhelmed the culture and structures of mid-century Britain. Despite their differences, these two streams had two crucial points in common. Both were hedonistic, and both were individualistic, albeit in different ways. I shall call them respectively *market* individualism and *moral* individualism. The high priest of the first, the *market* individualism of the right, was Friedrich Hayek; he and his many votaries and associates sought an economic regime based on unfettered competition. The second, *moral* individualism, was vaguely left in rhetoric, but more reminiscent of the antinomians of the sixteenth century, who thought they were exempt from moral rules, than of any coherent ideology. Notable examples of and influences on it included the psychoanalytic therapist R. D. Laing, the social anthropologist Edmund Leach and the critical theorist Herbert Marcuse. It was contemptuous of tradition and hostile to the nuclear family.

The market individualists were first in the field, so I shall look first at them, and particularly at Hayek. He was by no means the only market individualist of note. Others included Milton Friedman, the Chicago-based apostle of monetarist economics; the American Virginia School of public-choice theorists whose members held that state failure was more frequent than market failure; the maverick British Conservative Enoch Powell, whose monetarist philippics against the Heath Government mesmerized the House of Commons (and particularly the Conservative benches) in debate after debate; and Sir Keith Joseph, who recanted the collectivist policies he had pursued as a minister under Heath, and called on the Conservatives to 're-create the conditions which will again permit the forward march of *embourgeoisement* which went so far in Victorian times'.[47] Three think-tanks – the Centre for Policy Studies that Joseph set up in 1974 to 'convert the Tory party',[48] the Institute of Economic Affairs headed by Arthur Seldon and Ralph Harris, and the Adam Smith Institute headed by Madsen Pirie – spread the market individualist message through pamphlets, meetings and assiduous networking. But Hayek's writings were the spring from which almost all market individualists drank.

He was one of the most complex and subtle social thinkers of the age. He was an iconoclast, whose admirers turned him into an icon; a utopian, whose Utopia lay in the past. No brief summary can do him justice. He was born in Vienna in 1899, served briefly in the Austro-Hungarian army towards the end of the First World War, and studied law and economics at the University of Vienna. After research as a junior member of the so-called 'Austrian School' of economics, he was appointed to a chair in economics at the London School of Economics at the age of thirty-two. At LSE, he made a modest name for himself as a professional economist, but he was unknown to the general public. Then, in 1944, he published a passionate, gloom-laden, yet strangely exhilarating tract for the times, *The Road to Serfdom*.[49]

It made him famous overnight. Its pages crackled with barely suppressed rage; its target was the dream of a better, less selfish and more just society that suffused the public culture of wartime Britain. 'Nine out of ten' of the lessons that contemporary reformers drew from the war, he wrote, were 'precisely the lessons which the Germans did learn from the last war and which have done much to produce the Nazi system'. Many of these lessons were socialist: Fascism and Nazism were not, as conventionally assumed, reactions against the socialist trends of the preceding period, but their logical results. Those trends were everywhere visible in Britain. They were the primrose path to tyranny.

Two features of the wartime dream were particularly obnoxious to Hayek. The first was the insidious call for economic planning to replace the 'blind' forces of the market. Market forces *were* blind: that was their beauty. They reflected the innumerable, unpredictable choices of individual buyers and sellers operating under the rule of law, the 'great achievement of the liberal age'. In a planned economy, the rule of law would cease to exist. It was manifested in general rules which were not aimed at 'the wants and needs of particular people', but in a planned economy the state would have to address such wants and needs as they arose. It would have to choose which of them should have priority over others. Its choices would be arbitrary and ad hoc; and they would have to be imposed on the people by state coercion. Planning promised security, but it would deliver 'the security of the barracks'.

Equally obnoxious was the deliberate disparagement of 'all activities involving economic risk'. These too were characteristically German. Even in Britain, the younger generation had grown up in a world where commerce had come to seem disreputable. In Germany that attitude had gone much further. The widely held view that German militarism was due to the excessive influence of the armed forces was over-simplified. In truth, it stemmed from the widespread belief that it was better to be a functionary than an entrepreneur. (Though they would not have called themselves 'functionaries' this was what most of the professional service elite did believe.) Historically, the supreme British virtue had been a 'cultivation of the spontaneous'. Tragically, collectivism was progressively destroying the institutions and traditions that had embodied it. For a foreign admirer of the English genius it was 'one of the most disheartening spectacles of our time to see to what extent some of the most precious things which England has given to the world are now held in contempt in England herself'.

Six years after *The Road to Serfdom* was published, Hayek left the LSE, first for the United States and then for Germany. Two magisterial works appeared after his departure from Britain, *The Constitution of Liberty* in 1960 and the three volumes of *Law, Legislation and Liberty* between 1973 and 1979. They lacked the dashing *brio* of *The Road to Serfdom*, but partly because of their ponderous intricacy they became the lodestars of the market-individualist flotilla. Yet their message was more ambiguous than it seemed at first sight. Some of the themes of *The Road to Serfdom* reappeared, in a more elaborate form – chief among them the notion of 'spontaneous orders' brought about by human action but not by human design. Law and language were spontaneous orders; and so, above all, were markets. No authority designed, or could conceivably have designed, any of them. They emerged from unplanned, uncontrolled and uncontrollable human interactions over long centuries. As such, they were nurseries of freedom and of human flourishing.

Because of this, socialist strictures on the market order were not just misconceived; they were profoundly dangerous. Indeed, the watered-down post-war socialism that had replaced the red-blooded socialism of earlier decades was more dangerous than its predecessor. Socialists had abandoned their old dream of nationalization, but their new dream of a redistributive welfare state posed as grave a threat to the spontaneous order of the marketplace. Such a state would have to discriminate between its citizens in order 'to insure that particular people get particular things'. In doing so, it would inevitably 'lead back to socialism and its coercive and essentially arbitrary methods'.

The philosophical justification for state redistribution, Hayek declared, was a tissue of absurdities. Redistribution was supposed to achieve social justice, but there was no such thing. It was 'a mirage', a 'quasi-religious superstition'. It had nothing in common with 'the principles of just individual conduct' that classical liberalism had extolled. Unlike individual persons, whole societies could not be just or unjust: societies were not people. In a free society, with free competition, by definition uncontrolled by any single will, outcomes were the unsought consequences of myriads of independent transactions. Some people did well, others did badly. But this was not the result of merit or demerit; it was the result of a mass of free exchanges between autonomous economic agents responding to market signals. In such an order, there could be 'no answer to the question of *who* has been unjust'. Though the term social justice was vacuous, however, attempts to secure it were not vacuous at all: they struck at the heart of a free society. The distributive justice that socialists sought could not be reconciled with the rule of law; its pursuit stemmed from 'the atrocious idea that political power ought to determine the material position of the different individuals and groups'.

The Hayek of these strident negations concealed a sadder, more wistful Hayek, whose social vision was essentially tragic. Central to it was the notion of what he called the 'Great Society': a society without a single, directing centre that had evolved over long millennia. That society, with its spontaneous orders, was not just unsought; in a profound sense it was unwanted. The freedom it gave to its members had a bitter taste. The impersonal, general rules that guaranteed it ran counter to many of humanity's deepest instincts. For 50,000 generations *Homo sapiens* had roamed the earth in small face-to-face bands; in these human beings had developed the neural structure they still possessed.

The transition from these hunter-gatherer bands to urban civilization and eventually to the Great Society entailed a wrenching, acutely painful break with the values learned during the long millennia since the species had first appeared. Because it was so painful, the break was incomplete. The values of the small group are still deeply embedded in our natures; the impersonal, general rules of the Great Society which have been superimposed on them seem thin and bloodless by comparison. Our hearts tell us to go back to the morality of the small group; only our heads tell us to resist. In the battle between head and heart, the latter all too often wins: hence socialism and all its manifold temptations. However, we cannot go back. Whether we like it or not – and most of us don't – we are caught in the iron cage of the Great Society.[50] That is our tragedy.

There is also a second tragedy. Hayek puts it like this. We did not design the market order. We stumbled into it. Its extraordinary growth was made possible by the gradual spread of rules learned by 'a population consisting chiefly of independent farmers, artisans and merchants and their servants and apprentices who shared the daily experiences of their masters'. These

> held an ethos that esteemed the prudent man, the good husbandman and provider who looked after the future of his family and his business by building up capital, guided less by the desire to be able to consume much than by the wish to be regarded as successful by his fellows who pursued similar aims . . .
>
> At present, however, an ever increasing part of the population of the Western World grow up as members of large organizations and thus as strangers to those rules of the market which have made the great open society possible. To them the market economy is largely incomprehensible; they have never practised the rules on which it rests and its results seem to them irrational and immoral.[51]

Hayek's Utopia was the lost age of the prudent man, building up capital to win the approval of like-minded fellows, but he held out no hope of a return to it. On his showing, the onward march of large organizations and their denizens was irresistible. There was no way out of the collectivist age with its superstitious dreams of economic planning, just distribution, freedom from repression and permissive education, beyond a certain stoic irony. Man, he wrote, *'is not and never will be the master of his fate; his very reason always progresses by leading him into the unknown and unforeseen where he learns new things'* (italics in the original).

There was a paradox in all this which still lies at the heart of the market individualist world-view. For Hayek, the philosopher of market individualism, stoic irony had an alluring grandeur about it. For market individualists embroiled in struggles for power and political support, like the think-tankers and politicians mentioned above, it would have been a fatal handicap. For them, the task was to retrieve the lost Utopia of the market order; and that meant retrieving the values that had sustained it. Only one agency could do this: a powerful and intrusive state. In Andrew Gamble's language, 'the strong state' would be both midwife and nursemaid of 'the free economy'.[52]

But this strong state would be quite different from the Arnoldian state of the post-war era. To use a phrase coined by the legal philosopher and historian Philip Bobbitt it would be a 'market state'[53] resolutely sweeping away the cultural and institutional obstacles to a market order.

As later chapters will show, the story of Britain's moral and political economies since the collapse of the Keynesian social-democratic settlement is, in essence, the story of how this paradox played out. For the moment, what matters is that it did not weaken the drive and élan of Hayekian market individualism; if anything, it strengthened them. The contest between market individualism and the post-war order was, in reality, no contest. The old elites and their ethos had lost the battle before it started. Policy makers, like nature, abhor a vacuum. Hayekian market individualism rushed in to fill the vacuum of doctrine and policy that the crisis of stagflation brought in its train. In England, though not in Scotland or Wales, it still holds the field. Though Hayek was no Mammon worshipper, and though few Mammon worshippers read Hayek, his ideas lent a spurious respectability to Mammon worship. They also underpin a public doctrine that rules out any but cosmetic changes to the existing order.

MORAL INDIVIDUALISTS ON THE MARCH

The moral-individualist story is more complicated. Improbably, it starts at the beginning of the last century, in the elegant surroundings of Cambridge University. There the young philosopher G. E. Moore wrote the most famous book of his long career, *Principia Ethica*. Moore was a captivating figure; 'beautiful and slim', according to Bertrand Russell, and with 'an intellect as passionate as Spinoza's'.[54] He was a member of the Cambridge Conversazione Society, commonly known as the Apostles, a self-selected coterie of the cleverest undergraduates and dons from the grandest colleges. The Apostles took *Principia Ethica* to their hearts; Keynes, who was one of them, remembered later that it had seemed 'exciting, exhilarating, the beginning of a renaissance, the opening of a new heaven on a new earth'.[55] The new heaven was very different from the old heaven of the Victorian clerisy and their twentieth-century successors. It was a private, almost narcissistic place, with no room for arduous struggle in the public sphere or for an ideal of civic virtue. For Moore, only states of mind were valuable in themselves, and the most valuable were 'the pleasures of human intercourse and the enjoyment of beautiful things'. Morality was individual, not collective. What mattered was unflinching private honesty, not the strenuous discharge of public duty.

Mooreite ethical narcissism flowed, by way of the Apostles, into the Bloomsbury Group of *avant garde* artists and writers, who called themselves 'Bloomsberries'. Only a small minority embraced full-blooded Mooreism (Virginia Woolf and E. M. Forster are examples), but thanks in large part to the 'Bloomsberries' it helped to shape the culture of twentieth-century Britain. Its effect on biographical fashion was particularly marked. The 'tombstone' biographies of the nineteenth century, such as the life of Gladstone by the Liberal statesman John Morley and the life of Lord Salisbury by his daughter, Lady Gwendolen Cecil, were written in the spirit of Ecclesiastes: 'let us now praise famous men'. The underlying assumption was that activity in the public sphere was inherently worthy and public men admirable.

However, the age of the tombstone biographers came to a shuddering halt at the end of the First World War, when Keynes's friend and fellow Apostle Lytton Strachey published his iconoclastic bestseller *Eminent Victorians*, a collection of sparkling, mocking and sometimes cruel biographical essays on nineteenth-century worthies ranging from Cardinal Manning to Florence Nightingale. Unlike many bestsellers, it left an enduring mark on the public culture. It epitomized a post-war mood of scepticism about the pretensions of the famous. For the sceptics, the public sphere ceased to be a realm where honourable men engaged in worthy activity, and became an arena for coarse-grained and self-serving egoists.

In style, the moral individualists of the second half of the twentieth century could hardly have been more different from the 'Bloomsberries', but their values were closer to Moore's than met the eye. For them too self-deception was the only sin, and they too thought the structures of the past fettered the human spirit. They had no great teacher like Hayek or Moore to look up to, and no coherent doctrine commanded their allegiance. They scattered their fire over a multitude of superficially unrelated targets. Yet certain themes appeared again and again, albeit in a variety of different idioms. Like the Apostles and the 'Bloomsberries' they were for sincerity and authenticity above all; they prided themselves on facing unpalatable truths without fear or favour; and they delighted in rubbing society's faces in such truths as rudely as they could.

A favourite target was the family. For R. D. (Ronald David) Laing, families were the breeding grounds of schizophrenia. Laing grew up in a tenement block in south Glasgow and started his career as a conventional clinical psychiatrist. He soon switched to psychoanalysis, however; and as a psychoanalytic therapist, gripping lecturer and prolific writer he became a cult figure for the rebellious young of the 1960s. As such, he experimented avidly with LSD, and lauded cannabis as 'simply a delightful experience'. (In view of what we now know about the connection between cannabis and schizophrenia this was an astonishingly irresponsible thing for a therapist to say.) Madness, Laing wrote, was 'a sane response to an insane situation'. Orthodox psychiatrists were 'mind police'; the hospitals in which their patients were incarcerated were prisons. Mothers were particularly blameworthy. 'The initial act of brutality against the average child', he exclaimed in an Institute of Contemporary Arts lecture in 1964, 'is the mother's first kiss.'[56] The true role of the family was to brainwash the children, so as to 'turn them into imbeciles like ourselves'. Tragically the enterprise was successful.

> By the time the new human being is fifteen or so, we are left with a being like ourselves. A half-crazed creature, more or less adjusted to a mad world . . .
>
> The Family's function is to repress Eros: to induce a false consciousness of security: to deny death by avoiding life: to cut off transcendence: to believe in God, not to experience the Void: to create, in short, one-dimensional man: to promote respect, conformity, obedience: to con children out of play: to induce a fear of failure: to promote a respect for work: to promote a respect for 'respectability' . . .
>
> This is also known as selling one's birthright for a mess of pottage.[57]

Schizophrenics were those who refused to sell their birthrights. Their 'voyage' was not an illness to be cured: it was a 'natural way of healing our own appalling state of alienation called normality'.[58]

In his notorious 1967 Reith Lectures, Edmund Leach, Provost of King's College, Cambridge, added a non-too-subtle coda. Despite the god-like powers science had given us, he insisted, we were trapped in a vicious circle of fear of and violence towards 'the *other*'. In the eighteenth century, mad 'others' had been caged 'like wild beasts'. Even now criminals, lunatics and the senile were shut away from society and subjected to 'unconstrained' violence. Worse yet, present-day society was marked by 'rabid hostility' towards the young. From all sides, British youth was accused of being 'wild beasts with whom we cannot communicate'. But, in truth, the young were blameless. They were right to rebel against the conformist absurdities of their parents' generation. The true author of society's ills was the isolated modern family, unsupported by neighbours or kinsfolk, where 'parents and children huddled together in their loneliness', fought each other. Not only were the young right to rebel against their parents, but they were also right to reject the 'out-of-date clutter' purveyed by traditional scholarship. The over forty-fives were not fit to teach anybody anything. 'Only those who hold the past in complete contempt are ever likely to see visions of the New Jerusalem'. History was bunk, and so were its teachers.

Herbert Marcuse – an émigré from Nazi Germany to the United States in the 1930s, and another cult figure of the 1960s – went further. For him, the entire Keynesian social-democratic settlement was bunk. As much as free-market capitalism, it was based on repression, on the denial of Eros and the supremacy of Thanatos, Freud's death instinct. The powers that be had 'a deep affinity to death; death is a token of unfreedom, of defeat'.[59] That quotation comes from *Eros and Civilization*, first published in 1956; in it Marcuse held out a vague and cloudily expressed hope that the chains of Thanatos might be broken and a utopian future of erotic bliss assured. In *One-Dimensional Man*, published eight years later, he was more gloomy.[60] The welfare state was a warfare state; the '*trente glorieuses*' were not glorious at all. They were stifling and dehumanizing. They had given birth to a 'one-dimensional society': a society that squashed potential rebellions 'with Technology rather than Terror'.

The one-dimensional society was the realm of a 'one-dimensional man', alienated, regimented, cosseted and manipulated. Even sexuality had become an instrument of repression. Libido had extended its sway, but Eros had been denied. The rampant sexuality of contemporary novels and films was 'wild and obscene', and therefore harmless. The traditional working class offered no hope; it had become a force for repression instead of for revolt. Salvation could come, if at all, only from the 'substratum of the outcasts and outsiders, the exploited and persecuted of other races and other colours, the unemployed and the unemployable'.[61] It was among them that authenticity was to be found, and through them that the society of repressive tolerance might, just possibly, be overturned.

Much of this belonged to the realm of fantasy. Laing's unverified (and unverifiable) belief that schizophrenia was bred by the family has inflicted great harm on suffering people. His rhetoric about stone-age babies and the brutality of the mother's kiss encouraged disturbed young people to become even more disturbed. In a minor key, the same was true of Leach's cringing attempt to side with the young against the old and the ignorant against the knowledgeable. Most fantastic of all was Marcuse's cloudy melange of Marx and Freud, with its implied message that the young were denied the erotic bliss that was their due, and that their only hope was to drop out of a Thanatos-dominated society and make common cause with the outcast and the marginal.

But even fantastic ideas matter, and these ideas mattered more than appears at first sight. Robert Skidelsky's summation of the mood of the time is a little indulgent but it is a valuable corrective to the condescension of posterity.

> Anyone who was young in the 1950s and 1960s is bound to be ambivalent about the fruits of progress. Conservatives have attacked these decades as a mere outburst of egotism and licence, but they were more than that, at least in self-perception. There was hope – naïve in retrospect, but sincere at the time – that the unleashing of erotic energy would create a new form of community based not on power or money but on love (a version of the old Christian fellowship, only with sex and drugs added) and unlock creative powers repressed by convention and class. This was absurd, of course, but it is better to be a deluded

romantic when young than cynical from the start, like the subsequent generations so often seem to be.[62]

That mood helped to fuel Beer's romantic revolt. It hung in the air over the student rebellions of the 1960s that spread across the developed West, from Berkeley to Berlin and from the Sorbonne to Stanford. But it was more complicated than Skidelsky's summation suggests. The student rebels were lyrically communitarian, but at the same time hyper-individualistic. The communities of love were self-chosen; that was part of the point. As such, they were shifting, fluid and evanescent. The rebels' legacy is correspondingly complex. Britain is a far kinder and more tolerant place today than it was at the mid-point of the last century: to take just one example, gay marriage would have seemed both loathsome and inconceivable sixty years ago. There can be no proof, but it seems probable that the rebels of forty years ago helped to foster the cultural changes which led eventually to the more tolerant climate of today. Yet the rebels' world-view was fundamentally solipsistic. For them, the individual was the solitary captain of her own soul, steering by her own, unique moral compass. She was entitled to make whatever choices she wished, without regard to conventional restraints or old traditions. Albeit in an attenuated form, these assumptions entered the bloodstream of the public culture. Their legacy can still be detected in almost every sphere of life, from the most intimate to the most public.

BROTHERS BENEATH THE SKIN

As that implies, market and moral individualists were brothers beneath the skin. For both, individual satisfaction was sacrosanct and both railed against collective constraints. Both disdained the bonds of community. Both were quintessentially utopian, dreaming of an impossible future of perfect freedom. Both forgot that the deliberate pursuit of happiness invariably disappoints: that happiness is a by-product of attempts to reach other, less banal, goals. Above all, both were enmeshed in paradox. The first stood for libertarian individualism in the economy, but for order in a limited state and traditional morality in personal conduct. The second championed order in the economy, but libertarian individualism in the personal sphere. Market individualists assumed that free choice in the economy would go hand in hand with respect for traditional morality. Moral individualists assumed that the ethic of 'doing your own thing' could be confined to the private sphere, while economic life was organized on (unspecified) collectivist lines. Not surprisingly, both assumptions turned out to be false. Hedonism was indivisible.

For both groups, the old elites and the old values they adhered to were patronizing and discriminatory. For market individualists there were no such things as fair shares, a fair price or a fair wage; as Hayek taught, the notion of social justice was a 'mirage'. The market was self-validating. Whatever consumers wanted and entrepreneurs could supply, they were entitled to get. Moral individualists reached essentially the same destination by a different route. As the Communist historian Eric Hobsbawm later wrote of the rebellious young of the 1960s, 'they did not seem to be much interested in a *social* ideal . . . as distinct from the individualist ideal of getting rid of anything that claimed the right and power to stop you doing whatever your ego and id felt like doing'.[63] Old moral codes, old authorities and old loyalties, they insisted, should not be allowed to stand in their way. If the results included family breakdown, drug addiction and media prurience that could not be helped.

Gradually, the old elites were humbled, while the old structures dissolved or lost their authority. Slowly, incompletely, but unmistakably, today's hedonistic and relativist culture elbowed aside the old culture of honour and duty. The ties that had bound began to fray, most obviously the ties of family and faith. Where 90 per cent of infants had been baptized in the early post-war years, the 2011 census showed that only 55 per cent were self-described Christians while 40 per cent professed no religion at all. The traditional family came under increasing strain. Between 1980 and 2005, the number of births outside marriage rose from 12 per cent of the total to 43 per cent. Over a quarter of the marriages of 1971 ended in divorce after twenty years as against 2 per cent of the marriages of 1926 and 7 per cent of the marriages of 1951. The proportion of children living in single-parent households tripled between the early 1970s and the mid-2000s. Jobs were no longer for life (not that they had been for life before the long post-war boom). Trade union membership and party affiliation plummeted along with churchgoing. For a while, the heir to the throne became a figure of fun. The judiciary was subject to incessant attack by politicians and the media. MPs were found with their hands in the till. The civil service and the professions remained in being, and still attracted excellent recruits. But they lost their mystique.

The fall of the old elites did not usher in a non-elitist nirvana. All that happened was that new elites, most of whose members had little or no sense of public duty, took their place. Money and celebrity became society's chief yardsticks of merit and achievement, endlessly celebrated by gawping media. Murdoch's *Sun*; television programmes like *Who Wants to be a Millionaire?* and *The Apprentice*; endless media gossip about the love lives of famous footballers; the *Sunday Times* rich list; and the honours bestowed on Paul Ruddock, Alan Sugar, Richard Branson, Michael Levy and Philip Green all purveyed the same message: the rich were better than the poor and the very rich better than the rich. The rich and famous were the best of all. One of the results is a thin, intellectually and morally impoverished culture of amnesia. To that I turn in the next chapter.

3

Amnesia Conquers History

How selfish soever man may be supposed, there are evidently
some principles in his nature, which interest him in the fortune
of others, and render their happiness necessary to him, though
he derives nothing from it, except pleasure of seeing it ... That
we often derive sorrow from the sorrows of others, is a matter
of fact too obvious to require any instances to prove it; for this
sentiment, like all the other original passions of human nature,
is by no means confined to the virtuous and humane ... The
greatest ruffian, the most hardened violator of the laws of
society, is not altogether without it.

Adam Smith, *The Theory of*
Moral Sentiments, 1759

W. G. Sebald's masterpiece, *Austerlitz*, paints a harrowing picture of the psychic devastation that amnesia can bring. On the eve of the Second World War the hero, Jacques Austerlitz, then rising five, arrives at Liverpool Street Station on a *Kindertransport* carrying Jewish children from German-occupied Prague. He is brought up by fundamentalist Christian foster parents, who treat him as their son and cause him to erase his memories of his past. He forgets his native Czech; he forgets his early years in Prague; and he has only faint and fleeting memories of his real parents. In a profound sense he is a lost soul. He doesn't know where he came from, or who he is. Eventually he finds out, but his journey to discover his past is long, traumatic and anguished. When the novel ends we can't tell if he will recover.

What has Sebald's novel to do with present-day Britain? The answer is simple: everything. *Austerlitz* is fiction, but it is also a metaphor for fact. Extreme amnesia is one of the worst fates that can befall an individual human being. It can mean loss of personality; loss of communication; and loss of identity. The same applies to societies, indeed to countries and to nations. A nation that forgets – or is forced to forget – its history ceases to be a nation. True, national histories are political constructs, subject to contestation and revision, not unassailable truths; the sites of memory that evoke them are chosen to convey a message and not just to tell a story. But this does not affect the central point. Partial and contestable though they are, national histories are a fundamental part of nationhood. That is why conquerors, from ancient Babylonians to modern Israelis, so often try to erase the histories of the conquered, and why the conquered, from exiled Jews to dispossessed Palestinians, try desperately to cling to them. Without their histories, peoples perish.

LOST SOULS

That thought gives the story I told in the last chapter a new dimension. Mid-twentieth-century Britain was a homogeneous, history-heavy, union state. It was made up of four nations (five if you count the two communities of Northern Ireland as separate nations), but though these had their own, proud histories, they shared the overarching history of the Union. Britain was largely Christian, largely Protestant, and overwhelmingly white. It was also imperial. In the early post-war years, the myths and symbols of the empire on which the sun had never set were everywhere. Regimental battle honours from half-forgotten colonial wars, Rudyard Kipling's Indian tales, G. A. Henty's schoolboy adventure stories, the ties of ethnicity that bound the 'mother country' to the self-governing white Dominions, and globes still spattered with red[1] all told an imperial story. So did the four-mile long Victory Parade through London in June 1946, with its detachments from India, the colonial empire and the self-governing Dominions, and with Commonwealth prime ministers such as Mackenzie King of Canada and Field Marshal Smuts of South Africa on the reviewing stand. For at least 200 years, empire had been of Britain's essence, and for the moment it still was.

Except in Northern Ireland, the divide between the manual working class and the rest of the population was much more obtrusive than any national divides; and for most of the time the class divide was transcended by a common feeling of Britishness. One reason was that the history of the British working class was one of collaboration as much as of confrontation. Working-class Toryism – a fiercely patriotic and earthy tradition – left as strong an impress on the British labour movement as did working-class liberalism or socialism. ('Blue Labour' is its latest manifestation.) In truth, Britain never had a sharply defined, cohesive working class of the sort that the German and Swedish social democrats mobilized in their respective countries. In Britain there were a number of different working classes, with different histories, spawned by the sporadic, unsystematic, higgledy-piggledy evolution of the country's industries. A vast gulf of status and income divided highly skilled groups like engineers, shipbuilders, printers, building tradesmen, and boot and shoe operatives, arrayed on high days and holidays in good coats and large watch chains, from unskilled gas workers, dockers and farm labourers.[2] The Labour movement was an extraordinary patchwork quilt, defying logic and making nonsense of tidy generalizations. In some places, at some times, it roared like a lion. In other places at other times, it cooed like a dove. Its leaders sometimes talked of social transformation, but what it really wanted was *recognition*: a place in the sun. Thanks partly to Ernest Bevin and partly to the impersonal imperatives of total war, it won that prize under the Churchill wartime coalition. It kept it for most of the post-war period.

The old elites that helped to win it the prize were steeped in history. The clerisy and the professional service elite were acutely conscious of their membership of a centuries-old tradition of thought and imagination, going back to ancient Athens and Rome, not to speak of ancient Jerusalem. Their members had been taught Greek and Latin from an early age and most of them spoke at least one living continental European language as well. Many spoke several. The majestic cadences of the King James Bible were lodged deep in their minds. When Beveridge wrote of slaying the giants of 'Want, Ignorance, Idleness, Squalor and Disease' he might have been an Old Testament prophet denouncing sacrilegious kings. In 1945, when the future head of the Foreign Office, Sir Orme Sargent, wrote that Britain was 'the Lepidus in the triumvirate with Mark Antony and Augustus' he could be sure that his fellow mandarins would understand the allusion. Much the same was true of the working-class elite. Though Ernest Bevin never worked in a mine or factory or on a dockside, and became a trade union organizer by accident, he was wonderfully sensitive to the quirks and contradictions of working-class history; and as Foreign Secretary he talked of great predecessors such as 'Old Palmerston' and 'Old Salisbury' as though he had known them personally. ('Old Palmerston' was a particular favourite.) Aneurin Bevan and Arthur Horner never forgot the Marxist history they had encountered as young men, though Bevan rejected direct industrial action for parliamentary politics at an early stage in his career.

The same was true of many (though not all) of the structures of mid-century. The origins of marriage and the family were lost in the mists of time. The Church of England certainly dated from Henry VIII's break with Rome, and uncertainly from 597 CE when Augustine, the Pope's emissary to England and later the first Archbishop of Canterbury, landed on the shores of Kent. As every schoolgirl used to know, the English Parliament, which had effectively taken over the Scottish Parliament in 1707, was founded by Simon de Montfort in the thirteenth century. (Few realized that he was a French nobleman as well as an English one.) The House of Windsor was an ersatz creation, dating only from 1917, when the royals thought it politic to abandon their true surname (Saxe-Coburg-Gotha) in favour of an English one. However, the monarchy as an institution could plausibly claim to date from 1660, when the short-lived, but astonishingly creative English experiment in republican rule came to an end.[3] Less plausibly it claimed descent from William the Conqueror and even from obscure Saxon warlords before the Norman Conquest. The Co-operative movement claimed descent from the Rochdale Pioneers in the 1840s. The Trades Union Congress was founded in 1868. Bevin's Transport and General Workers' Union was descended from Ben Tillett's Tea Operatives' and General Labourers' Union founded in

1887 and the National Union of General and Municipal Workers from Will Thorne's Gas and General Workers' Union founded in 1889. Most of the big private-sector firms mentioned in the last chapter were newer, though Courtaulds was founded in the eighteenth century. However, they were all part of the social as well as the economic landscape.

Now all is changed: 'changed utterly' as Yeats's immortal line in 'Easter 1916' puts it. (Whether a 'terrible beauty' has been born is a matter of opinion.) The empire has vanished and the myths and symbols that once sustained and were sustained by it are barely memories. As the last chapter showed, Britain has become a post-Christian rather than a Christian country. Though the Muslim proportion of the population is well below those of France and the Netherlands, it has risen from 3.0 per cent of the total to 5.0 per cent since 2001. Britain is still largely white, but no longer overwhelmingly so. The 2011 census shows that 86 per cent of the population of England and Wales is white, down from 91 per cent in 2001. More than a million people are of mixed race. In London less than half the total population is white.

Though the union state survives, its future is more uncertain than at any time since the dark days of 1940. For the first time in more than 300 years a Scottish Parliament sits in Edinburgh. For the first time ever a Welsh Assembly or Senedd sits in Cardiff. At the moment of writing, the Scottish National Party, which stands for Scottish independence, has a majority in the Edinburgh Parliament; a referendum on Scottish Secession from the United Kingdom is due in September 2014; Plaid Cymru (the 'Party of Wales') is the third Welsh party, but from 2007 to 2011 it was the second; as such it joined a coalition government with Labour. Irrespective of the outcome of the Scottish referendum, the union is unlikely to survive for much longer in its present form. The two non-English nations of Great Britain are moving further and further away from England, in popular sentiment as well as in public policy. As a result, the union state is no longer the unquestioned focus for the loyalties of the political communities over which it presides. What Abraham Lincoln once called 'the mystic chords of memory'[4] no longer hold the peoples of Great Britain and Northern Ireland together. On the contrary, they pull them apart.

A greater uncertainty hangs over the future relationship between Britain's union state and the core states of the European Union. On the right, a myth of glorious, insular self-sufficiency swamps memories of the long centuries of British involvement in the cultural, religious, ideological, political and military history of the European mainland. To read the tabloid press or listen to Eurosceptic speeches in the House of Commons, one would think that the Dutchman William of Orange had never been King of England; that George I had not been a German princeling; that the *echt* Englishman, George Orwell, had not fought in the Spanish Civil War alongside Spanish republicans and against Spanish Fascists; and that hundreds of thousands of British men and women had not been killed in world wars triggered by ethnic conflicts in East/Central Europe. The myth of insular self-sufficiency has little appeal to the centre and the left, but neither of them has challenged it emotionally or ideologically. In the debate over Britain's future relationship with the continent of which she is part, Europhobes speak to the heart and Europhiles only to the head. 'Brexit', British secession from the European Union, is no longer a distant dream for some and an equally distant nightmare for others; it is a real possibility. If it happens, the odds on the survival of the union state will be poor: Scotland and Wales would probably wish to stay in the European Union even if England and Northern Ireland seceded.

Most of the apparently solid structures of the post-war period have fallen on evil days; some have disappeared. The monarchy is in better fettle than it was a decade ago, and the Church of England can still voice the conscience of the English nation in a way that no other institution can match. Yet as the last chapter showed, marriage and the family are in a parlous state. Trades unionism barely exists outside the public sector. The nationalized industries that Herbert Morrison lauded have been sold off. (By one of the strangest ironies of recent times, however, RBS, Northern Rock and Lloyds TSB were effectively nationalized to stave off total failure during the 2008 credit crunch. A further irony was Virgin Money's subsequent takeover of Northern Rock.) Of the big private-sector firms of mid-twentieth-century Britain, only Harland and Wolff survives. Cars are still manufactured in Britain, but by Japanese firms. Corus, the successor to British Steel, itself the successor to the great private steel companies of seventy years ago, has been taken over by an Indian conglomerate.

The British no longer know where they have come from or who they are. The very word 'British' has become problematic. In Scotland and Wales older identities, long antedating the creation of the British state and empire, have come in from the cold. There are signs – tentative and uncertain for the moment – that something similar is starting to happen in England. The British, insofar as they still exist, are becoming a people of Austerlitzes: confident enough on the outside, lost souls beneath. One reason is that the changes described in the last three paragraphs have swept away the moorings of custom, practice and shared morality that gave the notions of 'British' and 'Britishness' an anchorage in public sentiment. Another is that the market and moral individualists, who undermined the elites and structures of mid-century Britain, repudiated history. They did so in very different ways. Market individualists constructed a strange kind of anti-history: the history of a quasi-biblical 'Fall' from rigorous individualistic virtue to sloppy collectivist vice. Moral individualists shared an uneasy contempt for history as such, and above all for collective histories. For them, individuals were free-floating, tradition-less and history-lite, free of the bonds of the past and with no obligations to the future. But these differences hardly mattered. What did matter was that both groups scorned the histories that had made mid-century Britain what it was. The cultural revolution they helped to inspire was a revolution against history, memory and shared identity: tailor-made for the history-less new elites of money and celebrity.

The end result has been a tense, febrile society, in which the past is not just a foreign country, but an inconceivably distant one. The human need for continuity is flouted at point after point. Even in churches, the magical seventeenth-century prose of the King James Bible is rarely heard; it has been replaced by the tedious committee-speak of the Revised Standard Version and its 'New Revised' successor. (In fairness it should be noted that the King James Bible was itself the work of a committee.) History is still taught in schools, but only just. In any case, most schoolchildren encounter it as a random collection of unrelated topics: Henry VIII this year, the Holocaust next. Everywhere the hunt is on for a mysterious entity known as 'relevance' – a meaningless concept, better rendered as 'fashionable'. An incurious 'presentism' – combining a lack of historical sense, a pervasive contempt for the wisdom of the past, a fascination with novelty simply because it is new and a propensity to over-react to every ephemeral focus-group finding or tabloid whim – saturates public debate and shapes policy-making. History no longer counts; life started yesterday, or at the very most the day before yesterday. The tinny 'Young Country' and 'Cool Britannia' rhetorics of the New Labour regime when it came into power were particularly depressing cases in point. Unhistorical studies of globalization and the 'Third Way' have poured from the presses. Idealistic protesters and volunteers, committed to radical change, all too often imagine that sincerity and passion can change the world with no help from historical understanding.

As for policy making, a notable example of presentism is the Private Finance Initiative, a costly mechanism for funding public projects by mortgaging the future, which has burdened many hospital trusts with heavy debts and in some cases bankrupted them. Other examples include the flood of ill-considered anti-terror laws that followed 9/11, and repeated attempts to reconstruct the health and education services. (I shall have more to say about these in the next chapter.) However, the Iraq and Afghanistan wars are the grossest examples of what presentism means in practice. No one with any knowledge of the murky manoeuvres that carved what is now Iraq out of the defeated Ottoman Empire after the First World War could possibly have thought it a good idea to try, by force of arms, to turn that artificial, riven state into a beacon of democracy for the Middle East. No one who had studied the defeats inflicted on British forces in Afghanistan in the nineteenth century would willingly have dispatched troops, with no knowledge of the local languages and culture, to that harsh terrain with its warrior ethos. Was there really no one in the White House or No. 10 Downing Street who remembered Kipling?

> When you're wounded and left on Afghanistan's plains,
> and the women come out to cut up what remains,
> jest roll to your rifle and blow out your brains
> and go to your Gawd like a soldier.

ECONOMICS ABANDONS HISTORY

Not many bankers, hedge fund strategists or economics professors have blown out their brains on Afghanistan's plains, but as I shall try to show in the rest of this chapter, presentism has had a more baleful effect on policy towards, and debate about, the mesmerizing mysteries of the financial sector than on anything else. For the great economists of the past, from Adam Smith to John Maynard Keynes, economics was essentially a historical, philosophical and moral discipline. Smith was a moral philosopher before he was an economist. (He was Professor of Moral Philosophy at Glasgow University.) The book that made him famous was his *The Theory of Moral Sentiments*, from which I took the epigraph to this chapter. Smith's great insight was that the division of labour boosted productivity and therefore 'opulence'. Yet in *The Wealth of Nations* he savaged its effects on workers who spent their whole lives 'in performing a few simple operations' and in doing so became 'as stupid and ignorant as it is possible for a human creature to become'.[5] More generally, his moral philosophy and economics were both grounded in a sweeping historical narrative, beginning with the fall of the Roman Empire, and taking in the growth of towns in the later Middle Ages, the discovery of America and the banks of early-modern Amsterdam, to mention only a few.

The so-called 'historical school' predominated in nineteenth-century German economics. In early-twentieth-century America, historically oriented 'institutionalists' such as Thorstein Veblen and John Rogers Commons were leading figures in academic economics. In nineteenth-century Cambridge, economics was originally part of the Moral Sciences Tripos. Henry Sidgwick, one of the greatest moral philosophers of the age, was also an economist. William Cunningham, a belligerent disciple of the German historical school, and one of the founding fathers of economic history as an academic subject, taught both economics and history at Cambridge in the late nineteenth century, and held a chair in economics at King's College London. A passage in one of his journal articles should be emblazoned on the walls of every modern economics department.

The underlying assumption against which I wish to protest is . . . that the same motives have been at work in all ages, and have produced similar results, and that, therefore, it is possible to formulate economic laws which describe the action of economic causes at all times and in all places.[6]

Alfred Marshall, one of Keynes's heroes and perhaps the greatest British economist of the late nineteenth and early twentieth centuries, differed sharply from Cunningham, but he too was influenced by the German historical school as well as by a moral commitment to understand the causes of poverty and its degrading consequences. As the last chapter showed, Keynes himself was an ambiguous figure. He was not just the greatest British economist since Adam Smith: he was also a public moralist whose theories were rooted in strongly held ethical beliefs, personal experience and historical reflection. He was a stock market speculator whose speculations taught him more about the economic role of investors' 'animal spirits' than he could ever have learned from books, an admirer of the arch-historicist Edmund Burke and a philosophical Mooreite. 'If there is no moral objective in economic progress', he wrote, 'then it follows that we must not sacrifice, even for a day, moral to material advantage – in other words we must no longer keep business and religion in separate compartments of the soul.'[7] In practice, he failed to integrate his Mooreite ethics into his economic theory, but he designed the latter to serve the former. He wanted a society in which valuable states of mind would flourish, and he thought it would come into being when the economy finally became productive enough to sustain it. Sordid money worship would eventually procure a society in which only the pathological would worship money.[8]

In the second half of the last century, however, powerfully influenced by the distinguished American economists Kenneth Arrow and Paul Samuelson, both of them Nobel Prize-winners, mathematics overwhelmed history, ethics and philosophy. (In our own day, Amartya Sen holds a Harvard Chair in both Economics and Philosophy, but he is an exception.) For the most part, economists succumbed to a strange kind of physics envy. Economics, they began to think, should and could emulate the beautiful, timeless precision of a true science, purged of the messy, the contestable and the contingent. Its theories would be 'parsimonious', yet all-encompassing. They would yield the kind of understanding that Newton's and Einstein's had yielded. The result was a form of disciplinary lobotomy. History and morality in one lobe of the brain were sundered from finance and economics in the other. Economic history was gradually extruded from the academic discipline of economics. In some places, it survived as a lowly handmaiden to 'real' economists. In others it had to emigrate to history. The complex and inherently contingent history of economic thought was almost forgotten. Students studying economics paid no more attention to Smith or Mill than students of physics paid to Galileo. When applicants for jobs in the British Government Economic Service were asked what relevance history had for economists, they could not answer.[9]

The economics profession – and far more the so-called 'quants' who colonized the financial sector in the 1990s and 2000s, armed with sophisticated mathematical techniques for calculating risk – became captive to a peculiarly dangerous form of presentism. Economists, investment bankers, hedge fund managers, central bank heads and financial regulators persuaded themselves that the booms and busts that had been capitalism's most obvious hallmarks for centuries were no more. From the early 1980s onwards, the long struggle to tame capitalism went into reverse. The passionate debates that had accompanied its taming were forgotten, while the ethic which had inspired its tamers was trashed. The end result was a new kind of untamed capitalism, sleeker and less obviously exploitative than the capitalism of Mr Merdle and Melmotte, but driven by a similar dynamic and legitimized by an updated version of the laissez-faire doctrines of Dickens's and Trollope's day.

In the heady climate that followed, the quants and their ingenious financial engineering appeared to have banished risk for ever. Seemingly no one remembered Keynes's crucial distinction between risk, which is, in principle, calculable, and uncertainty, which is not. (Gambling at roulette is risky; the prospects of another change of regime in Egypt are uncertain.) By definition, the quants could not banish uncertainty; and since uncertainty plays at least as large a part in economic life as risk, this was a fatal error. Tragically, no one noticed. The path to a never-never land of continuous economic growth and ever-rising living standards seemed open. A gigantic bubble, powered by a toxic mixture of greed and self-deception on all levels of society, floated into the skies. Mammon has never had more acolytes. Some were rich, but as we saw in the introduction, it is self-deception to think they all were. There were plenty of Mammon worshippers among the squeezed middle and even among the struggling poor.

Apart from its exceptionally frenzied character, there was nothing particularly odd about the bubble. Bubbles have strong family resemblances. The sequel is a different matter. The economic crisis of 2008–9 was the second most shattering in the long history of capitalism, surpassed only by the Great Depression of the 1930s. It might have been expected to trigger departures from the pre-crisis orthodoxy. After all, that happened in the thirties: Roosevelt in the United States and Hitler in Germany both abandoned the conventional wisdom of what was then the recent past. (Mention of Hitler is a reminder that new departures can be malign as well as benign.) The New Deal administrations in America devalued the dollar by going off gold, launched major public-works programmes, established the Tennessee Valley Authority to promote economic development in the hard-hit Tennessee Valley, introduced a minimum wage, gave statutory protections to trade unions and passed a Social Security Act that set up a system of universal retirement and unemployment insurance.

The Nazi regime in Germany also initiated large-scale public-works programmes, notably including an impressive motorway network, and effectively insulated Germany from the pressures of the global economy through autarchic foreign-trade policies. Even 1930s Britain, conventionally seen as a slave to old orthodoxies, left the gold standard and abandoned free trade, cornerstones of its political economy since the nineteenth century. It also kept interest rates low, formed a sterling bloc, which quickly became the largest currency and trading bloc in the world, and managed the exchange rate. Not by accident, it recovered from the Depression more quickly than did most of its competitors.

Nothing comparable has happened this time. No substantial political leader has echoed the exhortation to 'drive the money changers from the temple' in Franklin Roosevelt's First Inaugural. In the political world and among most of the commentariat, the question is how to get back to business as usual, albeit with modifications. Keynesians on the left want to get back through budgetary 'stimuli'. Fiscal conservatives on the right want to do so through spending cuts and balanced budgets. These differences matter. The right's alternative echoes the 'Treasury View' of the 1920s that blocked all attempts to lower unemployment through a programme of public works, on the curious grounds that increased government spending would crowd out the investment which putative future private investors might conceivably wish to make at some unknown point in the future. Keynesians put their faith in the orthodoxy of the post-war period, forgetting that it fell apart during the stagflation of the 1970s and early 1980s.

However, the differences conceal a larger similarity. The two groups disagree about the route, not the destination. Though neither admits it, both want to get to the same place: to the imaginary sunlit uplands of ever-rising living standards. Neither has acknowledged the harsh truth that in a finite world, with finite resources and threatened by environmental catastrophe, living standards as today's common sense understands them cannot go on rising for ever: that, as the Labour politician Anthony Crosland once put it in a different context, the party is over. Neither has seen that one of the most urgent tasks facing the erstwhile party-goers is to revisit the connection between economic and moral life that preoccupied the clerisy of the nineteenth and early twentieth centuries, not to mention the authors of the Book of Deuteronomy, St Thomas Aquinas and Martin Luther. Among Keynesian political leaders, there is talk of 'good' capitalism. Unfortunately, no one has pointed out that good capitalism is impossible without good people, living good lives, or that in a culture suffused with hedonistic individualism the very notion of a good life is problematic.

Left and right alike are searching for a philosopher's stone that will finally bring the prize of continuous economic growth within reach. Both assume that a more humane, better regulated, less myopic version of the untamed capitalism which has straddled the developed world since the collapse of Communism will do the trick. Both have forgotten (or perhaps never knew) that regulation does not take place in a political, philosophical or moral vacuum. Regulators are necessarily guided by an ethic of some kind, even if they cannot put it into words. The choice of ethic is a supremely political matter which should be publicly debated and democratically determined, not left to technocrats or bureaucrats. Will Hutton, now Principal of Hertford College, Oxford, as well as a leading economic commentator, and the Skidelskys father and son have tried to initiate such a debate;[10] and, as will appear in later chapters, the same is true of a variety of social movements and campaigning groups. But the response from the political world is a deafening silence.

THE LESSON OF OZYMANDIAS

These are potentially deadly cases of memory loss. One example is particularly alarming: the paladins of untamed capitalism seem unaware of the list of once-confident cultures that were brought down by environmental folly. In much-quoted, yet increasingly ominous lines, Shelley's immortal poem 'Ozymandias' describes an inscription on the half-buried statue of what had been a great king.

> 'My name is Ozymandias, king of kings:
> Look on my works, ye Mighty, and despair!'
> Nothing beside remains. Round the decay
> Of that colossal wreck, boundless and bare
> The lone and level sands stretch far away.

For Ozymandias read Sumer, once the centre of the earliest literate, urban civilization in human history. Thanks to a flaw in the Sumerians' irrigation system, rising concentrations of salt in the soil caused a disastrous fall in wheat and barley yields; that in turn led to a falling population and foreign conquest. Man-made deforestation and soil erosion (and perhaps consequent climate change) destroyed the brilliant Maya civilization in Central America that had nurtured 'great art and architecture' before its fall, and furnished its kings and nobles with a 'luxurious lifestyle'.[11]

On remote Easter Island in the Pacific, prolonged and systematic destruction of forest cover left no trees standing. Food supplies dwindled and the islanders turned to cannibalism to stay alive. In around 300 years the population fell by 70 per cent. When Captain Cook visited the island in the late eighteenth century, he described the islanders as 'small, lean, timid and miserable'.[12] Norse settlements, with a total population of some 5,000, survived on the western coast of Greenland for around 500 years from the end of the tenth century. They died out early in the 'little Ice Age' that started in the fifteenth century. Cold alone did not kill them off, however: the Inuit population of Greenland experienced the same weather conditions, but survived. The true gravediggers of Norse Greenland were the stubborn and myopic conservatism that prevented it from adapting to environmental change and its chieftains' unwillingness (or inability) to acknowledge the dangers that threatened their community before it was too late. The parallel with the world of the twenty-first century is too close for comfort.

The good news is that our civilization commands inconceivably greater resources of skill, capital and scientific knowledge than were available to the Sumerians, Mayas, Easter Islanders and Norse Greenlanders. Unlike them, we know that our environment is already under threat, that the most serious threats are man-made, that we cannot afford to ignore them and that they can be averted only by human action. Despite fierce disagreements about the best way to avert them, we also know, at least in principle, what goal to aim at: to limit the rise in the global temperature to 2 degrees Celsius. Unfortunately, there are two alarming pieces of bad news as well. The first is that, unlike the threats that faced Sumer, Central America, Easter Island and Greenland, the threats we face affect the entire planet. Salination in Sumer had no effect on Egypt; systematic deforestation on Easter Island left the forests of Siberia undamaged. But if the Greenland or Antarctic ice caps melt completely (and they are already melting at an alarming rate) it is hard to see how civilization could survive. To put it simply, we have no place to hide.

The second alarming piece of bad news is that governments, their advisers and the peoples they represent all speak with forked tongues. In Europe (though not in the United States, China or India), outright climate change deniers are thin on the ground, but even in Europe debate on the subject has a curiously unreal air about it. 'Yes,' we all say, 'climate change is a serious threat'; 'Yes, we must take action to avert it.' But 'No, there is no case for panic'; 'No, we do not need to cut our current levels of consumption or change our way of life.' All too often, ministerial speeches and official papers treat climate change policy as a low-cost add-on: one more item in a range of policies and by no means the most salient of them. In a mordant study, the economist Dieter Helm, Professor of Energy Policy at Oxford, argues convincingly that our response to the threat posed by climate change is hopelessly inadequate. By analogy with the credit crunch of 2008, he shows that the world now faces a 'carbon crunch', from which there is no pain-free exit. Current industrial structures in the developed world and most developing economies, he points out, are 'overwhelmingly carbon-based'.

> Power stations, oil refineries, gas and electricity networks, cars and road transport, industrial plants, and aviation – these all embed carbon in the economy. Decarbonizing requires the co-ordinated replacement of almost all of the capital stock – of the world.
>
> The nearest analogy is the conversion of peacetime economies in the 1930s to wartime economies by 1940, but even this fails to do justice to the scale of the transformation required . . .
>
> . . . *[D]ecarbonization cannot be done with zero pain.* [Italics in the original.][13]

MEETING THE CHALLENGE

We ignore Helm's challenge to complacency at our peril, but meeting it will not be easy. Though Helm does not use the term, he has called for a radical change in the moral economy and the orthodoxy associated with it, and not only in the economic structure. Just as unprecedented state intervention procured the transition from a peacetime to a wartime economy in the 1940s, decarbonization on the scale Helm describes is inconceivable unless state power constrains market forces more radically than at any time since 1945. For that to happen, the market fundamentalist moral economy of today will have to give way to something more akin to its solidaristic predecessor. By the same token, the doctrine that underpins the untamed capitalism of the last thirty years will have to be challenged at its heart.

Sociologists and political scientists have pinned a convenient, but confusing, label on this doctrine: 'neoliberalism'. It is confusing for a number of reasons. One is that there have been so many varieties of liberalism since the term was coined in the early nineteenth century that no neat generalization covers them all. Liberals have been for 'freedom', but 'freedom' is a coat of many colours. In real-world political conflicts, positive freedom, 'freedom to', can differ radically from negative freedom, 'freedom from'. In nineteenth-century Britain, liberalism was a rather leaky umbrella covering a vast caravanserai of Whig noblemen, small traders, dissenters, successful professionals, teetotallers, trade unionists, radical intellectuals and leasehold tenants as well as the occasional business magnate. Some of the liberals of that era can fairly be seen as the intellectual ancestors of today's 'neoliberalism'. The free-trade campaigner Richard Cobden is one example; another is the ferocious opponent of all forms of social reform Herbert Spencer. But, in Britain, the liberal mainstream flowed in a very different direction. As we saw in the last chapter the later John Stuart Mill championed a form of market socialism and argued that property rights could legitimately be overridden for the sake of the public good. There is a clear line of descent from him, through the so-called 'New Liberals' of the early twentieth century who advocated extensive state intervention in the name of positive freedom, to the even more interventionist Keynes and Lloyd George in the 1920s and 1930s. Though they did not use the phrase, all of these sought to tame capitalism and to embed Karl Popper's synthesis of freedom and security in British soil. The doctrine that goes by the name 'neoliberalism' today could hardly be more different.

It is sometimes said that what is now called neoliberalism derives from the so-called 'Ordo-liberals' of post-1945 West Germany, who sought a non-socialist alternative to the nexus of state controls and industrial cartels that had typified the Nazis' political economy.[14] There is some truth in that, but it is mixed with a heavy dose of irony. Under Ordo-liberal inspiration, post-war West Germany did see significant market-friendly economic reforms – notably including a law against cartels – but the end result was the social-market economy that I mentioned briefly in the last chapter: a form of collaborative capitalism that worked through consensus seeking and power sharing. Workers were represented on company boards; strong industrial trade unions collaborated with employers; the Federal Government shared power with *Land* (or state) governments; coalition governments of big parties and small ones were the norm at both the federal and the *Land* level. Federal Germany was unquestionably capitalist, but it was not neoliberal as the term is understood today.

For all these reasons I shall argue that a better term for miscalled neoliberalism would be 'Chicagoan', after the so-called 'Chicago School' of economists whose most prestigious base has been the University of Chicago. (In the United States Chicagoans are sometimes called 'freshwater' economists to distinguish them from their 'saltwater' rivals on the eastern and western seaboards.) Chicagoans have championed so-called neoliberal doctrines with dedicated fervour and intellectual ingenuity. Known in toto as the 'Washington Consensus', these doctrines have shaped the thinking of the International Monetary Fund, the World Trade Organization, the bond markets, the credit rating agencies, and the governments and financial services of most of the developed world for the best part of a generation. The economic vision that encapsulates them was exported to post-Communist Russia, often by travelling intellectual cowboys, ignorant of Russian history and culture and chiefly anxious to make a fast buck. The consequences for the Russian state and people included impoverishment for most and gross enrichment for a few. Through the institutions of global economic governance, the same vision has been imposed on the world's poorest countries with even more destructive results.

Currently, it constrains the policies of the European Central Bank, the European Commission and most (though by no means all) of the European Union's member states. It has become a constricting prison of the mind and less obviously of the soul. Its inmates include most of the movers and shakers of the contemporary world as well as many of those they move and shake. The great question of our time is how to break out of it.

A CATHEDRAL BUILT ON SAND

The first essential is to examine the intellectual system of which the reigning economic orthodoxy is part. At its heart is a hero (or heroine): a calculating, rational, freely choosing, egoistic individual, endowed with perfect foresight and pursuing her interests in perfectly free, perfectly competitive markets. Provided the market *is* perfectly free and competitive, provided market actors have equal access to information, and provided these actors *are* rational, resources will be allocated with perfect efficiency and market outcomes will accord with the preferences of the sum total of economic agents. Armed with these axioms, Chicagoan economists have insisted that the future is predictable, that unemployment is voluntary and that rewards reflect the marginal productivity of their recipients. Since free competitive markets are by definition perfectly efficient, any interference with the price mechanism by governments, or interest groups or naïve do-gooders will detract from efficiency, and therefore from welfare.

Closely linked with these axioms is our old friend, Hayek's spontaneous order. For the Chicago School and its offshoots, markets are, in some mysterious sense, natural in a way that states are not. For Chicagoan economists, markets evolve; they are born, not made. Attempts to force them into a predetermined mould will be self-defeating. They are self-regulating; they should be left to their own beneficent devices.

This elaborate edifice soars skywards like a magnificent Gothic cathedral, but it is built on sand. Hayek's notion of the spontaneous order certainly has something in it. The farmers' market where my wife and I buy most of our vegetables and all our bread, to say nothing of freshly caught fish, wobbly eggs and superb goat's cheese, is a perfect example of a spontaneous order. However, the supermarket where we buy most of the rest of our food is the local branch of a big chain, with immense market power, not only in Britain but in far-flung countries that supply it – often by air – with out-of-season fruit and vegetables. The truth is that in the fast-moving, technology-driven world of today, the very term 'market' is misleading. It conjures up a picture of individual buyers and sellers striking mutually satisfactory deals, like the buyers and sellers in a Middle Eastern *souk*, or in the great fairs of medieval Europe. Most modern markets are not like that. They are arenas where *firms*, headed by CEOs whose remuneration packages encourage them to fixate on the share price, battle for market share and ultimately for survival.

Chicagoan economics treats firms as though they were individuals, but in reality they are *organizations* with their own cultures, hierarchies, strategies and brands. For the great American business historian Alfred Chandler, the 'organizational capability' of the firm – its 'collective physical facilities and human skills' as organized within the enterprise – held the key to success or failure; and these facilities and skills had to be carefully co-ordinated and integrated.[15] Adam Smith's well-known metaphor of the 'invisible hand' that leads markets to benefit society without conscious volition on the part of market traders[16] tells only part of the story of the market economy. To complete the tale, the visible hand that governs the firm must also be taken into account.

The old left assumption that firms don't 'really' compete with each other is false. They compete vigorously; and sometimes they gobble up their competitors. The disappearance of many of the household names of mid-century Britain is proof of that. But they have nothing in common with the abstract individual of Chicagoan theory. To all intents and purposes, they are *polities*. They are governed through complex processes of bargaining and discussion and, in the last resort, by authoritative fiat. Thanks to the market power they wield, the really successful ones are actors in the overarching polity of the nation as well. They seek favours from governments, and governments depend on them for such goods as high employment, economic growth and – not least – the favourable poll ratings that high employment and economic growth have procured. The relationship between the two is unequal, however: governments need firms more than firms need governments.

This applies most of all to big and successful transnational companies, many of whose headquarters are domiciled in the micro-states or tax havens that Nicholas Shaxson dubs 'treasure islands'.[17] To think of BP, HSBC, Vodafone, GlaxoSmithKline, Barclays, British American Tobacco or Richard Branson's Virgin Group as if they are individuals is patently ludicrous. The resources that many such firms command dwarf those of many member-states of the United Nations. They are mighty agglomerations of economic and political power, latter-day equivalents of the chartered companies of the early-modern period like the East India Company, the Hudson Bay Company and the Muscovy Company.

Whatever the market order that took shape in early-nineteenth-century Britain may have been, its emergence was certainly not spontaneous. Karl Polanyi's 68-year-old study of the process is still unsurpassed. He called it the 'Great Transformation'. He showed that it was driven by a doctrinaire and assertive state, determined to root out the values, assumptions and practices of the existing economic order in the interests of a laissez-faire Utopia, much as colonial regimes did their best to force the peoples they conquered to behave in ways that accorded with classical political economy. For Polanyi, markets were embedded in society; if the free market of laissez-faire theory were to function properly, society had to be remodelled in accordance with market imperatives. 'There was nothing natural about *laissez-faire*', he wrote; 'free markets could never have come into being merely by allowing things to take their course ... *laissez-faire* was not a method to achieve a thing, it was the thing to be achieved.' It was achieved, he argued, by energetic and unprecedented state intervention.

> The road to the free market was opened and kept open by an enormous increase in continuous, centrally organized and controlled interventionism. To make Adam Smith's 'simple and natural liberty' compatible with the needs of a human society was a most complicated affair ... [T]he introduction of free markets, far from doing away with the need for control, regulation and intervention, enormously increased their range. Administrators had to be constantly on the watch to ensure the free working of the system. Thus even those who wished most ardently to free the state from all unnecessary duties, and whose whole philosophy demanded the restriction of state activities, could not but entrust the self-same state with the new powers, organs and instruments required for the establishment of *laissez-faire*.[18]

Not only was the state the midwife of the market order of nineteenth-century Britain, it was also the nurse that guided it on its way – often, it must be said, with prompting from powerful market actors.[19] Much later, the mighty state that governed Britain during the Second World War nurtured the scientific and engineering developments that enabled markets in plastics, jet aircraft, computers and pharmaceuticals to flourish when the war was over. Later still, the World Wide Web – the brainchild of Sir Tim Berners Lee – was developed at CERN, the Geneva-based European Organization for Nuclear Research, founded by twelve European states. In truth, states and markets have been inextricably linked for centuries.

It is worth remembering that Adam Smith, the supposed father of *laissez-faire* economics, was no enemy of state intervention. He was against what he called the 'commercial or mercantile system', in other words state manipulation of foreign trade to protect domestic producers against low-cost imports. 'If a foreign country can supply us with a commodity cheaper than we ourselves can make it,' he wrote briskly, 'better buy it of them with some part of the produce of our own industry, employed in a way in which we have some advantage.'[20] He excoriated public regulations that encouraged producers to collude against the public interest. In an immortal passage in *The Wealth of Nations* he noted acidly:

> People of the same trade seldom meet together, even for merriment and diversion, but the conversation ends in a conspiracy against the public, or in some contrivance to raise prices. It is impossible indeed to prevent such meetings, by any law which could be executed, or would be consistent with liberty and justice. But though the law cannot hinder people of the same trade from sometimes assembling together, it ought to do nothing to facilitate such assemblies.[21]

In practice, Smith complained, the law did just that, discriminating unjustly in favour of some producers and against others. But Smith, the foe of state interference with foreign trade and state-facilitated cartels, was also Smith the friend of state provision of public goods. He focussed on three such goods: national defence, justice and public works that would benefit the entire society 'in the highest degree', but would not yield sufficient individual returns to attract private investment.[22] For Smith, in short, economic development could not be left to free competition alone; it was also a matter for the state.

Today's markets are constituted by states, sustained by states, regulated by states, protected by states and sometimes imposed by states. Market individualists sometimes sneer at what they call 'the nanny state', but without the state's laws, police officers, courts, prisons, patents, Fraud Offices, food and drug regulations, air safety controls and rules forbidding insider trading, there would be no markets. There would only be robbers, embezzlers and pirates. (Even as things are, there are plenty of pirates about.) In short, the crude realities of economic life elude the categories of Chicagoan economics. The doctrines that legitimize untamed capitalism tell us virtually nothing about the way in which it works.

THE CHICAGO CULT

Then why have these doctrines dazzled so many for so long? One reason is that Chicagoan economics is a cult. It offers its members comradeship, excitement and the joy of battle against the unregenerate. They live their intellectual lives in an enclosed world, sufficient unto itself, with its own prizes, hierarchies and saints. Once inside the cult, it seems almost treacherous to defect. Another reason, insufficiently acknowledged by non-Chicagoans, is that the doctrines are aesthetically satisfying, at least for those with crossword-solving minds. It is fun to see how far they can be pushed and to reconcile inconvenient facts with them. A third reason – and I suspect the most important – is that they chime with the spirit of the age which they have helped to create. They purport to explain the demise of the tamed capitalism of the recent past and to justify the untamed capitalism of the present. They offer us a whipping boy, or rather a queue of whipping boys: government, the state, politicians, the old elites, pampered public servants and feckless scroungers, against all of whom suppressed anger and resentment can easily be turned. They tell us that consumption is good and taxes bad. In doing all this, they give the beneficiaries of untamed capitalism a seemingly inexhaustible supply of rhetorical and ideological ammunition.

This makes it all the more important to subject the doctrines to close forensic examination. In truth, we do not decide our preferences in autistic isolation from the rest of our society; nor do we stick to them like limpets through all the buffetings of changing cultural tides. They are fluctuating and inconstant, drawn from myriads of sources: friends, acquaintances, advertisers, tweeters, bloggers, Facebook 'friends', the people next to us in the bus queue and the feverish novelty-hunting of the internet among them. In the real world markets are neither perfectly free nor perfectly competitive. The crucial Chicagoan assumption that sellers and buyers are always equally well-informed is simply wrong. In some markets they are, or nearly so: the farmers' market that my wife and I patronize is a good example. We can taste the goat's cheese and inspect the tomatoes before we buy them. But the more complex the product, the less symmetrical will information be. Inveterate technophobes like me know nothing like as much about the computers they buy as the salespeople in PC World. The mortgage market whose imperfections brought Northern Rock to grief was rife with asymmetries of information: badly paid would-be home owners could not possibly know as much as the firm which tempted them with absurdly favourable terms. The financial instruments that American banks sold on to German ones before the bubble burst were so complex that neither sellers nor buyers fully understood them.

Quainter still is the Chicagoan axiom that rewards reflect productivity. According to the High Pay Commission, the pay of top executives in a range of FTSE companies increased by amounts varying from just under 730 per cent to nearly 5,000 per cent in the thirty years after 1980.[23] It is beyond belief that their productivity can have increased by anything approaching that figure. (Average wages in the country as a whole increased threefold over the same period.) Moreover, the future is not predictable. If it were, no one would pay any attention to the ratings agencies whose findings can determine the fates of nations, and the wild gyrations of the bond markets they provoke would not be taking place. One of the favourite arguments of Chicagoan free marketeers is that undistorted competition promotes technological progress. Yet the Chicagoan paradigm has no place for inherently unpredictable technological innovations – or, for that matter for political crises, revolutions or wars, all of which have been part of the history of modern capitalism since it began. On a deeper level, market behaviour, like other kinds of behaviour, is *reflexive*. Market agents do not suddenly lose their eyesight when they enter the marketplace. They watch to see what other agents are doing, and they change their own behaviour in response, rewriting the future in the process. Equally, Chicagoans take no account of what economists call 'externalities' – the social and environmental costs of free competition that are not included in market prices. (Polluting chimneys, carbon dioxide emissions, oil-smothered water birds, lost bio-diversity and depleted aquifers are all examples.)

Above all, the heroine at the heart of the whole system – the rational, egoistic, calculating individual, relentlessly pursuing her own, private interests – is a phantom. The first thing to notice is that 'rational' as used by Chicagoan economists (and not only by Chicagoans) is a distinctly slippery word. It sounds cool, neutral and dispassionate: ideally suited to a science analogous to physics. In reality it is nothing of the sort. It is prescriptive as well as descriptive: a mealy-mouthed substitute for 'good'. When Chicagoan economists tell us that a certain sort of behaviour is rational, they mean that it accords with the axioms of Chicago School economics, and is therefore right. That is why, in a phrase coined by Joseph Stiglitz, so many economists are 'irrationally committed to the assumption of rationality'.[24] Abandon that assumption, and economics is no longer a science.

The trouble is that the Chicagoans' 'assumption of rationality' is full of holes. It tells us little about how we actually behave. It says that we choose our aims, and pursue them consistently. Sometimes we do, often we don't. We lurch from one aim to another, like a drunkard lurching from one lamppost to the next. We have to cope with unpredictable contingencies and face unforeseen dilemmas. In such situations the notion of consistency has no meaning. Sometimes, consistency may be irrational. White explorers in the Australian desert starved to death because they thought the plants the aborigines ate were inedible. They were consistent, but they might have survived if they had (inconsistently) fraternized with the Aborigines and followed their example. The Norse Greenlanders consistently bred livestock instead of fishing for their food, as the Inuit did. Their society died out as a result when the little ice age began.

THE WILL-O'-THE-WISP OF REASON

The notion of an unrooted 'rationality', applicable to all cultures, is a bewitching will-o'-the-wisp, bequeathed to us by the *philosophes* of the eighteenth-century French Enlightenment. It is not difficult to understand why it appealed to them. They were rebelling against an old order cluttered with archaic relics of the feudal past. The relics were no longer seriously oppressive, but that made them all the more irksome. Reason, pure, limpid, impersonal and imperious Reason, gave the rebels a seemingly unchallengeable standard against which to judge the old order and find it wanting. Gertrude Himmelfarb puts it well: reason was the *philosophes*' 'mantra, a token of good faith and right-mindedness', with the 'same absolute, dogmatic status as religion'.[25] An extraordinary dithyramb by the celebrated *philosophe* the Baron d'Holbach conveys the flavour:

> Show us, then, O Nature! that which man ought to do, in order to obtain the happiness which thou makest him desire. Virtue! Animate him with thy beneficent fire. Reason! Conduct his uncertain steps through the paths of life. Truth! Let thy torch illumine his intellect, dissipate the darkness of his road.[26]

But the French Enlightenment was just that: French. Its claim to universality was bogus. Himmelfarb argues convincingly that there were at least three Enlightenments: the British, the French and the American.[27] These 'three Enlightenments', she writes, represented 'alternative approaches to modernity, alternative habits of mind and heart, of consciousness and sensibility'.[28] Of the three, she thinks, only the French gave pride of place to Reason with a capital 'R': to reason as the source of 'universal principles independent of history, circumstance and national spirit'.[29] As Himmelfarb depicts it, the central theme of the American Enlightenment was liberty:[30] the political liberty that the founding fathers of the American Republic debated in the papers collected in *The Federalist*[31] and sought to embody in the intricate checks and balances of the United States Constitution. For her, the British Enlightenment was different again. It was sceptical in temper, respectful of history, latitudinarian in religion rather than dogmatically hostile to it, and gave priority to the 'social affections' of benevolence and sympathy. Adam Smith's *The Theory of Moral Sentiments* and Edward Gibbon's *The Decline and Fall of the Roman Empire* were characteristic examples.

Its greatest ornament was the Whig statesman and polemicist Edmund Burke, champion of the voiceless millions of Bengal against the rapacity of the East India Company, ally of the American colonists in their quarrel with the British Crown and enemy of the Protestant Ascendancy and the cruel penal laws it imposed on the Catholic majority in his native Ireland. He was also Europe's most formidable critic of the French Revolution. Because of that he has been seen as a black reactionary, hostile to Enlightenment values. In truth, he was as much a man of the Enlightenment as Voltaire and Diderot, but of a different Enlightenment from theirs.

He was no study-bound philosopher. His ideas tumbled out of him in passionate speeches and writings directed to particular questions as they emerged from the flux of events. Yet certain themes recurred again and again in his long career. He was for the specific against the universal; for empathetic understanding against *a priori* rationalism; and, above all, for experience and history against unhistorical theorizing. 'Impracticable' virtue, he wrote, was 'spurious'. Laws mattered less than 'manners' or what we now call culture; good government depended on empathy with and respect for the manners of the governed. Government was not a business for 'sophists, economists and calculators' seeking to reconstruct society and inherited manners in accordance with the dictates of an abstract Reason. In real life, reason counted for much less than the experience 'of nations and of ages'. The *philosophes*' contempt for the past was 'cold', 'muddy' and 'barbarous'. Looming behind it was the hangman.

We shall meet Burke again in the final chapter of this book. For the moment, two inferences stand out. The first is that the notions of 'rationality', 'reason' and 'rational behaviour' have always been contestable. Not only did Norse and Inuit Greenlanders differ over what it was reasonable to eat, but the British and French Enlightenments differed over the role of reason in human affairs. The second inference is that the Chicagoan conception of 'rational' economic behaviour is not a timeless truth. It is a trope of rhetoric.

HOMO SAPIENS VERSUS *HOMO ECONOMICUS*

In truth *Homo sapiens* has little in common with *Homo economicus*. The solipsistic, egoistic, calculating individual posited by social contract theorists like Locke and Hobbes, by their utilitarian rivals like James Mill and Jeremy Bentham, and by a long line of economists, by no means confined to the Chicago School, is another phantom. Like our primate ancestors and relatives, we are genetically programmed for sociability, and equipped with an enormous repertoire of social skills. We learn early in our lives how to pick up unspoken cues, to imitate others and to discuss with them. Our preferences are not shaped in glorious isolation, and nor are they fixed and determinate. They are fluid, drawn from a myriad of fluctuating sources. We have always learned whom to trust and who can't be trusted through continuous interaction with the other members of our society. We have always followed social norms, often sanctified by a religious or ideological authority; and we have always hungered for recognition and respect from our fellows.[32] Like our closest primate relatives, the chimpanzees, we have always had a strong propensity for violence, but the war of all against all that Hobbes imagined was a terrifying spectre, not an anthropological reality.

During the boom, these truths were forgotten. They have now returned to haunt us. Like its predecessor in the 1920s and 1930s, the 2008 crisis showed that markets cannot regulate themselves, and that only government can pick up the pieces when self-regulation fails: much-maligned state intervention just managed to save the world from a second Great Depression after bank failures had procured a potentially deadly credit crunch. The crisis also showed that a favourite trope of neoliberal rhetoric – that 'a rising tide floats all boats' – is self-serving humbug. Not only has wealth not trickled down from the ultra-rich to the rest; the gap between the rest and the rich has steadily widened, as subsequent chapters will show. Meanwhile the masters of the universe in the hedge funds and investment banks have turned out to be wealth destroyers, not wealth creators. 'Rational economic actors' were not just conspicuous by their absence in the run-up to the 2008 crisis. As George Soros has suggested, the true drivers of the booms and busts of the last twenty years were stampeding 'electronic herds' lurching from wild over-optimism to self-fulfilling pessimism. As well as staggering inequalities, their activities eventually procured a catastrophic fall in employment and output. The ecological, cultural and, above all, moral consequences of untamed capitalism have been more damaging still. The environmental costs it brings with it threaten the destruction of civilized life. As Chapter 5 will show, the inequalities and humiliation it breeds have helped to erode the public trust without which government by consent, and for that matter a properly functioning market order, are impossible.

Above all, it has coarsened our moral lives. It has flouted the ethical principles encapsulated in all three Abrahamic religions as well as in the teachings of the world-wide humanist movement. It has fostered money worship, selfishness and callousness. Its message is that altruism and public spirit are surplus to requirements; that to survive and prosper we must model ourselves on the 'self-serving and self-interested individual'[33] posited by Chicagoan theory. The better angels of our nature survive, but they have taken a heavy hit.

REVISITING MARX

No single school of thought or political tradition can offer an adequate explanation of the crisis or an alternative to the Chicagoan world-view that has now collapsed. That said, I believe that, in one crucial respect, Marx has more to say to our post-crisis world than Keynes, or Hayek, or their followers. That suggestion may raise eyebrows. Perverted versions of Marx's teaching have been prayed in aid by some of the most evil regimes in human history, but he was no more responsible for Stalin or Mao than Christ was responsible for the Holy Inquisition or Muhammad for today's jihadist atrocities. Now that Marxism is no longer the official religion of a superpower, he can at last be seen as the flawed but astonishingly penetrating genius he really was, rather than as an icon or anti-icon.

Marx was wrong about many things. His vision of capitalist production begetting its own negation 'with the inexorability of a Law of Nations' and of socialized labour bursting the 'capitalist integument' asunder has not been realized, and probably never will be. Murderous wars, in which workers from one country have slaughtered workers from others, have made nonsense of his belief that the working class had no fatherland. But he and his friend and collaborator Friedrich Engels were supremely right about the essential dynamic of capitalism: the voracious, unceasing, Promethean and world-transforming search for profit that they described in urgent, passionate and sometimes almost intoxicating prose in *The Communist Manifesto*.[34] The *Manifesto* was published in 1847 when Marx was twenty-nine and Engels twenty-seven. As befits its authors' youth, it breathes a spirit of exhilarating optimism, cocksure self-belief and outrageous *chutzpah*. Marx and Engels purported to speak for a Europe-wide Communist movement, whose spectre haunted the entire continent, and to exorcize which 'All the powers of Old Europe' had formed a Holy Alliance. In two of the most famous political sentences of the last 200 years, they ended with an audacious rallying cry that can still set the pulse racing: 'The proletarians have nothing to lose but their chains. They have a world to win.'

The truth was more prosaic. The powers of Old Europe were blissfully unaware of the spectre of Communism (not surprisingly, since no such spectre existed), while proletarians were nowhere to be found, except in parts of Britain and Belgium and a few pockets elsewhere. The *Manifesto*'s optimism and audacity, however, stemmed from the authors' conviction that they had uncovered the revolutionary essence of industrial capitalism, then still in its infancy; and in this they were not just right, but astonishingly prescient. Their critique of capitalism echoed Carlyle. The bourgeoisie, they wrote, had destroyed the traditional ties of the past, and 'left no other nexus between man and man than naked self-interest, than callous cash payment'. It had 'converted the physician, the lawyer, the priest, the poet, the man of science, into its paid labourers'. The workman had become 'an appendage of the machine'.

Unlike Carlyle, however, they eulogized capitalism as vigorously as they excoriated it. The bourgeoisie, they wrote, had

accomplished wonders far surpassing Egyptian pyramids, Roman aque-
ducts, and Gothic cathedrals; it has conducted expeditions that put in
the shade all former exoduses of nations and crusades . . .

Constant revolutionizing of production, uninterrupted disturbance
of all social conditions, everlasting uncertainty and agitation distinguish the bourgeois epoch from all earlier ones. All fixed, fast-frozen
relations, with their train of ancient and venerable prejudices and opinions, are swept away, all new-formed ones become antiquated before
they can ossify. All that is solid melts into air, all that is holy is pro-
faned, and man is at last compelled to face with sober senses his real
conditions of life, and his relations with his kind.

These wonders did not stop at national frontiers. They encompassed the
globe. In its search for expanding markets, the bourgeoisie had to 'nestle
everywhere, settle everywhere, establish connections everywhere'.

In place of the old wants, satisfied by the productions of the country, we
find new wants, requiring for their satisfaction the products of distant
lands and climes. In place of the old local and national self-sufficiency,
we have intercourse in every direction, universal interdependence of
nations . . .

The bourgeoisie, by the rapid improvement of all instruments of production, by the immensely facilitated means of communication, draws
all, even the most barbarian, nations into civilization. The cheap prices
of its commodities are the heavy artillery with which it batters down all
Chinese walls, with which it forces the barbarians' intensely obstinate
hatred of foreigners to capitulate. It compels all nations, on pain of
extinction, to adopt the bourgeois mode of production; it compels
them to introduce what it calls civilization into their midst, i.e. to
become bourgeois themselves. In one word, it creates a world after its
own image.

The most remarkable thing about these passages is that the developments they describe were barely in their infancy. Like ace cameramen
contriving to photograph tanks manoeuvring in the murk of battle,
Marx and Engels captured the inner essence of industrial capitalism
at a time when its future was still swathed in confusion. More clearly
than any of their contemporaries and most of their successors, they

saw that capitalism was both inherently revolutionary and inherently imperialistic. They did not foresee the tamed capitalism that prevailed after the Second World War, but there is no better guide to the untamed capitalism of today than their *Manifesto*. It is also a powerful corrective to the amnesiac political culture of our time. In the next chapter I shall look at the disturbing implications of its authors' prescience for the public realm.

4

The Market State
Invades the Public Realm

Anything that we have to learn to do we learn by the actual doing of it: people become builders by building and instrumentalists by playing instruments. Similarly we become just by performing just acts, temperate by performing temperate ones, brave by performing brave ones.

Aristotle, *The Nicomachean Ethics*, translated
by J. A. K. Thomson, 1955

No man is an Iland, *intire of it selfe; every man is a peece of the* Continent, *a part of the* maine; *if a* Clod *bee washed away by the Sea, Europe is the lesse, as well as if a* Promontorie *were . . . any mans* death *diminishes me, because I am involved in* Mankinde; *And therefore never send to know for whom the* bell *tolls; It tolls for thee.*

John Donne,
Meditation XVII, 1623

In successive weeks in November and December 2010 student protesters crowded into Parliament Square and immobilized large swathes of central London. They were following an old tradition. From the Peasants' Revolt in the fourteenth century to the two-million-strong march against the Iraq War in the twenty-first, London has been a magnet for demonstrations by the powerless and rebellious. Compared to the grievances that had triggered these historic events, the students' grievance seemed banal. They were protesting against a then prospective (now actual) threefold increase in the tuition fees charged by England's publicly funded universities. (Scotland and Wales have followed a different path.) The protesters' cause was worthy, but hardly commensurate with opposition to unjust taxation or an illegal war. Yet the demonstrations dramatized fundamental questions – about the purposes of higher education and its contribution to the public good and, on a deeper level, about the integrity of Britain's public realm.

Sadly, these questions hardly figured in the dispute that followed the protests. The disputants focussed almost wholly on the likely impact of the proposed fee increase on potential students from different social backgrounds; the questions mentioned above were virtually ignored. Yet they loom unmistakably in the background; and will be the stuff of this chapter. First, I try to tease out the inner meaning of the fee increase itself. Then I turn to the wider and more pressing questions concerning the public realm and the public good.

BARBARIANS AT THE GATE

The Government's decision to increase student fees was the child of a supposedly independent review of higher-education funding that Peter (Lord) Mandelson, then Business Secretary in Gordon Brown's hapless government, set up in 2009. The chairman was Lord Browne, sometime CEO of BP; to judge by their CVs the rest of the team were more at home in the world of university administration, management consultancy and policy advice than in the lecture hall or library.

The review appeared in October 2010. Its key proposals became law a year later. It was a remarkable document, suffused with a naïve economism which would have shocked Adam Smith, to say nothing of Keynes or Hayek. It made an occasional bow to the notion of a public interest, but it interpreted the notion in an odd way. It said nothing about the public good or the public realm. At its heart lay the assumption that a university education is a private good, enjoyed by individual consumers, like an expensive car or a generous annuity. For its authors, the point of university teaching was not to introduce young people to the life of the mind, to foster critical thinking or to turn out responsible and public-spirited citizens. It was to make the taught richer than they would otherwise have been. As the review put it:

> On graduating, graduates are more likely to be employed, more likely to enjoy higher wages and better job satisfaction, and more likely to find it easier to move from one job to the next. Participating in higher education enables individuals from low income backgrounds and their families to enter high status jobs and increase their earnings ... Over the course of a working life the average graduate earns comfortably over £100,000 more, in today's valuation and net of tax than someone with A levels who does not go on to university.[1]

For Browne and his team, the conclusion was obvious: like other private goods, university education should be traded in a competitive market where economically rational buyers and sellers could strike mutually beneficial deals. Unfortunately, they complained, the market for higher education was distorted by state subsidies, state price fixing and state control over student numbers. As a result, neither universities nor potential students could behave like the rational economic actors they should have been. The consequence was a horror story. British universities were losing out to foreign competitors. British employers found that graduates lacked 'communication, entrepreneurial and networking skills'. Because of this, the UK was falling behind in the global 'race for the top'.

The reviewers' solution was to remove the alleged distortions which had prevented the market for higher education from working properly. Instead of block grants from the state, universities should be forced to rely on student fees to fund their undergraduate teaching. Prospective students should be free to choose which universities and departments to patronize; they would choose the ones that offered the best deal in the hard terms of future earning power. Departments that gave good deals would expand; departments that gave bad ones would go out of business. The competitive pressures of free student choice would 'drive up quality' throughout the system.

Four fifths of the way through their review, however, Browne and his colleagues suddenly entered a caveat that made nonsense of its underlying assumptions. In 'priority' courses, they announced, 'targeted' public investment should override market forces.

These may be courses that deliver significant social returns such as to provide skills and knowledge currently in shortage or predicted to be in the future. Students may not choose these courses because the private returns are not as high as other courses, the costs are higher and there are cheaper courses on offer, or simply because these courses are perceived as more difficult.

Typically the courses that may fall into this category are courses in science and technology subjects, clinical medicine, nursing and other healthcare degrees, as well as strategically important language courses.[2]

What the Browne review was really saying was that it is in the public interest for universities to continue to teach medicine, science and technology, but not in the public interest for them to teach the humanities and social sciences. The serious business of the academy is to produce highly polished cogs for the nation's economic machine; graduates in English literature or history or politics are unfit for that all-conquering purpose. Universities may teach non-priority subjects if they wish, and can find students willing to study them and to pay for doing so, but such subjects are decorative add-ons to the academy's core function: to help UK plc best its competitors in the global marketplace. It is hard to decide which is more shocking: the barbarous assumption that the prime function of the academy is to enable the United Kingdom to do better in a global race against other nations, or the intellectual confusion running through the whole argument.

The notion of a global race stems from a fallacy. It is a twenty-first-century equivalent of the mercantilist theories that Adam Smith exploded 250 years ago. International trade is not a zero-sum game in which one player's gain is another's loss as mercantilists imagined; if the Chinese economy grows faster than Britain's, the British are not one whit worse off. Besides, even if there were such a global race, and the United Kingdom were losing it, it would not follow that British universities should change their ways. Modern universities (and British ones more than most) belong to a world-wide republic of letters. Students flock to this country from other countries; British academics research and teach in foreign universities; British research findings are consulted by researchers in foreign universities, from Vladivostock to the Bay Area of California; publication in the British journal *Nature* is the gold standard for scientific research. The Open University (one of Britain's most successful universities) is a world-leader both in distance and in lifelong learning, with 200,000 students, by no means all of them British.

Plenty of things are wrong with British universities: perverse assessment exercises that distort research priorities, leading to more publications of lower quality; an Anglophone fixation that gives a higher priority to contacts with the United States than to contacts with the rest of Europe; and a failure to think through the consequences of the huge expansion in the student population that has taken place in the last forty years (from 8.4 per cent of the age group in 1970 to 49 per cent today). But none of these would be put right by adopting the Browne review's prescriptions.

That leads us on to the intellectual confusion at its heart. As noted above, the reviewers assumed that university education is a private good. The truth is more complicated: universities provide both private and public goods. An individual student, enrolling on a university course, does so to acquire a private good or goods – not just higher than average earnings over her lifetime, as the Browne reviewers imagined, but goods that don't even figure in their review, such as intellectual excitement, stimulating friendships and the joy of discovery for its own sake, among many others. But university *graduates* are public goods. They enrich the entire society, not just in narrow economic terms, but culturally, intellectually and, not least, politically. Graduates in physics, or mathematics, or engineering, or Mandarin contribute to the vitality and dynamism of their society and not just to its ability to compete in an alleged global race to the top. Exactly the same is true of graduates in history, or philosophy or politics.

If democracy is above all a matter of public reasoning, as Amartya Sen believes (I think rightly), then a capacity to reason is crucial to it. You can't teach reasoning skills in the abstract, but you can show students what they are and encourage them to practise them. In its mission statement, Harvard College (the undergraduate programme of Harvard University) declares that it

> encourages students to respect ideas and their free expression, and to rejoice in discovery and in critical thought; to pursue excellence in

a spirit of productive cooperation, and to assume responsibility for the consequences of personal actions. Harvard seeks to identify and remove restraints on students' full participation, so that individuals may explore their capabilities and interests and may develop their full intellectual and human potential. Education at Harvard should liberate students to explore, to create, to challenge, and to lead.[3]

If Harvard College realizes that university education is a public good, as its mission statement shows it does, why did Browne and his colleagues fail to do so? Why does their review contain no hint of the values of free expression, critical thinking and productive co-operation that Harvard College extols so eloquently? Why could they not see that a prime function of any university is to help its students develop the qualities of mind and heart without which democracy as public reasoning is impossible?

The answer is plain: the intellectual confusion mentioned above reflects a deeper moral confusion. Browne and his colleagues were captive to the assumptions of the market fundamentalist moral economy which is now in crisis. They could not see that university education is a public good because the notions of *the* public good, in the singular, and of the public realm as the realm of the public good, were alien to them. As the rest of this chapter will show, they were not alone in that.

THE PUBLIC REALM

At this point enter the wider questions concerning the public realm and the good society. The 'public realm', as I understand it, is far more than the realm of governments, political parties, elections, policy-making and political debate, though they undoubtedly belong to it. It is the realm of service, equity, professional and public duty, as opposed both to the market realm of buying and selling and the private realm of love, family and friendship. It should not be confused with the public sector. It is not a sector of any kind: it is a dimension of social life cutting across sectoral boundaries. It is a space, protected from the adjacent market and private realms, where strangers encounter each other as equal partners in the common life of the society. The ethos of the public realm is Aristotelian: solidarity, its key value, comes with practice, just as bravery and temperance did for Aristotle. Fundamental to it is the assumption that the public interest is more than a bundle of private interests.

It is rooted, I believe, in the instinctive conviction – hauntingly expressed in Donne's phrase, 'No man is an island' – that we are members one of another. That conviction has an unmistakable religious dimension. (It was certainly unmistakable for Donne, Dean of St Paul's when he wrote his *Meditations*.) Jewish religious practice presupposes a Covenant between the entire Jewish people and the Almighty. Muslims owe allegiance to the world-wide 'ummah' that embraces all Muslims, wherever they may be. In medieval Europe, the weekly Eucharist was a collective experience that made Donne's vision live in the hearts of the participants. In today's secular societies, however, the religious dimension of the public realm matters less than Adam Smith's 'moral sentiments', discussed in the last chapter. As Smith knew better than most, we are market agents. But he also knew that neither the exchange relations of the marketplace nor the private attachments of kinship and friendship embrace the whole of our social lives. Family mattered to him enormously. (He was the only son of a widowed mother, and was devastated by her death at the age of ninety.)[4] But in his discussion of the 'moral sentiments' he showed that, for him, the bonds of sympathy which help to hold society together included far more than private ties. If Smith of *The Wealth of Nations* is the patron saint of the market economy, his other self, Smith of *The Theory of Moral Sentiments*, is the patron saint of the public realm.

A complex structure of duties and rights sustains the bonds of sympathy that preoccupied the second Smith. The rights in question include the generalized 'human rights' promulgated in declarations like the UN's Universal Declaration of Human Rights of 1948 and the European Convention on Human Rights that appeared two years later. These human rights include, among many other things, the right to life, prohibition of torture and slavery, the right to a fair trial, the right to freedom of expression and association, and the right to freedom of thought, conscience and religion.[5]

But they are not the only rights that sustain the bonds of the United

Kingdom's public realm. Supplementing them are more specifically British rights, such as the right to strike; the right to free health care; the right to safe working conditions; the right to equal pay for equal work; and the right to free primary and secondary education. Most of these British rights have foreign analogues, but that does not detract from their British origins. They did not emerge peacefully from the womb of philosophical or legal argument. They were secured through political action and debate – by the clerisies I discussed in Chapter 2; by popular agitation, often led by the working-class elite which also figured in Chapter 2; and by political leaders as various as the Conservative R. A. Butler, the socialist Aneurin Bevan and the Liberal David Lloyd George.[6] They are rooted in a tradition that goes back to the so-called Levellers of the seventeenth century, who challenged the rights of property in the name of the common people. In a phrase that echoes down the centuries, the Leveller supporter Thomas Rainborough declared that 'the poorest he that is in England hath a life to live as the greatest he'. If the patron saint of the public realm is the Adam Smith of *The Theory of Moral Sentiments*, its motto is Rainborough's call to arms.

Rights presuppose duties. In one of the most lucid and challenging contributions to debate on these matters, Onora O'Neill argues convincingly that duties are logically and morally prior to rights. 'Active citizens who meet their duties', she writes, 'thereby secure one another's rights.'[7] If citizens are too passive, too self-indulgent or too strongly influenced by the hedonistic individualism of our day to perform their duties, talk of rights will be so much hot air; and, though O'Neill does not use the term, the survival of the public realm will be in jeopardy. In his inaugural address as President, John F. Kennedy famously urged his fellow Americans, 'ask not what your country can do for you, ask what you can do for your country'.[8] That could serve as a maxim for the public realm. It is a gift of history, precious but also vulnerable. We, and not just remote elites, are responsible for its health; it is up to all of us to make sure it survives and prospers. We demean ourselves if we try to shuffle off that primordial responsibility onto others.

THE GOODS OF THE PUBLIC REALM

The public realm engenders and protects precious forms of human flourishing – above all mind- and heart-expanding public debate and collective action in a common cause – which cannot be bought and sold, or found in a narrow circle of friends and kinsfolk. Its goods include publicly provided water that is safe to drink, fair trials, free elections, accessible health care, national defence, welcoming public spaces, honest police officers, public libraries, safe food, impartial public administration, disinterested scholarship, community groups, the minimum wage, the Pennine Way and the rulings of the Health and Safety Executive, to mention only a few.

Some of these are public goods in the strict economist's sense: goods that, by their very nature, have to be supplied to everyone if they are to be supplied to anyone. As noted in the last chapter, Adam Smith thought national defence, justice and public works of great benefit to society that would not attract private investment were public goods in that sense. To Smith's list present-day economists would add clean air, the police force, street cleaning and the fire and rescue service, among other things. But this does not apply to all the goods in my list: it would be technically possible to restrict access to St James's Park to visitors who are willing to pay for it, or to restrict access to public libraries to paying readers. Yet this technical possibility is beside the point. The goods of the public realm may or may not be tradable technically: the point is that, if they are traded, they will no longer be public. In Ruskin's language, they would forfeit the 'moral sign' attached to them if they could be bought and sold. Access to them would no longer be a right. They would be commodities available only to paying customers.

Two critically important conclusions follow. The first is that the boundaries of the public realm may shift over time. Of the goods of the public realm listed above, free elections in any meaningful sense date from the introduction of the secret ballot in 1872 and the Corrupt and Illegal Practices Prevention Act of 1883, designed to stamp out bribery in elections. Impartial public administration was a product of the Northcote–Trevelyan Report discussed in Chapter 2. A modern and (reasonably) honest police service dates from Sir Robert Peel's tenure of the Home Office in the 1820s. The Pennine Way is the child of the post-war Labour Government's legislation setting up a series of National Parks. The Health and Safety Executive was established in 1974.

The second conclusion follows from the first. No timeless, universally agreed rules or set of *a priori* principles can tell us where the boundaries of the public realm should lie. Argument, contestation, persuasion – Amartya Sen's 'public reasoning' – determine its shape. The reasoning takes place in the media, in blogs, in bus queues, in the internet journal *Open Democracy* and on Facebook, as well as in Parliament and the courts; it may lead to legislation, but it can be just as effective if it only simmers in the hearts and minds of those who take part in it. The process of reasoning is open-ended. It is impossible to imagine a civilized society – or for that matter a genuinely free market – without a public realm. The private ties of family and friendship are fundamental to human life; so are the exchanges of the market realm. Yet without a robust and confident public realm to complement them, the private and market realms are likely to become nests of predators, preying on those who lack private influence or market power. The Sicilian Mafia is an example of the first, Northern Rock's pertinacious mortgage salesmen of the second. But the constitution of any particular public realm is always open to argument.

WHO BELONGS TO
THE PUBLIC REALM?

As this suggests, its boundaries are hazy. State employees like policemen, government officials, judges and soldiers normally belong to the public realm. Private equity fund managers, software designers and pop musicians generally (but not invariably) inhabit the market realm. Certain professionals straddle the divide between them. Barristers are market traders, selling their wares in a competitive marketplace. That is not all they are, however. They also have duties to the court, above all a duty not to mislead it: if a defence counsel discovers that her client is guilty, she is duty-bound to drop the case. Before universities were funded by the state, academic salaries came from fees and endowment income. But academic duties included the promotion of disinterested learning and free inquiry, and the transmission of high culture to the young. These duties decreed a meritocratic examination system and ruled out the sale of degrees. Academics did not suddenly enter the public realm when state funding for universities began in 1918; they had been part of it before. The same is true of certain individuals. A prime example is Sir Tim Berners-Lee, whom we met in the last chapter. He has worked for private profit-making companies as well as for the government-created and publicly funded CERN; the World Wide Web, which he invented, has helped to create an international public realm of immense cultural and economic significance.

THE PROFESSIONAL ETHIC

In short, the ethics that motivate professionals matter more than the source of their incomes. But this apparently simple proposition raises thorny questions. What is the professional ethic? How did it originate? What role does it play in social life?

Certain things are reasonably clear. Whatever professions may or may not be, they are, in the language of English common law, combinations in restraint of trade. They restrict entry, they try to fix prices and they lay down the standards of quality that their goods are supposed to meet. In this way, they command a rent, in the sense defined by the great pioneer of classical political economy, David Ricardo: in effect, a payment for the use of a scarce resource. But unlike many rent seekers, they perform an indispensable social function. The economists Michael Dietrich and Jennifer Roberts put it well. Professionalism, they argue, is a response to the inescapable reality that, in markets for professional services, information is bound to be asymmetrical. That asymmetry, they write, 'may disrupt the principle of *caveat emptor* [buyer beware]'.[9]

Consumers of professional services can't know enough to beware. Unless they are prepared to trust the producers they will condemn themselves to a state of paranoid catalepsy whenever they need professional help. If I spent my time 'bewaring' before consulting an eye surgeon about an incipient cataract or a surveyor about possible subsidence beneath my house I would soon be a nervous wreck. The cumbersome machinery of audits, assessments and league tables which has become an ever-more intrusive feature of professional life in the last twenty-five years or so has not displaced – indeed cannot displace – the bedrock of duty and trust on which the relationship between professional and client necessarily rests.

Hence, advanced societies face a dilemma. They need professional services, and the more advanced they become the greater their need. But only professionals can judge the quality of professional services. Quantitative box ticking can complement professional judgement, and throw light on weaknesses that professionals ought to look at, but it is not a substitute for the judgements of quality that only professionals can make. Onora O'Neill puts it well.

> Teachers aim to teach their pupils; nurses to care for their patients; university lecturers to do research and to teach; police officers to deter and apprehend those whose activities harm the community; social workers to help those whose lives are for various reasons unmanageable or very difficult. Each profession has its proper aim, and *this aim is not reducible to meeting set targets following prescribed procedures and requirements.*[10] [My italics.]

The need to trust is inescapable. Professionals are not all saints; some of them sometimes cut corners. Occasionally a small minority of them betray their trust. But at the moment of truth – consulting a school teacher about a child's progress, consulting a barrister about the best way to deal with a libellous allegation, consulting an architect about adding a conservatory to one's house – the client *has* to trust her professional adviser. In the same way, society as a whole *has* to trust professionals as a whole. In effect, it makes an implicit bargain with the providers of professional services. Professionals are allowed their rents; in return they are supposed to abide by a professional ethic of equity and service that prevents them from exploiting their clients and degrading the quality of the goods they supply. Professionals who betray their trust and break the rules that embody their ethic can be disciplined by their peers, and in the last resort expelled from their profession.

THE PUBLIC REALM AND TRUST

That leads us to a wider point. Markets cannot work properly without trust. If market actors don't or can't trust each other, there is no market; there are only pirates or gangsters, preying on the weak and unwary. Yet, though the market realm depends on trust, it can't engender trust all by itself. Markets depend, among other things, on the rule of law, enforceable contracts, enforceable property rights and an efficient fraud squad – all quintessential products of the public realm. It is these that make it possible for market actors to trust each other; without them markets would not exist.

What is true of trust in the marketplace is equally true of trust in the polity. The goods of the public realm also include liberty – not in the familiar sense of freedom to pursue private interests, but in the classical republican or 'Roman' sense of freedom from domination.[11] In principle at least, republican liberty goes with democratic self-government. If ordinary citizens don't trust their political representatives, democratic citizenship and the integument that binds leaders to led will wither. Citizens will trust their leaders if they think public institutions are governed by an ethic of equity and service, as by and large most citizens did in the early post-war years. But if the public realm succumbs to invasion by the market or private realms, as it did when Members of Parliament used parliamentary expenses to line their own pockets; or if political leaders surround themselves with dependent courtiers instead of disinterested and independent-minded public servants,[12] citizenship becomes an empty shell and public trust withers. As Chapter 6 will show, there is not much doubt that this is now happening in Britain.

SOPORIFIC COMPLACENCY

A look at the historical background will help to explain why. In Britain, the public realm in the sense put forward here grew slowly. Its origins can be traced back to the Glorious Revolution and the Bill of Rights of 1689. Lord Bingham's summary is as resonant as it is masterly: 'No monarch could again rely on divine authority to override the law. The authority and independence of Parliament were proclaimed; the integrity of its proceedings was protected and there could be no standing army in time of peace without its sanction. The power to suspend laws without the consent of Parliament was condemned as illegal. So was the power of dispensing with laws or the execution of laws.'[13] It was left to the Victorians, however, to carve out an unmistakable public realm from the adjacent private and market realms, and to erect strong barriers against incursions into it.

Two themes ran through their achievement: the reconstruction of the state and the narrowing of the market. Gladstone and his contemporaries dismantled the ancient structure of 'Old Corruption', and asserted the values of equity, service and civic duty against the clinging embrace of connection and patronage. By the end of the nineteenth century the patronage-ridden, nepotistic state of 100 years before had been effectively replaced by an efficient, modern state, equipped with a (fairly) corruption-free Parliament and a bureaucracy recruited and promoted on merit. Successive Reform Acts had widened the circle of political citizenship to embrace around 60 per cent of the adult male population, as against 9 per cent before the process started. The introduction of the secret ballot and the prohibition of corrupt practices in elections had struck further blows against intimidation and vote-buying. The abolition of the purchase of commissions in the army had helped to procure a professional officer corps; the Northcote–Trevelyan reforms had created a professional state bureaucracy.

The municipalization of public utilities in the great industrial cities of the Midlands and the North and the statutes listed in Dicey's account of the transition from individualism to collectivism discussed in Chapter 2 ran in parallel with such political reforms. By the turn of the nineteenth and twentieth centuries, a regulatory state with the capacity and will to discipline market power in the public interest was a feature of the landscape. Public authorities deserved much of the credit for its emergence, above all local ones. New industrial towns and cities such as Manchester, Leeds, Bradford, Bolton and Sheffield, as well as older ones like Newcastle, Liverpool and Birmingham, were centres of civic pride, civic activism and civic enterprise, symbolized by magnificent town halls that mimicked Gothic cathedrals or Renaissance palazzi.

Initiatives by churches, chapels, friendly societies, individual philan-thropists, co-operatives and trade unions were equally important. So was that leitmotiv of nineteenth- and early-twentieth-century British history, an extraordinary growth in the number of professional occu-pations with corresponding qualifying bodies. In 1800, there were seven such bodies, four for the Bar and three for medicine. By the out-break of the First World War there were sixty-six.

The story continued well into the twentieth century. The social reforms of the Liberal Government of 1905–14 laid the foundations of the welfare state completed by the wartime coalition of 1940–45 and the Labour governments of 1945–51. The professions, which had spearheaded the growth of the public realm in the second half of the nineteenth century, became more sizeable, more numerous and more confident. By the 1950s, the public realm seemed unassailable. The welfare state had been consolidated on the lines set out in the Beveridge Report. The economic approach that Keynes had advo-cated between the wars was a feature of the landscape. Few dissented from John Stuart Mill's belief that property rights could be modified or abolished if it were in the public interest to do so. Most of the pol-itical class, most officials and most influential commentators took it for granted that the so-called 'mixed economy' – an economy with a substantial publicly owned sector alongside a much larger private one – should continue indefinitely.

The results were cruelly ironic. The champions of the public realm succumbed to a soporific complacency. Marx, it seemed, had been proved wrong; tamed capitalism and the solidaristic moral economy that went with it would continue indefinitely; the institutions and practices of the public realm were beyond reproach; ideological conflict had ceased. In 1956, Anthony Crosland, social-democratic theorist and future Labour minister published his magnum opus, *The Future of Socialism*, arguing that capitalism had been so thoroughly transformed that it was a moot point whether it still deserved the name; even 'businessmen', he exclaimed, now accepted 'the doctrine of collective government responsibility for the state of the economy'.[14] In 1960, the American sociologist Daniel Bell proclaimed the 'death of ideology'; throughout the Western world, he argued, there was a con-sensus 'in favour of the welfare state and mixed economy'.[15] In 1965, the economist Andrew Shonfield opined that the extraordinary success of post-war capitalism was due to 'long-range national planning'.[16] All three patently assumed that the political and moral economies they depicted were set in stone.

SAILING BY GOD AND GUESS

Confident predictions have rarely been so comprehensively belied. It turned out that Marx had not been proved wrong. In spite of his manifold mistakes, the insight into capitalism's revolutionary voracity that ran through *The Communist Manifesto* was a much better guide to the world after stagflation than anything offered by the middle-way theorists of the post-war years. As Chapter 2 showed, the solidaristic moral economy that seemed a permanent feature of the landscape in the 1950s was engulfed in crisis twenty years later. Capitalism's taming turned out to have been skin deep; its dramatic return to the wild has been the dominant theme of global politics for the last thirty years. The institutions and practices of the public realm no longer looked irreproachable. The crisis of stagflation was also a crisis of the state. Like medieval barons defying a feeble king, over-mighty vested interests ranging from trade unions to Ulster Loyalists made it impossible for governments to govern as they thought best; it became fashionable to ask if Britain had become ungovernable.[17] Last, but not least, ideology rose again, like an angry phoenix from the ashes.

On the left, an amalgam of class-war proletarianism and statist socialism became the vehicle for an assault on the Keynesian social democracy of the recent past, led by the charismatic Tony Benn. But he and his followers found few takers. Their nostrums – more nationalization, workers' control of industry and autarchic insulation from an ever-more interdependent global economy – sounded more like a cry of mourning for a bygone age than a trumpet blast heralding a new one. The right – passionately backed by virtually all the print media – had the ideological field to itself. Yet the right's alternative ideology was not as clear-cut as it sometimes seems in retrospect. It drew its inspiration from Hayek; on one famous occasion, Margaret Thatcher, the right's answer to Tony Benn, plonked a well-worn copy of Hayek's *The Constitution of Liberty* onto a table and declared, '*This* is what we believe.'[18] But Hayek's teachings were signposts, not a route map. They didn't tell harassed ministers and officials what to do when they were faced with the unpredictable contingencies of political life. Like almost all successful political leaders Thatcher sailed by God and by guess, seizing unforeseen opportunities as they arose.

She was an extraordinary mixture of courage, guile, panache, demonic energy and an unsleeping will. Partly because of this, a thick coating of myth obscures the true nature of her extraordinary reign. For example, it is often said that she was an unusually successful vote-winner. The truth is that she never won anything approaching 50 per cent of the popular vote. Her biggest parliamentary majority (in 1983) was won with a mere 42.4 per cent of the total vote. In contrast, Anthony Eden's middle-way Conservative Party won 49.7 per cent in 1955. North of the border, she and her policies aroused an 'astonishing animosity' that helped to fuel what became an irresistible demand for a Scottish Parliament.[19] In the 1987 election, the Scottish Conservatives held only ten of the twenty-one Commons seats they had won in 1983. In the early years of her government she also had to contend with a multitude of hostile ministers; in the summer of 1980, 'Jim' Prior, the Employment Secretary, told Hugo Young of the *Sunday Times* that Thatcher hadn't 'really got a friend left in the whole Cabinet'.[20]

Another myth is that under Thatcher's governments popular attitudes became more favourable to the free market and less favourable to old-style Keynesian social democracy. The opposite is true. Simon Jenkins has summarized a mass of opinion surveys. There was no majority in the opinion polls, he writes,

> for her assault on the unions, for utilities privatization, or for cuts in top-rate taxes. In 1988 opinion was actually more favourably disposed to welfare socialism than when she came to power. In 1976, Gallup had found a majority for the Thatcherite policy of curbing inflation over reducing unemployment, by 54 per cent to 36 per cent. By 1986 this had reversed to 13:81.[21]

That said, the central themes of the age of Thatcher – which, as

Jenkins shows, covered the prime ministerships of John Major, Tony Blair and Gordon Brown as well as hers[22] – were defined under her government. Two themes stood out: one moral and philosophical, the other institutional and political. For Thatcher and her followers Donne was wrong: individuals *were* islands unto themselves; the notion that we are members one of another was a smokescreen for collectivist molly-coddling. Thatcher's alternative vision was summed up in her immortal dictum: 'there is no such thing as society. There are individual men and women and there are families.'[23] Not to be outdone, David Young, corporate grandee turned Conservative politician, declared that the essence of the Thatcher project lay in 'the restoration of the age of the individual'.[24]

The political and institutional theme is closely related to the moral and philosophical one. Asocial individualism went hand in hand with a relentless centralism, eerily reminiscent of Thomas Hobbes, the great seventeenth-century philosopher of absolute rule. For Hobbes, only an all-powerful sovereign could overcome the self-destructive passions of men, and make society possible. For Thatcher and her closest colleagues, only an untrammelled state could cut through the clinging institutional and cultural foliage that impeded progress towards the market order of their dreams. Intermediate institutions standing between the state and the citizen – self-governing professions, local authorities, universities, trade unions and the BBC – were suspect at best and subversive at worst. (For some of Thatcher's followers, the same was true of the Church of England, the most formidable intermediate institution of them all.)[25] Thatcher hated socialism and all its works, but her attitude to the state and its relationship with such intermediate institutions was closer to the doctrinaire centralism of early Fabian socialists than to the relaxed and tolerant flexibility of the Conservative tradition.

Much as the central state of early-nineteenth-century Britain had sought to reconstruct society in the interests of Karl Polanyi's 'great transformation' to laissez-faire,[26] the Thatcher governments sought to use the 'market state' described by Philip Bobbitt[27] to wage a war for hegemony on behalf of what they called an 'enterprise culture' and against what they saw as the defeatist culture of the past.[28] They used two instruments – privatization and marketization. Privatization, the sale of public assets to private purchasers, was the more conspicuous. Marketization, a process of rhetorical and behavioural colonization that intruded market norms and market practices into the public realm, was the more effective.

The privatization process was remarkably haphazard. Privatization did not even figure in the Conservatives' 1979 election manifesto. The first major privatizations – those of British Telecom and most of British Gas – did not take place until Thatcher's second term. In her third term, what had been a trickle to start with became a flood. British Petroleum, British Steel, the water authorities, British Airports, and electricity generation and distribution were all sold off. Under Major, British Rail, British Coal and nuclear energy joined the list. Altogether, the Thatcher and Major privatizations raised the staggering total of £65.6bn. The face of the British economy was changed, if not for ever then certainly for as far ahead as anyone could see.

How far privatization changed the body of the economy as opposed to the face is not so clear. John Kay's balance sheet is downbeat, but on the whole favourable. 'Privatised businesses', he writes, 'have not thrived in the private sector', but they had not thrived before privatization. All privatized companies, he adds, 'start from behind'. Privatized undertakings operating in competitive markets have done reasonably well, but that could have been achieved by changes in governance, without changing ownership. Consumers have benefited, though not by much.[29] The effect on the public realm is ambiguous too. The nationalized industries that the Major and Thatcher governments had sold off had been part of the public sector, but as noted above the public sector and the public realm are not the same things. The bonds of sympathy that Adam Smith thought fundamental to human society were not embodied in the nationalized industries before privatization any more than in privately owned firms. Besides, some of the privatized undertakings were natural monopolies (railways and water companies are examples). Only regulation could ensure that they did not exploit their customers, and the regulators were bound to be skilled professionals discharging public duties – quintessential inhabitants of the public realm.

MARKETIZATION:
A TRANSFORMATIVE PROJECT

The marketization story is very different. Privatization and marketization are easily confused, but they are not the same. Privatization refers to the sale of publicly owned undertakings to private purchasers. Marketization goes wider and deeper. It refers to the introduction of market mechanisms and market norms into activities hitherto run on non-market lines. It has covered a vast range of activities, but it is much more than a series of ad hoc responses to discrete problems. It is a coherent project, aimed at radical social transformation.

Among its most remarkable features is a curious linguistic revolution. Slowly, gradually, but inexorably the language of the marketplace has displaced the language of service and citizenship. Passengers have become 'customers'. Public-service job losses procure increased 'productivity'. Academics in search of promotion boast of being 'entrepreneurial'. Funding cuts are now 'efficiency gains'. Public services are 'delivered' to their users. Policies designed to further marketization are 'reforms'. Professionals, notably including professional public servants, have to be 'incentivized' to give of their best.

Here Joseph Stiglitz's scorn for the fetish for *individual* incentives is as pertinent as it is biting. 'Is it conceivable', he asks, 'that a doctor performing heart surgery would exert more care or effort if his pay depended on whether the patient survived the surgery or if the heart valve surgery lasts for more than five years? Doctors work to make sure each surgery is their absolute best, for reasons that have little to do with money.' And he goes on:

> Most employers recognize that teamwork is absolutely essential to the success of the company. The problem is that *individual* incentives can undermine this kind of teamwork . . .
>
> The prevailing approach to behaviour in standard economic theory focuses on rational *individualism*. Each individual assesses everything from a perspective that pays no attention to what others do, how much they get paid, or how they are treated. Human emotions such as envy, jealousy or a sense of fair play do not exist or, if they do, have no role

in *economic* behaviour ... To noneconomists, this approach seems nonsensical – and to me, it does too.[30]

The economic individualism that Stiglitz excoriates was not confined to economists. Early in her prime ministership, Thatcher famously declared, 'Economics are the method, the object is to change the heart and soul.'[31] Not since Cromwell and the rule of the 'Saints' in the 1650s had a British government attempted anything as ambitious. In pursuit of changed souls, Thatcher and her colleagues advanced on several fronts, linked by an overarching logic. In almost every area of social life, the core executive of ministers and high officials[32] at the apex of the state sought to hobble, humble and where possible to reconstruct the galaxy of institutions whose practices and values held back the tide of Hayekian market individualism and ran counter to the imperatives of the capitalist renaissance of the time.

THE GROVEL COUNT

High on the list of such institutions was the professional, career civil service. Here, Thatcher trod carefully. She did not launch a head-on attack on the whole institution. Instead, she did her best to wean it away from the fundamental Northcote–Trevelyan principle that civil servants should have 'sufficient independence' to 'influence' ministers as well as assisting them. She took a closer interest in promotions than any previous Prime Minister had done. In a narrow party sense, charges that she politicized the service were wide of the mark; some of those who benefited from her patronage were Labour in politics. But she undoubtedly changed the culture of Whitehall. To use a phrase coined by Lord Bancroft, the 'grovel count'[33] in Whitehall rose, as officials discovered that it was no longer wise to give ministers disinterested advice that they did not wish to hear. More important were the introduction of performance-related pay (a classic example of an individual incentive of the sort Stiglitz condemned) and individual contracts of employment. It would be wrong to exaggerate. Able and devoted officials still did (and do) their best to serve their country, just as their opposite numbers in the armed forces did and do. But they were no longer guardians of the public realm; willy-nilly they were agents of a market state.

Trade unionists were even more obnoxious to the marketizers than civil servants. For marketizers, the labour market was a market like any other. Unfortunately, it was rife with 'distortions' that prevented it from working properly. These had to be eliminated; and since trade unions were the prime distorters, their teeth had to be drawn. The teeth-drawing was astonishingly successful. In a series of statutes passed between 1980 and 1990, the Thatcher Government ended the unions' eighty-year-old immunity from civil suits arising out of trade disputes; protected trade union members from disciplinary sanctions against crossing picket lines; gave employers the right to dismiss unofficial strikers; removed legal immunities for industrial action in support of workers so dismissed and effectively abolished closed shops. (The last was a blow for individual freedom, but it was also a free rider's charter.) Trade union membership fell by around four million between 1979 and 1991. Over the same period, the percentage of the labour force in unions plummeted from 53 per cent to just over 34 per cent.[34]

The decline in union density was not solely due to government policy. It also reflected a marked decline in manufacturing employment: from seven million in 1980 to around five million in 1990.[35] But the Thatcher governments played a crucial part in the story. It was not always clear whether they wanted to destroy trade unionism or to foster a 'new unionism' co-operating with ministers, on the model of the electricians led by the sometime Communist Eric Hammond.[36] Yet the central theme of their policy was not in doubt. They hoped, through carefully judged salami tactics, to substitute individual rights for group rights and an individualistic employment culture for a collectivist one.

How far they succeeded is not clear. Today, as noted in the previous chapter, trade unionism barely exists outside the public sector, but unions still contribute significantly to public debate, as my final chapter will show. What is clear is that the Thatcher governments' hostility to the unions ran counter to the teachings of the two greatest economists in British history, Adam Smith and John Maynard Keynes. Adam Smith was no enemy of trade unions (or 'combinations' as they were called in his day). He deplored combinations of 'masters' to keep wages down, but defended combinations of 'workmen' to raise them – partly on the grounds that it was easier for masters to combine than for workmen to do so, and partly because the law allowed masters' combinations but prohibited combinations of workmen.[37] In twenty-first-century language, he believed that employers and employed should meet on a level playing field, and thought that unions would help to level it. Keynes's thoughts on the subject are even more pertinent today. In a mordant attack on Winston Churchill's policies as Chancellor of the Exchequer, published a year before the 1926 General Strike, he wrote:

> The truth is that we stand mid-way between two theories of economic society. The one theory maintains that wages should be fixed by reference to what is 'fair' and 'reasonable' as between classes. The other theory – the theory of the economic Juggernaut – is that wages should be settled by economic pressure, otherwise called 'hard facts', and that our vast machine should crash along, with regard only to its equilibrium as a whole, and without attention to the chance consequences of the journey to individual groups.[38]

The juggernaut theory never quite disappeared, but during the post-war years it was mitigated in the interests of fairness and social cohesion. Under the Thatcher governments it returned to favour. Its return is a prime cause of the growth of inequality to be discussed in Chapter 5; though there can be no proof, it has almost certainly helped to discredit the whole notion of collective action, not just in the workplace but almost everywhere. The most obvious result has been a powerful boost to Mammon worship.

THE WAR ON LOCAL DEMOCRACY

At a time when public memories of the strikes of the 1970s were raw, the trade unions were a soft target. Local government was a different proposition. Localism has been part of the British political tradition for centuries. The central state in London has never had high-level representatives on the local or provincial level, comparable to prefects in France or Italy. Outside the cities, what we now call local government was, for centuries, a matter for local gentry, sitting as justices of the peace. Conservatives had traditionally championed local authorities as bulwarks of local autonomy, resisting the statist tendencies of the Labour Party. (The first really serious assault on local democracy in the last century came under the post-war Labour Government, whose nationalization of public utilities and hospitals stripped local authorities of some of their most important functions.) But the market state and its managers were centralists by definition. Local authorities might be fine in principle, but in practice they impeded the march to marketization. Indeed, some authorities went out of their way to impede it: with astounding folly, certain far-left local authorities sought deliberately to use the powers of the 'local state' to negate central Government's economic policies.[39] Retribution was inevitable.

But it would be a mistake to think that exasperation with so-called 'loony left' councils was the chief source of the marketizers' antipathy to local government. The underlying reason was that local authorities belonged unmistakably to the public realm, which they had done so much to develop. Simply by existing, they challenged the marketizers' vision. Their nineteenth-century heyday was long gone, but they were still repositories of the non-market values of equity, service and professional duty. They were not all angels of rectitude, but serious scandals were rare. Yet from the marketizers' point of view, they were on the wrong side in the war for cultural hegemony. They had to be brought to heel.

They duly were. Thanks to central government's 'Right to Buy' legislation, around a fifth of council houses were sold off to their tenants in the course of the 1980s. This too has been seen as a blow for individual freedom, and in one sense it was. But it was also a blow against the property rights of the entire body of local-authority citizens, the ultimate owners of all council property, including houses. Since the Treasury appropriated a large proportion of the receipts from council house sales, moreover, the net effect of Right to Buy was to redistribute resources from the localities to the centre.[40] As well, the Government took power to 'cap' the rates, overturning a 400-year-old tradition that gave local authorities freedom to determine their own rates. The Greater London Council and the Metropolitan counties, both Conservative creations, were summarily abolished. Schools were encouraged to 'opt out' of local-authority control, and in doing so to opt in to control by the central state. Local authorities were compelled to deregulate bus services, and forbidden to subsidize public transport. The 1988 Education Reform Act transferred control of polytechnics from local to central government.

Functions previously performed by elected councillors were farmed out to more compliant bodies – in some cases, to private firms; in some to nominated bodies known as 'quangos' (quasi non-governmental organizations), appointed by ministers; and in some to central government itself. The effects on London government were particularly striking. By the mid-eighties, central government controlled London Transport, London's Docklands, London's land use planning, main roads, museums and galleries and suburban transport. In the Western world, only Paris was subject to a comparable degree of centralization.[41] In the early 1890s, Londoners elected around 12,000 citizens to serve on committees and boards that ran local services. In the early 1990s around 12,000 Londoners still sat on boards administering local services. The difference was that only 1,914 of them were elected.[42]

THE WAR ON PROFESSIONALISM

For the marketizers, professions, professionals and professionalism were as suspect as local government. Like the trade unions, they were market-distorting cartels. Worse still, the professions were carriers of – indeed formed by – an implicitly anti-market ideology. The professional ethic was premised on the assumption that professional goods could not be allocated on market principles. That ideology had to be rooted out if the marketizers were to win the war for cultural hegemony. The result was a systematic campaign to force professional groups, extending from doctors, teachers and academics to social workers and even policemen, into a market mould. The details varied from profession to profession, but the broad outlines were common to them all. In institution after institution professional autonomy was curtailed and professional judgement demeaned.

In a doomed pursuit of the chimera of perfect accountability, professional performance was increasingly subjected to trust-destroying audits. Here too Onora O'Neill gets to the nub of the matter with icy clarity.

> *In theory* the new culture of accountability and audit makes professionals and institutions more accountable *to the public*. This is supposedly done by publishing targets and levels of attainment in league tables, and by establishing complaint procedures by which members of the public can seek redress for any professional or institutional failures. But underlying this ostensible aim of accountability *to the public* the real requirements are for accountability *to regulators, to departments of government, to funders, to legal standards*. The new forms of accountability impose forms of *central control* . . .
>
> *In theory* again the new culture of accountability and audit makes professionals and institutions more accountable *for good performance*. This is manifest in the rhetoric of improvement and rising standards, of efficiency gains and best practice, of respect for patients and pupils and employees. But beneath this admirable rhetoric the real focus is on performance indicators chosen for ease of measurement and control rather than because they measure quality of performance accurately. Most people working in the public service have a reasonable sense not only of the specific clinical, educational, policing or other goals for which they work, but also of central ethical standards that they must meet. They know that these complex sets of goals may have to be relegated if they are required to run in a race to improve performance indicators . . . *Perverse incentives are real incentives.*[43]

More recently, the Francis Report on the appalling standards of care in the Mid Staffordshire Foundation Trust Hospital[44] has shown that perverse incentives (in this case to focus on financial targets rather than patients' wellbeing) can be deadly as well as real.

There was more. Control over school curricula was taken away from professional teachers and placed in the hands of an inevitably headline-conscious and short-termist Secretary of State. In the National Health Service a so-called 'internal market' eroded medical autonomy (and spawned a mass of quangos). The academic-dominated University Grants Committee, which had disbursed government funding to individual universities since the 1920s, was replaced by a Funding Council, on which academics were required to be in a minority. Universities were obliged to contract with the Council, a monopoly purchaser, to deliver specified services, of a specified quality, judged by ever-more elaborate appraisals. Even the police did not escape. Elaborate appraisal systems measured police performance against centrally determined targets; and to drive the lesson home, chief constables were put on fixed-term contracts.

There was no master plan, but a vision gleamed through the detail: political power would be concentrated in the hands of the central state and its agents; market principles would reign supreme elsewhere, except in the private sphere of friendship and family. The Thatcher and Major governments bequeathed that vision to their successors; despite differences of emphasis here and there, it has encapsulated the common sense of most of the political class, most of the commentariat and most of the business elite for the best part of a generation.

BACK TO PATRONAGE

This is not to say that the New Labour governments were carbon copies of the Thatcher and Major governments. For one thing, Blair had a rather wispy communitarian streak in his philosophical make-up, the residue of a youthful fascination with John Macmurray, the Scottish philosopher of personal fulfilment through 'community'.[45] Wispy communitarianism hardly mattered; two institutional departures from the Thatcher–Major legacy mattered a great deal. The first was an unintended consequence of Thatcher's disdain for Scottish opinion and indifference to (or possibly ignorance of) the specificities of Scottish history and culture. By the 1990s, a swelling demand for the devolution of Scotland was in full spate north of the border. In opposition, Labour signed up to Scottish devolution and, for good measure, to Welsh devolution as well. Two years after Blair took office in 1997, a Scottish Parliament was sitting in Edinburgh and a Welsh Assembly in Cardiff. The second oddity – an elected Mayor for London, accountable to an elected Assembly – stemmed from Blair's personal commitment. Albeit in very different ways, both changes created new sites of civic engagement and new spaces for public reasoning, strengthening the public realm in the process.

But in general the continuities between Thatcher and Blair were more salient than the contrasts. The New Labour governments were as suspicious of professionals as Thatcher's and Major's had been and no more friendly to trade unions. If anything they were more contemptuous of the Northcote–Trevelyan vision of a non-partisan, independent-minded civil service, duty-bound to give its political masters disinterested advice, even when it was unwelcome. No. 10 Downing Street swarmed with politically appointed advisers. (Where John Major's government made do with thirty-eight, Blair's first government had seventy-four.) In certain departments, unelected advisers, often with no experience of life outside the narrow confines of the Westminster and Whitehall village and invariably unaccountable to Parliament, had as much influence on decisions as junior ministers. On some issues members of the Prime Minister's Policy Unit, also unelected, were almost certainly as influential as Cabinet ministers, answerable to the House of Commons. One of the first things Blair did when he entered office was to give two political appointees – his press secretary, Alastair Campbell, and his chief of staff, Jonathan Powell – authority over civil servants. Parliament had no say in this portentous change in Britain's unwritten constitution, since it was made by Orders in Council. The long struggle to cleanse the state of patronage and favouritism had gone into reverse.

By the same token, the Blair governments were as contemptuous of local democracy as Thatcher's and Major's had been. Ministers launched a plethora of initiatives, designed to force local councils to dance to the centre's tune. OFSTED (the Office for Standards in Education), which had been set up under the Major Government, gained new powers at the expense of local education authorities. A small number of centrally funded 'academies', with private sponsors, were set up to promote 'innovation' and 'creativity' in areas where inner-city schools had allegedly failed to do so. Action 'zones', in which policy was determined by central government, were created 'with reckless abandon'[46] to deal with such matters as low educational achievement, poor housing and health inequalities. Not surprisingly, the Essex University democratic audit of the United Kingdom found that Britain was in breach of eleven of the thirteen major provisions set out in the

Council of Europe's Charter of Local Self-Government, which the Blair Government had accepted.[47]

Present-day equivalents of the 'practical men' whom Keynes mocked in the peroration to the *General Theory* would, no doubt, reply that there was a case for all these interventions. Practical men and women can almost always find a case for centralization: if they couldn't, centralizers would make no headway. But there is also a case for local democracy, and for those who prize republican liberty and the public realm it trumps the centralizers' case. It goes back to the insight offered by the French nobleman Alexis de Tocqueville in his masterpiece, *Democracy in America*: that American freedom rested on a complex network of civil associations of all kinds, local governments among them; and that, but for those associations, Americans might have succumbed to the tyranny of the majority. There is no way of telling if the New Labour governments were aware of de Tocqueville's insight; what is clear is that, even if they were, they paid no attention to it. They had internalized the centralist imperatives of the market state as thoroughly as their predecessors had done.

By the same token, they were equally wedded to the cult of private-sector managerialism. Ministers talked endlessly about the need to 'reform' the public services. Translated into ordinary English, that mantra meant that public institutions from schools, to universities, to hospitals and even to police forces should be managed as if they were private firms. Debate between the parties was conducted in the language of private consumer satisfaction. The question at issue was how to balance competing *private* claims – private claims to publicly provided goods, financed by taxation, versus private claims to privately provided goods, bought in the marketplace. Rightly or wrongly, political leaders increasingly took it for granted that it would be electoral death to argue that public needs should take precedence over private wants.

BARBARIANS TRIUMPHANT

The sequel tells essentially the same story. In New Labour's closing years, David Cameron made much of what he called the 'Big Society' but hopes that this implied a new respect for the public realm were soon belied. Just as New Labour followed where the Thatcher and Major governments had led, the Conservative–Liberal Democrat coalition has taken the path that New Labour staked out – only with extra passion. So far from slowing down, the attrition of the public realm has speeded up.

As Education Secretary, Michael Gove has been at least as contemptuous of professional opinion and at least as hostile to local democracy as any of his predecessors. He has sought explicitly to 'free' schools from local-authority control – in other words from control by democratically elected local politicians, close to the people and accountable to them. To that end, he has made one quantitatively minor, but qualitatively significant innovation: so-called 'free schools'. Free schools are funded by taxpayers, but (crucially) free of local-authority control. Groups wishing to set up free schools may consist of parents, charities, faith communities or businesses; the object of the exercise, according to David Cameron, is 'to open up schools to new providers and use the competition that results to drive up standards across the system'.[48] The echo of the Browne review is unmistakable.

Free schools are the light artillery of Gove's marketization. The heavy guns are a slew of new 'academies': descendants of the brain-children of (Lord) Andrew Adonis, sometime head of Blair's Policy Unit and subsequently New Labour schools minister. As noted above, academies under New Labour were supposed to be few in number, with a remit to improve standards in inner-city areas. Since they were funded and overseen by central government, they undermined local democracy, but the damage they did was not great. Gove's academies are a different matter. The stated intention is that all English schools will be academies in due course; by early 2013, 2,886 academies were open for business. To the obvious question – how could around 20,000 schools, each with its own funding contract, be overseen by the Department for Education in London? – there is, as yet, no answer. What is certain is that, if Gove's stated intentions are realized, he will have redistributed power from the localities to the central state on a scale never previously attempted. Entities called local authorities will doubtless still exist but they will have lost what has been their most important function since the then Conservative Government's Education Act of 1902.

Even Gove's marketizing zeal seems half-hearted in comparison with Andrew Lansley's when he was Health Secretary at the start of the Cameron Government. Within a few months of taking office, Lansley published a White Paper announcing what seemed at first blush a revolutionary reorientation of health policy. It was explicitly designed to 'liberate' the National Health Service (from what or whom was not stated), and clearly intended to promote competition between providers, both private and public, in a market for health care. The parliamentary bill giving effect to the White Paper was long, complex and virtually incomprehensible to non-experts. It encountered furious opposition, not just from the Labour Party, but from most of the Liberal Democrat rank and file, as well as from the BMA, the Royal College of General Practitioners, the Royal College of Nurses and the Royal College of Midwives. In the course of its slow passage through both houses of Parliament, hard-fought battles took place on innumerable detailed amendments, some of which were included in the eventual Act. When the dust of battle had subsided, however, it was clear that the fundamental principles of the White Paper had survived. Britain had taken a giant step away from the vision that had inspired the creation of the NHS, and towards a system in which the place of health care in the public realm will be, at best, problematic.

It is too soon to tell how these changes will bed down. But two points are already clear. One is that Lansley's apparent revolution was the culminating stage of a long-drawn-out process of incremental change, carried out under successive New Labour ministers. Colin Leys and Stewart Player have shown that from 2000 onwards a small group of ministers, advisers and officials in the Health Department and No. 10 Downing Street were intent on opening up a potentially lucrative health care market to profit-seeking private companies.[49] Each stage in the process followed logically from the one before, and prepared the way for the next one. Had that process not taken place, Leys and Player suggest, Lansley's apparent revolution would have been impossible. This is not to say that Lansley's changes don't matter:

they matter a lot. They amount to a transition from a managed market to an unmanaged one. But the latter would have been inconceivable if the former had not been in place.

The second point is both more complicated and more important. It has to do with the mentality and rhetoric of the marketizers, and with the social vision they encapsulate. At the heart of all three lies the totemic term 'choice': free choice by unconnected individuals, satisfying individual wants through market competition. As a gnomic phrase in the Government's health White Paper puts it, 'People want choice'. As so often the truth is much more complicated. Polling evidence shows that people believe that choice should be available, but it also shows that they don't value it for its own sake. What people want most of all is to be involved in their treatment and have their views treated with respect.[50]

But for the Coalition, even more than for New Labour, a reified 'Choice' with a capital 'C', which has little to do with the mundane choices of real-world parents, or patients or students, has acquired an almost iconic quality. It is, by definition, good. Resistance to freedom of choice is a sin, of which professionals who resist marketization are *ipso facto* guilty. There is nothing special about education or health care; they are commodities like any other, and competition between providers will ensure that consumers have the widest possible freedom of choice. The logic points not just to a swollen market realm, but to a market society, in which there are no limits to the empire of money.

We haven't reached that point yet. The public realm survives. Adam Smith's bonds of sympathy have not disappeared. Despite audits, box ticking and multifarious perverse incentives, professionals of all sorts do their best to abide by the ethics appropriate to their calling. Active citizens in tenants' associations, sports groups, faith groups and amenity groups still perform the civic duties that Onora O'Neill lauded at the beginning of this century; even more have a strong sense of civic duty even if they sometimes fail to live up to it.[51]

But the direction of travel is ominous. The Harvard political theorist Michael Sandel puts it well. 'The era of market triumphalism', he writes, 'has coincided with a time when public discourse has been largely empty of moral and spiritual substance.' And he adds, 'commercialism erodes commonality. The more things money can buy, the fewer the occasions when people from different walks of life encounter one another ... Democracy does not require perfect equality, but it does require that citizens share a common life.'[52] The vision of a common life – Donne's vision in modern dress – lay at the heart of the solidaristic moral economy of the post-war years, and helped to inspire the growth of the public realm. In the name of free choice we are turning our backs on that vision. One of the greatest tasks of our time is to renew it in a twenty-first-century idiom. To do so we must first examine the strange story of the free-choice cult, from the promise of liberation to the reality of servitude. To that I turn in my next chapter.

5

From Fate to Choice – and Back Again

'Two nations; between whom there is no intercourse and no sympathy; who are as ignorant of each other's habits, thoughts, and feelings, as if they were dwellers in different zones, or inhabitants of different planets; who are formed by a different breeding, are fed by different food, are ordered by different manners, and are not governed by the same laws.' 'You speak of –' said Egremont hesitantly. *'THE RICH AND THE POOR.'*

Benjamin Disraeli,
Sybil, or the Two Nations, 1845

Bow, bow, ye lower middle classes!
Bow, ye tradesmen, bow ye masses.
W. S. Gilbert and Arthur Sullivan,
peers' chorus, *Iolanthe*, 1882

On a rain-sodden day in June 2012, Elizabeth II celebrated her diamond jubilee as Queen. Unlike her great-great-grandmother Queen Victoria, the last British monarch to celebrate a diamond jubilee, she was neither Empress of India nor Queen of Great Britain and the whole of Ireland. Still (by the grace of God) she *was* Queen of Great Britain and Northern Ireland, as well as Head of the Commonwealth and Defender of the Faith. With her multiple palaces and archaic court rituals, she easily outclassed the other monarchs of Europe in grandeur, though not in intellectual or artistic accomplishment. She was the conduit for an unceasing stream of lordships, knighthoods, dameships, commanderships, orders and medals (many of them named for a long-defunct empire) with which political leaders rewarded their friends and the establishment rewarded itself. She was conscientious and dutiful to a fault; and despite the royals' unpopularity immediately after Princess Diana's death she had won a place in her people's hearts that seemed likely to endure. Yet she was the focal point of a culture of flummery that swathed the brute realities of inequality and exploitation in tinsel.[1]

In spite of the rain, the jubilee was an auspicious occasion. More than a million spectators watched from the banks of the Thames as a flotilla of 1,000 boats proceeded downstream from Battersea to a little beyond Tower Bridge. On the royal barge the imposing figure of Prince Philip stood ramrod-straight, arrayed in the medal-bestrewn uniform of an Admiral of the Fleet. Less ramrod-like, Prince Charles was also present, also in an Admiral's uniform. The young princes William and Harry, Catherine, Duchess of Cambridge, and Camilla, Duchess of Cornwall, completed the royal party. Lesser royals were scattered among lesser vessels. The general verdict was that the Brits had once again shown the world that they were unbeatable at pageantry.

For some, it was pageantry on the cheap. Two days after the river event, it emerged that a number of unpaid young people on job-seekers' allowances, who had been bussed into London to act as stewards, had had to sleep under London Bridge for the night before the pageant, and had then had to change into security clothes in public. Allegedly they had been deposited in a swampy campsite outside London after working a fourteen-hour shift in the pouring rain. Lord (John) Prescott, Deputy Prime Minister under the two New Labour prime ministers, and one of the few authentically working-class people to reach the front rank of politics in the last twenty years, savaged the Government for 'exploiting cheap labour'. A Downing Street spokeswoman airily replied that the incident was a 'one-off'. The managing director of Close Protection UK, the firm that had supplied the stewards, apologized for a 'logistics error'.

Not everything was cheap in jubilee Britain, however. That summer, undeterred by the recession, jewel-studded Nokia Vertu mobile phones were selling like hot cakes at £200,000 apiece.[2] A week before the jubilee, the glossy Friday supplement of the *Financial Times* advertised a range of delights: 'funky' Pandora LovePod rings for £615 in yellow gold and £635 in white gold; organza and straw millefeuille bicorn women's hats for £1,650; BB Magic Gold wrist watches for £27,000; muslin and silk-lace dresses for 12,860 euros; and Alfa Sea yachts for US$19m (VAT paid). The quip that modern society is divided between 'Haves' and 'Have Yachts' has rarely been more graphically illustrated.

THE PILLARS OF INEQUALITY

These contrasts frame a long and complex story, with many sub-plots. I hinted at the overarching theme at the end of the last chapter: the contrast between the promise of an idealized free choice that echoes through public debate and the reality of an oppressive fate. To grasp the logic and implications of that theme, however, at least four sub-plots need examining. One is the stubborn survival of the conception of unconditional property rights that John Stuart Mill attacked in his later years and that still underpins a peculiar – and peculiarly inegalitarian – Anglo-American form of capitalism. Another is the contrast between Britain's steady march towards greater economic equality in the middle decades of the last century and her precipitate rush away from it in the last thirty years. The third is the damage that growing inequality has inflicted, not just on the poorest in the land, but on British society as a whole. The fourth is the decline in public trust and political commitment which have accompanied it. I shall deal with all of these in this chapter, but I begin with property rights.

First, a platitude: Britain has never been an egalitarian society. The monarchy; the House of Lords; the Privy Council; centuries-old orders of chivalry like the Most Noble Order of the Garter and the Most Ancient and Most Noble Order of the Thistle; the comparatively parvenu Order of the Companions of Honour; and the Ruritanian absurdities of the honours list all denote and buttress an inherently inegalitarian culture, which has enabled new money to blend effortlessly with old money, and the upper reaches of the salariat to blend with both.[3] Shakespeare's Ulysses in *Troilus and Cressida* famously argues that inequality is the cement that holds society together. How, he asks, could

> Prerogative of age, crowns, sceptres, laurels,
> But by degree stand in authentic place?
> Take but degree away, untune that string,
> And hark what discord follows.

As the jubilee day showed, Britain's public culture still reeks of that assumption. There is no British equivalent of the American myth of homespun frontier equality or the French republican triad of '*liberté, égalité, fraternité*'. The British 'religion of inequality' and its 'great god Mumbo-Jumbo', as R. H. Tawney memorably called them, have deep, tough roots – deeper and tougher than even he realized. To defend inequality on the grounds that it accords with economic laws, he wrote, 'is to dance naked, and roll on the ground, and cut oneself with knives, in honour of the mysteries of Mumbo-Jumbo'. But, he added:

> the power of Mumbo-Jumbo, like that of some other spirits, depends on the presence of an initial will to believe in the minds of his votaries, and can, if only they are not terrified when he sends forth his thunders and his lightnings – the hail of his logarithms and the whirlwind of his economic laws – be overcome.[4]

As we shall see, Tawney's hopes have been betrayed. Mumbo-Jumbo and the 'religion of inequality' have at least as many votaries today as they did when he wrote eighty years ago and far more than when he died fifty-two years ago. Part of the explanation lies in the culture of flummery I mentioned a moment ago, but there is a deeper explanation as well. Among other things, Tawney's 'religion of inequality' is the legatee of a long-drawn-out, multiple revolution, at once cultural, ideological, social and political, that gave the propertied elite a secure title to rule in its own interests. In the course of that revolution, property owners brushed aside the surviving remnants of a pre-modern, essentially feudal conception of property, for which their claim to such a title would have been impious and unlawful, and fought off the rival claims of a would-be authoritarian Crown. In a now-classic study, the social historian Harold Perkin argues that the philosopher-in-chief of this revolution was John Locke, for whom the *raison d'être* of government and indeed of civil society was the preservation of property.

Perkin paints a vivid picture of the way in which the revolution worked itself out.

> Whereas the medieval conception of property, especially in land, was conditional, circumscribed and subject to the specific claims of God, the Church, the King, the inferior tenants, and the poor, the eighteenth-century concept was absolute, categorical, unconditional; and whether based with Locke, Blackstone and Adam Smith on a natural right anterior to society, or with Hume, Paley and Bentham on the principle of utility, it was secure from the envy of the poor and the covetousness of kings. Property gave to the owner the right to dispose of it exactly as he wished, short of actual fraud or physical injury to others. As the Dean of Westminster put it in 1798: 'Riches, you may think are abused; but have not the rich a right over their own wealth, to use it or abuse it? A man may be vicious, or a prodigal or a fool; but if he injures himself only, he is accountable to himself only, to his family or to God.'[5]

When the Dean of Westminster wrote, the social meaning of unconditional property was manifested most obviously in the wealth of the great landed magnates who dominated social and political life. In 1734 the gross rental income of the Duke of Bedford was £31,000 a year. In 1764 the Duke of Devonshire's was £34,000. (The purchasing power of the Duke of Bedford's £31,000 a year amounts to £3.9m in twenty-first-century money. As a proportion of average earnings it is equivalent to £53m today.) Rent rolls were only part of the story. A stream of bribes, pensions, sinecures and inflated official salaries topped up the wealth that the great magnates derived from their lands. At the beginning of the eighteenth century, the Earl of Nottingham made £50,000 from two spells as Secretary of State. At around the same time, the Duke of Chandos, Paymaster of the Forces, was said to have made £600,000 from his office.[6] Later in the century, Henry Fox, father of the scourge of George III, Charles James Fox, made a profit of £400,000 from the same office.

Daron Acemoglu and James A. Robinson usefully distinguish between 'extractive' political institutions, which allow rulers to cream off more of the social product than they contribute to it, and 'inclusive' ones, which don't.[7] The Dukes of Bedford, Chandos, Devonshire and their ilk were wealth extractors in excelsis.[8] Yet we should never forget that gross economic inequality did not prevent the slow growth of equality before the law; despite a brutal penal code, replete with savage punishments, the great landlords mentioned above had to assert their extractive power through open legal processes. Though they succeeded for most of the time, one of the most remarkable features of eighteenth-century Britain is that they sometimes failed.[9]

In externals the contours of twenty-first-century property rights have little in common with those of the eighteenth century. In essentials, the two are closer than most of us imagine. The notion of unconditional property rights easily survived the Dean of Westminster and the property owners for whom he spoke. As much as landed magnates, the capitalist owner-managers who helped to make Britain the first industrial society in history were the absolute owners of their property, with which they could do whatever they pleased. The property-less labourers they employed were 'hands' – commodities – with no more control over their working conditions than bales of cotton or hods of coal. Charles Dickens's horrified depiction in *Hard Times* has lost none of its power to shock.

> In the hardest-working part of Coketown; in the innermost fortifications of that ugly citadel, where Nature was as strongly bricked out as killing airs and gasses were locked in; at the heart of the labyrinth of narrow courts upon courts and close streets upon streets, which had come into existence piecemeal, every piece in a violent hurry for some one man's purpose, and the whole an unnatural family ... among the multitude of Coketown, generically called 'the Hands', – a race who would have found more favour with some people, if Providence had seen fit to make them only hands or, like the lower creatures of the seashore, only hands and stomachs – lived a certain Stephen Blackpool, forty years of age.

City magnates like 'Ned' Baring and Lionel Rothschild, the first Jew to sit in the House of Commons, were doubtless smoother than the owner-managers in the provinces, but there is no reason to believe that they viewed property rights in a different spirit.

The long-drawn-out growth of the public realm I described in the last chapter chipped away at the outer fortifications of unconditional property, but the inner ideological and institutional essence remained almost intact. Acts of Parliament compelled employers to do, or to refrain from doing, this or that, but in the areas untouched by law their property rights were still unconditional and absolute. (For all practical purposes wives were property too.) After the Second World War, as Chapter 2 showed, nationalization effectively abolished private property rights in certain industries; and, even in the private sector, big firms were run by professional managers who broadly accepted the solidaristic moral economy of the time and the Keynesian social-democratic settlement that went with it. But the 'mixed economy' that took shape in this period was mixed only in the sense that publicly and privately owned undertakings existed side by side. However socially responsible their managers might be, privately owned firms were still owned unconditionally by their shareholders, who alone had voting rights in company general meetings. As Chapter 2 showed, the trade unions could deal with employers on more equal terms than in the past, but they were not allowed – and in many cases did not wish – to penetrate the citadel of decision-making power and responsibility.

Because unconditional property rights have been part of the architecture of British and American capitalism for as long as anyone can remember, British and American economists, politicians and commentators tend to see them as intrinsic to capitalism as such. (This helps to explain why peripatetic American economic gurus, who took it for granted that market economies depend on unconditional property rights, gave disastrous advice to post-Communist Russia.) The truth could hardly be more different. As Chapter 2 showed, John Stuart Mill came to believe that, even in a market economy, property rights could be modified, or even abrogated, for the sake of the public good. The resounding papal encyclical *De Rerum Novarum* that Cardinal Manning helped to inspire echoed and amplified Mill. Working men, declared the encyclical, had been 'surrendered, isolated and helpless, to the hardheartedness of employers and the greed of unchecked competition'. The socialist alternative, to do away with private property, was manifestly unjust: 'every man has by nature the right to possess property as his own'.

What they did not have was the right to abuse the power that property gave them. It was 'shameful and inhuman' for employers to treat their employees 'as though they were things in the pursuit of gain'; to pay unduly low wages was 'a great crime which cries to the avenging anger of Heaven'. Equally, workers had a right to form associations to defend their legitimate interests.[10] Property rights, in short, were *conditional* on the performance of duties; and so were workers' rights. *De Rerum Novarum* laid the intellectual foundations of the Catholic social teaching of the twentieth century, embodied in the Christian Democratic movements that played a central role in shaping the economic culture of the central European democracies in the post-war period.

Its precepts were sometimes flouted in practice, but that is true of all the great political statements in the Western canon, from the American Declaration of Independence to the United Nations' Universal Declaration of Human Rights. The important point is that Catholic social teaching helped to engender the attitudes that still underpin the staggeringly successful post-war German social-market economy, with its long time horizons, industrial co-determination and, above all, its concern for human development.[11] (Catholic social teaching does not deserve all the credit for this: Konrad Adenauer's successor as Chancellor, Ludwig Erhard, often seen as the father of the social-market economy, was a Protestant.)

Germany did not become a paradise of financial wisdom. After the crash of 2008 it turned out that many German banks had been as foolish and greedy as British and American ones. But Germany's financial sector did not overshadow the rest of the economy in the way that Britain's did. The ethos and structures of the social-market economy remained intact, above all in the so-called *Mittelstand* composed of medium-sized, often family-owned manufacturing companies which account together for more than half Germany's GDP. John Studzinski, a former Morgan Stanley banker and subsequently head of the Investment Banking Division of HSBC, singles out three crucial features of the *Mittelstand*: a spirit of collaboration between employers and employees, fostered by works councils representing all the workers in a given enterprise; a determination to 'build for the long term'; and above all a particular ethos, for which,

> business is a constructive enterprise that aims to be socially useful. Making profit is not an end in itself: job creation, client satisfaction and

product excellence are just as fundamental. Taking on debt is treated with suspicion. The objective of every business leader is to earn trust – from employees, customers, suppliers and society as a whole.[12]

That ethos has helped to make Germany the unquestioned economic powerhouse of Europe. It has also made it one of the world's most egalitarian big economies.

Britain has seen occasional attempts to undermine the fortress walls of unconditional property rights. In the 1920s the Liberal 'Yellow Book' masterminded by Lloyd George and Keynes championed 'the worker's right to be a citizen and not merely a subject, in the world of production' and called for a Council of Industry representing workers as well as employers. In internal Labour Party disputes in the 1930s Ernest Bevin fought for workers' representation on the boards of future nationalized industries. In the 1970s Alan Bullock, distinguished historian and former Oxford Vice-Chancellor, chaired a Royal Commission on industrial democracy that recommended a rather pale version of German co-determination, in which trade union representatives would sit on company boards. In the 1990s, an unofficial Commission on Wealth Creation and Social Cohesion chaired by the Liberal Democrat peer Ralf Dahrendorf (and on which I served) championed 'stakeholder' capitalism – an economic system in which private firms balance the interests of a range of stakeholders, including employees, suppliers, distributors and local communities as well as shareholders, instead of pursuing shareholder interests to the exclusion of all the rest.

It was all in vain. Policy makers shrank from the hard, tedious, unglamorous task of building a consensus for a revised economic architecture and culture. Government after government dreamed of a magic bullet which would remedy the country's economic ills without continuous and consistent effort on the part of the political and administrative elites. Unconditional property rights held the field. Indeed, the decline of trade unionism, the privatization of publicly owned industries and, most of all, the onward march of the financial sector tightened their grip. As we shall see, the richest 1 per cent of the population gained substantially. The remaining 99 per cent lost.

THE STRANGE CAREER OF
THE GINI COEFFICIENT

Against that background the second of my sub-plots – Britain's steady progress towards and precipitate rush away from greater economic equality – falls into shape. During the Second World War, the British state faced an existential threat, more terrible than any it had faced before. To overcome it the Churchill coalition had to wage total war; and total war entailed the 'war socialism' I described in Chapter 2. The 'religion of inequality' that Tawney had savaged was thrown to the winds. As noted earlier, Britain became more egalitarian than it had ever been before or was ever to be again. The rich lost far more than the poor from the inevitable cut in private consumption. The standard rate of income tax reached 50 per cent; on top of that a levy on incomes above £20,000 a year, known as 'surtax', reached 48 per cent. In effect the richest taxpayers were paying 98 per cent of their incomes to the tax collector. Revenue from direct taxation on incomes rose twice as fast as from indirect taxation on consumption. Free school meals, cheap milk for children and expectant mothers and free cod liver oil benefited the working class more than the middle class. In real terms, wage incomes rose by 22 per cent from 1938 to 1949. Salary incomes fell by 22 per cent and incomes from property by 15 per cent.[13] In 1937 the top 1 per cent of income taxpayers received 12.6 per cent of post-tax incomes. Twelve years later the figure was 6.8 per cent.

Belying Labour fears that a Conservative victory in 1951 would mean a return to the bad old days before the war, the Conservative regime that held office in the 1950s and early 1960s did not slash welfare spending or abandon Keynesian economic management. Cuts in income tax benefited the middle class more than the working class, but earnings went up faster than prices, so that real wages increased. Social spending increased absolutely and held its existing share of GDP. The share of post-tax incomes going to the top 1.0 per cent actually fell; by 1959, the year of Harold Macmillan's famous boast that the British people had 'never had it so good', the figure was 5.5 per cent. (In 1969 it was 5.0 per cent.)[14]

The standard measure of income equality is the so-called 'Gini coefficient'. A coefficient of 0.00 would mean that incomes were totally equal, a coefficient of 1.00 that the entire income of the society belonged to one person. In 1961, the first year for which the figure is available, the coefficient was 0.261. It fell – though not by much – during the 1960s. By 1970, the year that Harold Wilson gave way to Edward Heath as Prime Minister, it was 0.259. It went on falling during the 1970s. In 1979, the year the Callaghan Government staggered to its doom, the Gini was 0.23. It rose a bit during Thatcher's first term, but by 1982, the year of the Falklands War, it was still only 0.261.

Then came Thatcher's 1983 landslide victory. In quick succession it was followed by the 'Big Bang' opening up the City to foreign competition, the great privatizations, the sweeping advance of marketization in sphere after sphere of common life, the rise of the 'grovel count' in Whitehall and, above all, the installation of the fetish of free choice and the free market at the heart of the state. With astonishing speed, Tawney's 'religion of inequality' returned to favour; the great God Mumbo-Jumbo acquired a vast new congregation; and the Gini started to rise remorselessly almost year by year. By 1987, the year of Thatcher's third victory, it was 0.305. In 1990, the year of her fall, it was 0.34. Inequality stayed on a plateau under Major, but it rose again under Blair, reaching 0.35 by 2005. It then fell a little, but it was still exceptionally high by European standards. According to Eurostat, the Luxembourg-based statistical service of the European Commission, the Gini coefficient in the United Kingdom was 0.33 in 2011, much lower than in the United States, but higher than in all EU member states except ex-Communist countries on the Union's eastern periphery (Bulgaria, Latvia, Romania) and Portugal and Spain on its southern periphery.[15]

The upward march of the Gini coefficient is only part of a bigger story. To gauge the social impact and human meaning of the capitalist renaissance of the last thirty years we should also ponder the astonishing rise of the super-rich. By 1999, the top 1.0 per cent of taxpayers received 10.2 per cent of taxable income, easily the highest figure since the end of the Second World War, and not very far short of what it had been in 1937.[16] The dynamics of income distribution within the top 1.0 per cent are even more striking. Chrystia Freeland quotes a study by the LSE economists Brian Bell and John Van Reenen. In 1998, Bell and Van Reenen showed, the top 2.0 per cent of the top 1.0 per cent received 11 per cent of that cohort's income; in 2008, it received 13 per cent.[17] The eighteenth-century Dukes of Bedford and Devonshire would have been at home (though they might have found the jewel-encrusted Nokia mobiles a little vulgar). Keynes, Beveridge, Bevin and Bevan might have wondered if they had lived in vain.

A 2008 study by the Institute for Fiscal Studies is more revealing still.[18] The 'very rich' and the 'very, very rich', as the IFS termed them, were 'racing away' from the rest of their society. (The 'very rich' are the top 1.0 per cent; the 'very, very rich', the top 0.1 per cent.) By 2004/5 the gap between those at the topmost end of the income scale and the rest of the population was enormous. The richest 0.1 per cent of the population comprised 47,000 people, just enough to fit into Manchester City's football ground. Their *average* pre-tax income was £780,000 a year, as against an average for all income taxpayers of around £25,000. The total pre-tax income of the 'very, very' rich 0.1 per cent was £37bn, or 4.3 per cent of total pre-tax incomes. The 'very rich' 1.0 per cent comprised 420,000 people out of nearly 30 million income taxpayers. Their average pre-tax income was a fraction more than £155,000. The average income of the 'very, very rich' was thirty-one times as much as that of the average taxpayer; and the average income of the 'very rich' six times as much. In a lecture to the Royal Statistical Society more recently, Professor Danny Dorling of Sheffield University showed that the richest 1.0 per cent of the population now take 15 per cent of total income, up from 6 per cent in 1979. As the share going to the richest 1.0 per cent grew, moreover, the share going to the 9.0 per cent immediately below them fell.[19]

One reason was the upward climb of top executives' pay. A survey by Manifest and MM&K in June 2012 showed that the pay of CEOs in FTSE 100 firms rose by an average of more than 12 per cent in the preceding year, while employees received virtually no pay increases at all. In the single year 2011 Bob Diamond, the CEO of Barclays bank, and the most highly paid individual in the country, received £20.9m of 'realizable remuneration' (in other words salary, bonus and any share options that could be cashed in during the year). On the same basis, Sir Martin Sorrell, CEO of the media and advertising company WPP, and the second on the list, received £11.6m. Others in the list of the top ten highest-paid executives included Sir Andrew Witty, CEO of Glaxo, with £10.7m; Peter Voser of Shell, with £9.7m; and the tenth on the list, Dame Marjorie Scardino of Pearson, with £8.9m.[20] In purchasing power, all of these remuneration packages outclassed the rental incomes of the great noblemen of the eighteenth century.

There is an important difference between then and now. Eighteenth-century noblemen went on the Grand Tour to acquire the polish appropriate to their station, and some of them built mansions in a continental style, but they were rooted in British soil, and drew their incomes from British estates. Many of them played leading roles in national politics. By contrast, the Diamonds, Sorrells and Wittys are part of a global community of super-rich with its own rituals, rivalries, ambitions, meeting places, consumption patterns and career trajectories. The community members have much more in common with each other than with lesser folk in the countries where they originated or whose passports they now carry. They are driven, insecure and footloose. Davos, the venue for the annual meetings of the World Economic Forum, means more to them than any national capital. For Aditya Mittal, CEO of ArcelorMittal and son of its founder, Lakshmi Mittal, 'you can achieve almost the same set of objectives whether you're in London, New York or a place like Singapore. You have access to talent, you have access to bankers, lawyers, you have access to good restaurants, good hotels.'[21] Above all, the global super-rich are players in a global market for executive talent – both as buyers and as sellers. In short, the upward climb of British executive pay is powered by global forces – above all in the financial sector.[22]

The story of marketable wealth – 'congealed income', as John Hills nicely terms it – is different in detail, but similar in essentials. It took time, he thinks, for the increased income inequality of the 1980s to be reflected in the distribution of wealth. In 1991, the richest 1.0 per cent owned only 17 per cent of marketable wealth. But by 2001 the figure was 23 per cent.[23] In a later study, Hills found that the richest 1.0 per cent owned £1.5m or more of net wealth per head not including pension rights and £2.6m or more including them. The figure for the top 10 per cent was £853,000 including pension rights. The bottom tenth owned wealth of £8,820 on average. The bottom 1.0 per cent possessed negative wealth: in other words fewer assets than liabilities.[24]

THE SWELLING BOIL

Unseemly as they are, these figures massively understate the true extent of inequality, though by how much it is impossible to tell. A long list of well-heeled British tax exiles, domiciled in more accommodating jurisdictions, includes such varied figures as the Barclay brothers, Nat Rothschild, Sean Connery and Stelios Haji-Ioannou, the founder of EasyJet. With unblushing *chutzpah*, Richard Branson, the epitome of the new elites of money and celebrity, recently boasted:

> Virgin's offshore status has been crucial to its development: it allowed money to move from business to business without massive tax liabilities. If we had not done it the way that we did, Virgin would be half the size that it is today.[25]

Branson plainly thought not just that Virgin was self-evidently entitled to avoid the taxes lesser mortals paid, but that everyone would agree that its right to do so was self-evident.

A report by the Tax Justice Network in July 2012 estimated that, in the world as a whole, at least £13tn is hidden in tax havens or 'secrecy jurisdictions', beyond the reach of any taxman and concealed from prying eyes.[26] How much of the loot belongs to British nationals is uncertain, but there is no doubt that a great deal of it does. Nicholas Shaxson has shown that, of the world's sixty secrecy jurisdictions, around half are part of a 'hub-and-spoke array of tax havens centred on the City of London'. In the inner ring are Crown Dependencies such as Jersey, Guernsey and the Isle of Man. Then come fourteen Overseas Territories ranging from the Cayman Islands to Gibraltar. These two rings, as Shaxson nicely puts it, 'combine futuristic offshore finance with medieval politics'. (For financial operators in Jersey, Shaxson was told, Gibraltar 'was where you put the real monkey business'.)[27]

The outer ring of the spider's web includes fully independent jurisdictions, such as Singapore, Dubai and Ireland, which are still closely connected to the City of London – the centre of a web of tax havens that girdles the globe. According to Russia's deputy prosecutor general, who is presumably no novice in such matters, the City is also 'a giant launderette for laundering criminally sourced funds'.[28] In another report Richard Murphy has added some intriguing details. British banks, he showed, have a total of 547 subsidiaries in seven British 'secrecy jurisdictions', including, among others, the inevitable Cayman Islands, Jersey, Guernsey and the Isle of Man. The 'big four' accountancy firms, KPMG, Ernst and Young, PWC and Deloitte, operate in all seven, as well as in the Turks and Caicos Islands, Anguilla and Montserrat.[29] The City of London is at one and the same time a state within a state, a powerful lobby group and a motor of inequality. It is also a swelling boil on the nether parts of the global financial system.

INEQUALITY'S STING

The third sub-plot comes into my account at this point. Inequality levies a heavy toll, socially, politically and psychologically. It is paid by the entire society, even including the rich, but the worst sufferers belong to the growing army of the poor that the rising rich leave behind them. Increasing poverty was as much a hallmark of the Thatcher governments as increasing inequality. The figures are striking: in the Thatcher years, the number of people living in poverty – in other words on incomes of less than 60 per cent of the median income of the nation – almost tripled.[30] The New Labour years saw a change: the poverty total fell somewhat, largely because of the governments' vigorous attempts to cut child poverty. (Among working-age adults without children, a group that Labour's tax and benefit reforms did not help, relative poverty increased.) There are two standard measures of poverty – after and before housing costs – and both peaked at the start of 1990s. However, the subsequent fall was not particularly steep. In 2009/10 more than one fifth of the population were living in poverty after housing costs and not quite one fifth before housing costs.[31] In 2007, *Social Trends* reported that the poverty rate in the United Kingdom was the eighth highest in the EU, after Italy, Ireland,

Portugal, Slovakia, Greece, Spain and Estonia. By 2010, the UK rate was the tenth highest, after Italy, Portugal, Greece, Spain, Estonia, Lithuania, Bulgaria, Romania and Latvia.[32] (Bulgaria and Romania did not join the Union until 2007.)

Of the major economies of the European mainland, none is as unequal as Britain; only Italy matches her poverty rate. On poverty as on inequality, Britain ranks with ex-Communist and ex-Fascist countries to the east and south of the Union's heartland, not with its stable and prosperous core. This did not happen because governments deliberately sought a unequal society. The Thatcher governments were not dismayed by the astounding growth of inequality on their watch, but insofar as they thought about inequality at all (which was not very far) they saw it as a consequence of policies pursued for other reasons. As the last chapter showed, they dreamed of an 'enterprise culture', and wanted to set the enterprising free to rise above the common herd, but for them inequality was a by-product, not the aim of the exercise. Much the same was true of New Labour. Like the Thatcherites, Blairites and Brownites were for equality of opportunity, not equality of outcome; but though they were unfazed by increasingly unequal outcomes, they did not seek them for their own sake. What they did seek – what all the governments of the last fifty years have sought – was Growth with a capital 'G': a bonanza of unceasing, uncontested economic growth, which would make everyone better off and take the sting out of inequality. In the 1970s, they hoped the bonanza would come from North Sea oil. In the 1980s, 1990s and 2000s they put their faith in capitalism's return to the wild: in capitalism shorn of the constraints imposed on it in the years after the Second World War and driven by a rapacious and (as we now know) occasionally criminal financial sector.

The results, to put it mildly, have not come up to scratch. For a while untamed capitalism did produce rapid growth, but inequality's sting did not abate. In a now famous study (which has been criticized, but convincingly defended), Richard Wilkinson and Kate Pickett show that inequality breeds dysfunctional societies and that, in the developed world, wealthy societies with high levels of inequality are more dysfunctional than less wealthy ones with lower levels of inequality.[33] The United States is a glaring example. She is one of the richest countries in the world, and also one of the least egalitarian. Despite her high standard of living as measured by GDP per head, life expectancy in America is lower than in almost all other developed countries. Despite the excellence of the great American Ivy League universities and state universities such as Berkeley, Michigan and Wisconsin, educational achievement is poorer. Mental illness, drug abuse, crime (particularly homicides), teenage births and obesity are more common than in less unequal societies. There are similar differences between individual American states, with the more unequal ones like New York and Louisiana doing worse than more equal ones such as Wisconsin or Vermont.

The United Kingdom is not in the same league as the United States, but among the developed economies that Wilkinson and Pickett mention she is an outlier on a range of social indicators as well as on inequality and poverty. Britain has less mental illness than the US, but more than Japan, Belgium, the Netherlands, France, Canada and New Zealand. Drug abuse and obesity are more common in Britain than in most other member-states of the EU, and life expectancy is shorter. The US heads Wilkinson and Pickett's list of teenage births per country, but Britain is second. Among the G7 Britain comes second in the proportion of fifteen- to 24-year-olds that are not in education or employment. Britain's prison population per 100,000 inhabitants is ninth in the EU; the other eight are all former Communist dictatorships, apart from Spain, which was a Fascist dictatorship not long ago. Among the twenty-five EU member states for which data are available, the British death rate from cancer among men was slightly lower than the EU average, but among women it was substantially higher.[34] By virtually all measuring rods, the United States is the most dysfunctional society in the rich developed world. Britain is the second most.

CHAVS, SLAGS AND SLOBS

The causal link between inequality and poverty on the one hand and these social ills on the other is not self-evident, but it is not difficult to grasp. In a society that equates wealth with worth, the poor soon become worthless. They become 'chavs', 'slags', 'slobs', 'scroungers' and 'yobs'. They are 'benefit cheats', they lack 'aspiration', they belong to an inert, yet menacing 'under-class'. Their very existence is an offence. It challenges a central premise of the ideology of untamed capitalism: that free choice in free markets benefits everyone. The poor ought not to exist. Since they do exist, and since the ideology of untamed capitalism is assumed to be true by definition, the only possible explanation is that they have failed to take advantage of the opportunities that free markets have given them: that they are to blame for their poverty. In days gone by a supposed distinction between the 'deserving' and 'undeserving' poor was a stock theme of public debate. Now there are no deserving poor: there are only the undeserving poor and 'hard-working families who play by the rules'.

In this climate it was acceptable for the Conservative social security minister, Peter Lilley, to tell a Conservative Party conference, in a nasty parody of Gilbert and Sullivan, that he had a 'little list of young ladies who get pregnant just to jump the housing list'. It was almost commonplace for the *Daily Telegraph* journalist James Delingpole to opine that 'rudderless urchins are routinely downing alcopops and cans of super-strong lager before they've reached their teens', or for another *Daily Telegraph* journalist, Janet Daley, to complain that even visits to the theatre are incomplete without 'a gang of boisterous, inebriated chavs who will disrupt the performance and may threaten you with assault if you upbraid them'.[35] The Labour MP Stephen Pound distils these anxieties unforgettably:

> I genuinely think that there are people out there in the middle classes, in the church, and the judiciary and politics and the media, who actually fear, physically *fear* the idea of this great, gold bling-dripping, lumpenproletariat that might one day kick their front door in and eat their au pair.[36]

On one level, the anxieties are not new. A hundred and fifty years ago, during the debates over extending the suffrage, the political elite took extraordinary pains to draw a line between the self-respecting, self-controlled upper working class and the 'residuum' of allegedly drink-besotted and violence-prone 'Roughs'. (More recently, David Selbourne resurrected the nineteenth-century spectre of the residuum in the shape of a loutish new class of 'plebeians', which had replaced the self-respecting proletariat of old days.[37]) However, there is an important difference between the nineteenth century and today. The 'Roughs' who haunted the imaginations of *bien pensant* mid-Victorian intellectuals were not – or at least did not remain – isolated social atoms. Many of them joined the National Reform League formed in 1865 to bring pressure on MPs to widen the suffrage. Many more took part in the great demonstrations that paved the way for the 1867 Reform Act. They or their children joined the unskilled 'general' trade unions of the closing decades of the century, like Ben Tillett's dockers and Will Thorne's gas workers. They defeated the employers in the London dock strike of 1889. They learned the disciplines of democracy and collective action in friendly societies, trade union branches and co-operative societies. They were sustained by a common culture and, albeit intermittently, by a social vision that made their fate comprehensible and held out the hope that it would one day be mastered.

Vestiges of that culture survive, but they are only vestiges; and the vision is barely a memory. Marx's dream of a formless mass of the dispossessed morphing into a class-conscious, disciplined proletariat has been turned inside out. Today's poor have little or nothing in common with Marx's proletarians. They are barely a class. They are social isolates, fending as separate individuals for themselves. There is no place for them in the narrative of 'meritocracy', 'opportunity' and 'ambition' that dominates our public culture on left and right alike; and they have no alternative narrative to counter it. In the race of life they are for ever also-rans. Poverty has always been humiliating, but we can safely assume that it is more humiliating in the lonely emotional wastelands of today than it was when those at the bottom of the social pile had solid structures to cling to and a collective dream of justice to give them hope.

At the extreme, as in Nazi concentration camps or the Abu Ghraib prison in Iraq or, for that matter, among the Roman soldiers who mocked and spat upon Christ before leading him away to his terrible death on the cross, humiliation can be used deliberately to break the spirit of the humiliated: to destroy the citadel of the Self. Nothing like that happens to the poor of twenty-first-century Britain. But extreme cases can illuminate more commonplace ones, like a lighthouse illuminating a dark sea; and I think the humiliations inflicted on Jewish prisoners in the camps, on Iraqis in Abu Ghraib or on Christ before his crucifixion can help us to understand the myriad lesser humiliations that accompany poverty in our time. In all the cases mentioned above the humiliators sought, knowingly and intentionally, to strip the humiliated of their humanity; to degrade them from human beings into objects with no thoughts or feelings. They were signalling that the humiliated were not to be taken seriously, that they were at once negligible, contemptible and absurd, that in a profound sense they were worthless.

Peter Lilley taunting teenage mothers or James Delingpole lambasting pre-teen urchins and their alcopops were not humiliating the poor directly, but the stereotype they appealed to conveyed essentially the same message. Besides, humiliation can take milder forms, and in a culture saturated with the twin assumptions that the poor have brought their poverty on themselves and that the only solution is to force them out of it with 'tough love', it is apt to do just that. In his formidably wide-ranging and penetrating study, *The Decent Society*, the Israeli moral philosopher Avishai Margalit suggests that the institutions of the welfare state, originally designed to rescue the poor from the humiliation of poverty, are often humiliating in themselves – albeit unintentionally.[38] In Britain, the Beveridgean welfare state – the welfare state envisaged in Beveridge's 1942 Report – substituted universal entitlements, available as of right to all citizens, for the means-tested 'doles' of the past precisely because the latter were *ipso facto* humiliating. Little by little, however, the Beveridgean welfare state has morphed into an unacknowledged workfare state that distinguishes between the deserving and the undeserving poor much as Victorian do-gooders did. This too is humiliating: the allegedly undeserving poor are the passive objects of state policy, not autonomous and equal citizens. The 2008 crisis and its aftermath have bred further humiliations. Today's rhetoric of 'strivers' versus 'shirkers' might have been designed to narrow the circle of full citizens and to humiliate those outside it.

Humiliation is stressful; it leads to, can indeed be equated with, prolonged and continuous low self-esteem, punctuated with self-hatred and occasional outbursts of rage. Wilkinson and Pickett report a *British*

Medical Bulletin account of the shame experienced by a working-class man when he encountered a middle-class woman in a Social Security office.

> [T]here were chairs and a space next to this stuck-up cow, you know, slim, attractive, middle class, and I didn't want to sit with her ... I became all conscious of my weight, I felt overweight, I start sweating, I start bungling, shuffling, I just thought 'no, I'm not going to sit there, I don't want to put her out', you don't want to bother them ... What it is, it's a form of violence ... right, it's like a barrier saying 'listen, low-life, don't even [*voice rises with pain and anger*] come near me! ... What the fuck are you doing in my space ... We pay to get away from scum like you' ... They are fuck all, they've got nothing, but it's that air about them you know, they've got the right body, the clothes and everything, the confidence, the attitude, know what I mean ... We [*sadly, voice drops*] ain't got it, we can't have it. We walk in like we've been beaten.[39]

The man's loss of self-worth is a good example of what Émile Durkheim called 'anomie': a state of 'normlessness' into which people sometimes fall when the moral ties that link them to their society and give meaning to their lives have snapped, and when no new ties have replaced them. That depiction resonates as powerfully today, after almost a generation of untamed capitalism, as it did when Durkheim offered it. Anomics belong nowhere; they are shut out, unrecognized, cast adrift. They inhabit a shifting psychic universe, where there are no internalized rules and no life-plans. Durkheim thought they were casualties of a laissez-faire economy, unconstrained by any moral rules binding employers to employees and manufacturers to customers, in which unbounded egoism carried all before it. He conceded that such an economy might be more productive than a regulated one, but he thought that was beside the point. Society, he wrote, 'has no *raison d'être* if it does not bring men a little peace, peace in their hearts and peace in their mutual relations. If industry can only be productive by disturbing that peace and unleashing warfare, then it is not worth the cost.'[40] Durkheim coined the term *anomie* when he was studying suicide, but it applies to more than that. Most of the social ills described by Wilkinson and Pickett stem from lesser forms of self-harm, like binge-drinking, smoking, gang warfare, drug taking, guzzling junk food, dropping out of school and perhaps unprotected sex. These are all mini-suicides, or perhaps cries for help.

INEQUALITY AND DISTRUST

That leads us to the fourth sub-plot: the decline of trust and political engagement. The process is complex; the language in which it is described is often opaque; and the questions it raises are conceptual minefields. Trust is like the proverbial elephant: we know it when we experience it (or at least we think we do), but we can't define it. What does it mean to say 'I trust you'? That I believe you will, in certain conditions, behave in certain ways, presumably ways I approve of? That I believe you will do this all the time, or only most of the time? Or does it mean that I have good reason to believe these things? And if so, what counts as good reason?

Opinion surveys find that huge majorities trust doctors and teachers while substantial majorities distrust business leaders and government ministers. But what precisely do these findings mean? Are all doctors equally trustworthy all the time? Patently not. If they were, the legal firms that specialize in medical negligence cases would have no clients. Are *all* business leaders untrustworthy? Some certainly are, but is James Dyson one of those? As for government ministers, survey respondents were asked if governments could be trusted to 'place the interests of the nation over the interests of their own political party'. But government ministers presumably think the interests of their party coincide with the interests of the nation: if they didn't they would not have joined their party in the first place.

Surveys measuring generalized trust, trust in anonymous others, encounter similar problems. A standard survey question asks, in one form or another, whether the respondent thinks either that 'most people can be trusted' or that 'you can't be too careful in dealing with people'. This question has been asked repeatedly in World Values Surveys; and the answers vary enormously between countries. In one survey, 65 per cent of Norwegians thought most people could be trusted as against 30 per cent of British respondents and 3 per cent of Turks. These percentages obviously need a health warning. It is not clear what the question is supposed to mean, and still less what respondents think it means. Who are 'most people'? Neighbours? People I encounter in a bus queue? The entire population? Is there really as big a difference between Norwegian and Turkish levels of trust as the survey data suggest? Or do the data merely show that different cultures understand trust in different ways?

But it would be a mistake to dwell on these difficulties. The central point is that trust matters. It matters so much that we can't afford to ignore the pollsters' findings about its level and resilience, even if we think the questions they ask are poorly designed. Without trust there could be no markets, no states, no medical services, no schools, no banks, no courts, indeed no organized societies. The German sociologist Niklas Luhmann puts it nicely: 'A complete absence of trust would prevent [one] even getting up in the morning.'[41] In fact, a complete absence of trust is inconceivable. Most of us *have* to get up in the morning; and when we go about our daily business we *have* to act on the assumption that unnumbered others, many of whom we don't know and will never meet, can be trusted to do their jobs properly.

Going about our daily business is one thing, however; taking part in collective action in a common cause is another. No matter how desperate our situation or strong our convictions, we don't *have* to take part in collective action. It may be sparked off by a solitary martyr, like the young stallholder in Tunis who burned himself to death at the start of the Arab Spring, but however inspiring they may be, solitary martyrs are just that: solitary. By definition, collective action is a group activity; and there will be no group if its putative members can't trust each other to take part.

Against that background, the falling levels of *public* or *social* trust – of trust in anonymous other people – to which recent survey evidence points take on an ominous colour. Two findings stand out. The first is that, in Britain, the level of public trust has fallen precipitately over the last fifty years. In 1959, 56 per cent of those sampled thought 'most people' could be trusted; by 1998 the figure was 30 per cent.[42] (It has hardly changed since.) There was an equally precipitate fall in the US: from 55 per cent in 1964 to 35 per cent in 1995. The second finding is more complicated. It is that there is a marked correlation between low levels of public trust and high levels of inequality. Wilkinson and Pickett show that the level of public or social trust is far lower in the United Kingdom than in the Netherlands and the four Scandinavian countries and significantly lower than in Austria, Germany, Canada, Switzerland, Ireland, Spain, Australia and New Zealand – apart from Spain, all of them less unequal than Britain. They also show that individual American states conform to the same pattern: comparatively high levels of trust in comparatively egalitarian states, and low levels in states with high Gini coefficients. Wilkinson and Pickett also quote a study by the political scientist Eric Uslaner showing that the trust level in the United States has fallen steadily since the late 1960s, in parallel with an equally steady rise in inequality.[43]

TRUST AND EMPATHY

It is not difficult to see why trust declines when inequality grows. Trust goes with empathy, with an ability to put ourselves in other people's shoes, to feel with them and not just for them. For the Cambridge psychologist and neuro-scientist Simon Baron-Cohen empathy is 'our ability to identify with what someone else is thinking or feeling, and to respond to their thoughts and feelings with an appropriate emotion'.[44] We are not all equally empathetic by nature: childhood experiences and perhaps genetic endowments can make a big difference. But natural capacity is not the only thing that makes empathy possible. Social propinquity is necessary too. It is hard, even impossible, to empathize with people whose economic or social circumstances are so different from ours that we cannot imagine their lives, or tell how they are likely to think or feel. It will be harder still if we think they hate, fear or despise us. The sad, defeated working-class man who started sweating, bungling and shuffling when he encountered a well-dressed woman in the Social Security office couldn't conceivably have empathized with her, and it is hard to believe that she could have empathized with him. Still less could they have trusted each other.

As well as empathy trust needs time – time to sort out cheats and discover how to deter them; time for the debates of the public realm discussed in the last chapter to bring strangers together; time for rituals of co-operation, to use a coinage of Richard Sennett's,[45] to emerge and develop. Research by the historian Tony Ashworth has yielded a telling picture of the way in which such rituals emerged among British and German forces facing each other in the trenches during the First World War. The soldiers on both sides had gone off to fight in a fervour of patriotic enthusiasm, but they soon found themselves bogged down in a static war of attrition with no resemblance to the dreams of glory that had inspired them when they first left for the killing fields. The front-line soldiers on both sides also found that they had more in common with each other than they had with their respective High Commands well behind the lines. For one thing, they were physically much closer to their opposite numbers than they were to their distant commanders: in some cases so close that they could shout at each other and even send each other messages hidden in grenades from which the explosive had been removed. For another, the ordinary soldiers on both sides had a common interest in staying alive, whereas the High Commands wanted them to inflict as many casualties on the enemy as they could.

In some sectors tacit agreements about when to fire and when to desist gradually emerged. For example, both sides wanted to eat their breakfasts in peace and soon realized that a tacit breakfast truce would be to everyone's advantage. Little by little more complex patterns took shape, as soldiers on each side came to see their opposite numbers on the other side as people with lives and predicaments like their own. A passage by Marek Kohn summarizing Ashworth's findings is worth quoting:

> The more one feels one has in common with someone, the more confident one is likely to be about their behaviour . . . Tacit truces had arisen from everyday habits such as that of regular mealtimes. They were sustained by a kind of familiarity not unlike that which creates a sense of neighbourhood in a peaceful locality. One British soldier told a brigadier that there was an 'elderly gentleman' with a long beard who often showed himself above the German parapet. The brigadier demanded to know why the soldier had not shot the German. 'Why, Lor' bless you sir', replied the soldier, ''e's never done me no harm'. Familiarity permitted the application of a moral code based on reciprocity. The soldier recognised the German as an individual, part of his neighbourhood.[46]

Kohn's use of the word 'neighbourhood' is bitterly ironic. In a fine work of reportage, Anna Minton shows how costly urban redevelopment schemes, spurred on by private developers allied to business-dominated quangos called 'Urban Development Corporations', are destroying old neighbourhoods, driving out some of their inhabitants to make way for more affluent ones and, above all, privatizing public space.[47] She starts with a vivid picture of the development of the docklands in East London. Canary Wharf station, she writes, is 'one of the most breathtaking stations on the London Underground'. In 'its sheer confidence, with its vaulted ceilings stretching up, it seemed, to the sky, it reminded me of the grandeur of Stalin's Moscow Metro'. When she emerged from the station she found herself in a pedestrianized square called Reuters Plaza, bounded by the pub chain All Bar One and the restaurant chain Carluccio's. Electronic ticker tape, with the latest information on international share prices, ran around half the square; to the north was a large plasma screen tuned to Reuters financial television news. Local residents of the Isle of Dogs were nowhere to be found. One of them told Minton that she didn't like going to Canary Wharf: 'It always gives me the fear.'

For Canary Wharf read a long list of similar developments: in Liverpool, Manchester, Salford, Leeds, Newcastle, Cardinal Place hard by Victoria Station, Westfield in London's Shepherd's Bush, and Paddington Waterside among many others. These are all variations on a common theme. The spaces are owned by highly leveraged companies, driven by the need to make profits. To do so, high-class shoppers (ABC1s in the jargon) must be attracted and low-class ones (C2DEs) deterred. Three results stand out. The first is a series of sanitized environments bristling with CCTV cameras: 'personality-free zones' as one of Minton's informants called them. The second is a climate of vague apprehension among the included and of resentment among the rest. Because these places are 'not for everyone', Minton writes, 'spending too much time in them means people become unaccustomed to – and eventually very frightened of – difference'. The third result was encapsulated in a comment by a manager of one of these developments:

> Bugger democracy. Customer focus is not democratic. You ask the customer what they want and you deliver it. The citizen is a customer and

the aim is to respond best to the needs of the customer. The second it becomes involved with politics, it becomes diluted down and the pure vision of the customer is lost.[48]

CHOICE BECOMES FATE

We trust people we believe are like ourselves. In an egalitarian society we can safely assume that strangers will be sufficiently like us for us to trust them. But as society becomes more unequal, it fragments. Empathy withers. The social world begins to look like Hobbes's terrible vision of the state of nature, where every man's hand is raised against every other man. Distrust grows; and its growth erodes the ties that bind society together. Those at the bottom of the pile can gape at those at the top, but they can't empathize with them. Those at the top don't gape at those at the bottom; they shudder with distaste or fear or both. The 'squeezed middle' look up with resentment, and down with trepidation.

Hence, one of the great mysteries of contemporary politics. In Britain, large majorities believe that the gap between rich and poor is too large. Yet support for redistributive policies, designed to narrow the gap, has declined. The figures are startling. For well over twenty years more than 70 per cent of the population have believed that the gap between high and low incomes is too large. But today only 32 per cent think the Government should redistribute income from the better-off to the worse-off. (In the mid-nineties the figure was 44 per cent.) Only one person in five thinks poverty is due to social injustice. One in three thinks it is inevitable, and just under one in three that it is due to laziness on the part of the poor.[49]

The fetish of 'Free Choice' has brought us to a destination we did not wish to go to, and do not like now that we have arrived. Indeed, as noted in the last chapter, we didn't choose 'Free Choice': it was chosen for us, by marketizing governments for which it was a self-validating mantra. Yet a pervasive inertia prevents us from escaping. We cannot escape as a multitude of separate individuals. To escape we would have to act collectively, but we can't act collectively if we can't trust each other. In a Hobbesian jungle, only mugs will devote time and energy to collective action. *Sauve qui peut* will become the motto of the canny and the careful, and little by little it will become part of the common sense of the age. Besides, state intervention to redistribute income has been denigrated as an impediment to choice and freedom for more than thirty years; and that denigration pervades the air we breathe. The choices our governments have made for us have procured an outcome that few of us wanted, legitimized by a public doctrine that rules out any possibility of fundamental change. The great argument for fetishized choice was that it would free us from the constrictions of fate. Instead, choice has itself become a kind of fate. In the next chapter I examine the implications for British democracy.

6

Charismatic Populism Smothers Democratic Debate

Seen in historical perspective, the attempt to combine the equality of civil and political rights, which is of the essence of democracy, with the inequality of economic and social opportunities, which is of the essence of capitalism, is still in its first youth. There is sufficient experience, however, to suggest that the result represents, at best, a transitional arrangement . . . It may well be the case that democracy and capitalism, which at moments in their youth were allies, cannot live together once both have come of age.

R. H. Tawney, Preface to 1938
edition of *Equality*

*You cannot hope
   to bribe or twist
thank God! the
   British journalist.
But, seeing what
   the man will do
unbribed, there's
   no occasion to.*

Humbert Wolfe,
Under the Fire, 1930

In different ways, both the last two chapters posed an ominous question: can British democracy survive the market state's invasion of the public realm, the seemingly ineluctable advance of a market society and the associated growth of inequality and decline of public trust? This chapter will locate that question in a broader historical and cultural context. I shall look at the trials and tribulations of democratic governance in present-day Britain against the background of an inevitably brief summary of the extraordinary career of democracy itself, both as an ideal and as a set of institutions and practices. Then I turn to the enemies of democracy, among them hubristic media, rent-seeking by the super-rich, and an increasingly populist political style. Looming in the background throughout is the question R. H. Tawney posed in the epigraph to this chapter: is it still possible to reconcile the economic inequality which is intrinsic to capitalism with the democratic promise of political equality?

Democracy's long but distinctly chequered career began 2,500 years ago in the almost inconceivably remote city state of Athens. Its citizens described their then unique form of government as '*demokratia*', rule by the many. The many did not include anything like the total adult population. Only Athenian citizens could take part in government; women, slaves and foreigners were excluded from full citizenship. Athenian citizens, however, really did govern themselves. They were not equal in wealth or status, but they *were* equal politically. Any citizen with the energy and self-confidence to do so could address the Assembly, composed of his peers; and the Assembly was, in present-day language, the 'legislature, judiciary and executive' at one and the same time.[1] Athenian *demokratia* was turbulent, factious, sometimes wildly irresponsible, but often magnificent.

In one of the greatest political speeches in the democratic canon, Pericles, perhaps the most famous of many famous Athenian leaders, summed up the Athenian vision of participative democracy in a passage that has echoed down the centuries.

> Our constitution is called a democracy because power is in the hands not of a minority but of the whole people ...
>
> Here each individual is interested not only in his own affairs but in the affairs of state as well: even those who are mostly occupied with their own business are extremely well-informed on general politics – this is a peculiarity of ours: we do not say that a man who takes no interest in politics is a man who minds his own business; we say that he

has no business here at all. We Athenians, in our own persons, take our decisions on policy or submit them to proper discussions: for we do not think that there is an incompatibility between words and deeds; the worst thing is to rush into action before the consequences have been properly debated.[2]

Since Pericles, the term the Athenians coined to describe their form of government has been used in a plethora of different ways. Democracy has never been a single, monolithic entity available for export to all parts of the world, as George W. Bush and Tony Blair imagined. It is plural, not singular; it depends on the tacit understandings of particular cultures at least as much as on formal rules. Today, the rulers of Putin's Russia describe their regime as a 'sovereign democracy'; the ayatollahs of Iran claim that theirs is an 'Islamic democracy'. Not so long ago the Soviet satellites in East/Central Europe insisted that they were 'people's democracies'. For Abraham Lincoln, democracy meant 'government of the people, by the people, for the people'. For the British High Tory Leo Amery it meant 'government of the people, for the people, with but not by the people'.

Not only has the meaning of the word been in continual dispute; so too has the desirability of the thing. For centuries, many of the best minds of Europe saw the very notion of popular government as alarmingly risk-prone at best, and impious folly at worst. Plato and Aristotle condemned it as an immoral and disruptive assault on the natural order. Hobbes thought that, if the 'democratical gentlemen' who fomented the seventeenth-century civil wars had their way, society would revert to the terrifying insecurity of the state of nature. The French Revolution, with its horrifying progress from plebeian frenzy to blood-soaked terror to Napoleon's dictatorship at home and aggression abroad, seemed to many to vindicate the familiar argument that democracy is bound to end in tyranny.

As memories of the Revolution faded such fears ebbed, but others took their place. As noted in Chapter 4, Alexis de Tocqueville, the great analyst of democratic rule, thought the rich array of civil associations that characterized American society would hold the danger of majority tyranny at bay, but even he feared that democracy might go hand in hand with a bland and mediocre conformism, which would smother dissent like a vast, all-embracing pillow. Already, he thought, the 'immense and tutelary power' of a monolithic public opinion posed a quite novel threat to the freedom that American civil associations protected.

> That power is absolute, minute, regular, provident and mild. It would be like the authority of a parent if, like that authority, its object was to prepare men for manhood, but it seeks on the contrary, to keep them in perpetual childhood: it is well content that the people should rejoice, provided they think of nothing but rejoicing . . .
>
> I have always thought that servitude of the regular, quiet, and gentle kind which I have just described might be combined more easily than is commonly believed with some of the outward forms of freedom, and that it might even establish itself under the wing of the sovereignty of the people.[3]

De Tocqueville's nightmare was the obverse of the Periclean dream: it pictured a dystopia, without the civic energy that had once sustained Athenian democracy, and still sustained its American successor.

That note has recurred again and again in political debate since de Tocqueville wrote. As I shall show in the next chapter, John Stuart Mill – a friend and to some extent a disciple of de Tocqueville – had similar fears, and concluded that popular government should be practised on the local level before it was attempted on the national. In nineteenth-century Britain many working-class radicals, who fought to extend the suffrage, wished to enfranchise only the 'manly' and independent-minded who could be trusted to carry out the duties of active citizenship, not the weak and dependent. Onora O'Neill's insistence that such duties come before rights is another example of the theme.[4] In a different way, so is Amartya Sen's claim that democratic rule depends on public reasoning.

The stubborn persistence of this theme from de Tocqueville's day to ours suggests that, though the *demokratia* of ancient Athens has gone for ever, it has not disappeared without trace. Somewhere in the prose of modern representative democracy, and even in the parodic monstrosities of Putin's Russia and the ayatollahs' Iran, there lurks a snatch of poetry: a faint, tantalizing memory of the Athenian agora where the world's first free citizens gave birth to the ideals of political equality and self-government. (That is why Putin and the ayatollahs have tried to steal the word.) As everyone knows, the prose and the poetry are far apart, but they feed into each other in surprising ways. The prose has subverted the poetry, and the poetry has legitimized the prose. That, argues the Cambridge political theorist John Dunn, is why, against all expectations, the word that the Athenians gave to their idiosyncratic form of rule now girdles the globe. 'What we mean by democracy', he points out, 'is not that we govern ourselves.' What we do mean is that the governments under which we live derive their legitimacy from us. They do so, Dunn maintains, by holding regular elections, 'in which every citizen can vote freely and without fear, in which their votes have at least reasonably equal weight, and in which any uncriminalized political opinion can compete freely for them'.[5] Modern representative democracy, he concludes, has transformed the meaning of democracy 'almost beyond recognition'. But that is why, against all the odds, it now girdles the globe.

Dunn's list – legitimacy drawn from the people; regular elections in which citizens can vote freely; free competition for the people's vote between 'uncriminalized' political opinions – comprises the most familiar and arguably the most important norms of modern representative democracy. At first sight they look undemanding, but some of their implications are quite challenging. Regular elections in which the people can vote freely will count for little if potential voters don't bother to go to the polls; if the turn-out falls below a certain point, the exercise may start to look like a pointless charade, and the notion that the government and the state draw their legitimacy from the people may cease to be believable. If non-voters belong disproportionately to lower-income groups, as is the case in the United States and Britain, the threat to legitimacy will be even greater. As for free competition between uncriminalized political opinions, that must imply a level playing field, on which the opinions of the ultra-rich compete on equal terms with the opinions of the rest of us – a wildly utopian notion in the era of growing inequality described in the last chapter.

Dunn's norms are not the only ones. Hovering fitfully in the democratic air is another norm, harder to put into words: a norm of *dialogue*, through which minds change (and are changed), new opinions and new possibilities emerge and the terms of political competition shift. This last norm, the norm of dialogue, owes more to republican

Rome, by way of Renaissance Italy, than to democratic Athens. It also owes a great deal to the Reformed tradition of Protestant dissent, with its disdain for priestly hierarchy and emphasis on congregational self-government. John Milton's blazing attack on censorship, *Areopagitica*, is canonical. It was published in 1644, at the height of the English Civil War. Like many tracts which have reverberated in political memories long after they were published, it was triggered by immediate events of great complexity. In 1643 the Presbyterian-dominated Parliament brought in a licensing order, designed to stamp out publications by the radical Protestant sects, which Milton saw as the true heirs of the Reformation and the best hope for a Royalist defeat. *Areopagitica* had a broad political, indeed revolutionary, purpose that went far beyond its ostensible topic.

STRENUOUS LIBERTY VERSUS BONDAGE WITH EASE

So far from promoting harmony, Milton insisted, censorship led only to the 'forced and outward union of cold, and neutral and inwardly divided minds'. Worse yet, it did violence to the character of the English people and the extraordinary ferment of ideas that made revolutionary London 'the mansion house of liberty'. England was 'a nation not slow and dull, but of a quick, ingenious and piercing spirit, acute to invent, subtle and sinewy to discourse'. London was full of 'pens and heads ... sitting by their studious lamps, musing, searching, revolving new notions and ideas'. Though the city was 'besieged and blocked about' and her 'navigable river invested', her people were

> disputing, reasoning, reading, inventing, discoursing, even to a rarity and admiration, things not before discoursed or written of ... and from thence derives itself to a gallant bravery and well-grounded contempt of their enemies ...
>
> Methinks I see in my mind a noble and puissant nation rousing herself like a strong man after sleep, and shaking her invincible locks; methinks I see her as an eagle mewing her mighty youth, and kindling her undazzled eyes at the full midday beam, purging and unscaling her

long-abused sight at the fountain itself of heavenly radiance, while the whole noise of timorous and flocking birds, with those that also love the twilight, flutter about, amazed at what she means.[6]

Milton's vision of liberty was both republican and national; indeed, he was appointed Secretary for Foreign Tongues under the Commonwealth. He was no democrat, yet his argument was implicitly democratic: poor as well as rich, unschooled as well as learned, could and did contribute to the subtle and sinewy discoursing he lauded. The wise and holy had no lien on truth. In an explosive phrase, he insisted that 'all the Lord's people are become prophets'.[7] But it was democratic in a special way. It did not point to a democracy of head-counting; it pointed to a democracy of vigorous and sustained deliberation and debate. Samuel H. Beer puts it well. For Milton, he writes, 'deliberation by the many is superior to the judgement of the few'.[8] As we saw in Chapter 2, A. D. Lindsay said much the same thing centuries later.

The norm of dialogue is more challenging than the norms listed by Dunn. No one compelled Milton's Londoners to spend time 'disputing, reasoning, reading, inventing, [and] discoursing'; they did so out of a sense of civic and religious duty, powered by an infectious intellectual and political excitement. The 'noble and puissant nation' Milton dreamed of presupposed citizens willing to engage in noble and potentially puissant actions; 'subtle and sinewy' discoursing presupposed subtle and sinewy discoursers. The tone and style of *Areopagitica* are luminous with hope: to Milton it seemed that the Lord's people and their incessant discoursing were on the march. But his hopes were betrayed. After Cromwell's death, the English republic fizzled out; the monarchy returned; for a while Milton went in fear for his life. In his tragic poem, *Samson Agonistes*, he drew an anguished moral. He put it into the mouth of his hero, the enslaved and humiliated Samson, imprisoned in Gaza.

> But what more oft in nations grown corrupt,
> And by their vices brought to servitude,
> Than to love bondage more than liberty,
> Bondage with ease than strenuous liberty.[9]

'Strenuous liberty' versus 'bondage with ease': that harsh contrast encapsulates Milton's republican vision of politics, a vision that goes back to Cicero and forward, at least in some of his moods, to George Orwell. For Milton, the return of the monarchy was not just a political defeat, it was a craven surrender of principle. Just as Delilah had handed Samson over to the Philistines, England had handed itself over to Charles II. In doing so, the English had demeaned their better selves. In an age when almost every political leader offers ease and hardly any dare to point out that the price of liberty is eternal vigilance, Milton's contrast cuts to the quick.

The norm of dialogue outlived the English Republic. (It also outlived Milton himself.) It has had a high place in the British political tradition for centuries. For it, politics is not just a struggle for power *between* opinions; it is also a struggle *for* opinion: a struggle to persuade, to win conscious and deliberate assent and not just passive acquiescence. Most of the great political leaders of our history – Charles James Fox, Edmund Burke and the Pitts father and son in the eighteenth century; Robert Peel, Gladstone and Disraeli in the nineteenth; Lloyd George, Churchill and Aneurin Bevan in the twentieth – have seen politics in this way. None of these thought of himself as a republican (though Bevan was a revolutionary Marxist as a young man). Yet the values implicit in the notion of politics as persuasion are closer to Milton's republicanism than appears at first sight. The dialogue that makes persuasion possible requires tolerance, generosity of spirit, intellectual honesty, a willingness to engage with others, a certain magnanimity and above all openness to new ideas.[10] Since Milton's day, we have learned – partly from thinkers such as de Tocqueville and John Stuart Mill, but even more from bitter experience – that it also requires a pluralistic polity in which power is dispersed, debate encouraged and majority tyranny held at bay.

DEMENTING TRIVIA

Here the hubristic media mentioned above move centre-stage. There has never been a time when the media were all lily-white: Humbert Wolfe's doggerel that I have used as one of the epigraphs to this chapter reminds us of that. In the early twentieth century the press lords Northcliffe, Beaverbrook and Rothermere swaggered about the political stage with unbridled egoism, intimidating politicians, debasing public debate and pushing their own, often eccentric causes. Northcliffe could claim some of the credit for destroying the Asquith Government in 1916; Beaverbrook could claim more for persuading Bonar Law to destroy the Lloyd George Government in 1922. The austere Liberal journalist A. G. Gardiner dubbed Northcliffe the 'dictator of the mobocracy'; in one the deadliest political phrases of the century Baldwin accused Beaverbrook and Rothermere of seeking 'power without responsibility, the prerogative of the harlot through the ages'. (That did not prevent Beaverbrook from being one of Churchill's boon companions or Aneurin Bevan from accepting his hospitality.)

But the press lords of that era flourished at a time when the public realm was expanding, when the old elites described in Chapter 2 were gaining new authority, when the foundations of the welfare state were being laid and when the solidaristic moral economy that prevailed after the Second World War was taking shape. Poverty, inequality and injustice were rife, but the super-rich were not 'racing away' from the rest of society as they are today. Equally, the print media were more diverse, politically and culturally, than they are now. The *News Chronicle* was a middlebrow paper, owned by the Cadburys and broadly Liberal in politics. Arthur Koestler covered the Spanish Civil War for it; the future Popular Front MP Vernon Bartlett was a staff member. *Reynolds News* (a Sunday newspaper, owned by the Co-operative Movement) and the *Daily Herald* were Labour. Taken together, the print media of those days added extra decibels to some of the voices that took part in the democratic dialogue at the expense of others, but they did not smother the dialogue itself.

Today, they have come dangerously close to doing so. A new race of rootless, global, multi-media moguls, with no national loyalties, has replaced the press lords of the past. In the fluid culture of the late twentieth and early twenty-first centuries, there is an insatiable appetite for easily digested information, titillation and opinion, the commodities in which they deal; and, as will appear later, their aggressive populism runs with the grain of the times. The most famous mogul is Rupert Murdoch, whose media empire's malefactions came to light in the phone-hacking scandal of 2011 and 2012. But, though the Murdoch empire's repeated attempts to subvert the police and its intimidation of actual or potential critics flouted the norms of British democracy, the eagerness with which senior politicians courted him was at least as damaging, and in some ways more so. Thanks to the assiduity of the Commons Culture, Media and Sport Select Committee, the *Guardian* newspaper and the Leveson Inquiry into the press that David Cameron reluctantly set up in 2012 the story is now well-known; only one or two salient points need discussing here.

The first is the extraordinary scale of the Murdoch empire's wrong-doing. Tom Watson and Martin Hickman show that confirmed or suspected News International phone-hacking victims total well over 200, ranging from Princes William and Harry, to Richard Branson, the murdered school girl Milly Dowler, John Prescott, and the Labour MP Chris Bryant by way of Alastair Campbell, Cherie Blair, the McCanns, whose daughter Madeleine disappeared in Portugal in 2007, families of soldiers killed in Iraq and Afghanistan and the actor Brad Pitt.[11] Between 2006 and 2012 the Metropolitan Police made eighty-six arrests in connection with the phone-hacking scandal. Rebekah Brooks, former *News of the World* editor and subsequently chief executive of News International, and Andy Coulson, also a former *News of the World* editor and subsequently David Cameron's director of communications, were charged with conspiring to intercept communications unlawfully. In September 2012 Rebekah Brooks and her husband Charles were charged with conspiracy to pervert the course of justice. When this book went to press, all of these were on trial at the Old Bailey.

In January 2013 Detective Chief Inspector April Casburn was found guilty of offering to sell inside information on the phone-hacking investigation to the *News of the World*. Fawning politicians were more blameworthy than venal policemen and policewomen, however. Tony Blair was a particularly prominent fawner. In 1995, just after his election as Labour leader, he was invited to address a conference of Murdoch's satraps in Australia and eagerly accepted. 'It is better to be riding the tiger's back', he explained, 'than let it rip your throat out.'[12] Not only did he fly half-way around the world to pay court to

Murdoch; he became godfather to Murdoch's daughter. Lesser fawn-ers included Peter Mandelson, David Miliband, James Purnell and Tessa Jowell, all of whom happily attended a grand summer event hosted by the Murdoch dynasty in the Cotswolds in July 2011, along with the Education Secretary, Michael Gove, the actress Helena Bonham-Carter and the television presenter Jeremy Clarkson.

David Cameron joined the fawners' chorus in 2008, two years before becoming Prime Minister. Like Blair, he courted Murdoch in person – only on a yacht off the Greek island of Santorini rather than in Australia. The most obvious result was the originally sinister but eventually farcical story of Murdoch's bid to acquire total control of the British Sky Broadcasting Group (commonly known as BSkyB). At first it looked as if the Government would wave the bid through, but the furore over the Milly Dowler phone-hacking affair forced Mur-doch to beat a humiliating retreat and withdraw the bid. It was a spectacular defeat, not only for Murdoch, but for Cameron as well.

But it is a mistake to make too much of Murdoch and his flatterers. All the mass-circulation papers view the world much as Murdoch views it. A notable case in point is the *Daily Mail*'s vicious and argu-ably anti-Semitic attack on Ed Miliband's father, Ralph Miliband, in October 2013. For all such papers, society is a Hobbesian jungle, where no one is safe, few are faithful and no one – least of all demo-cratically elected political leaders – can be trusted. Irrespective of the merits of the case, their motto is the alleged advice of the famous *Sun-day Times* editor, Harold Evans: 'Always ask yourself, when you interview a politician – why is this bastard lying to me?'[13] Even the quality press and broadcast media find it hard to stand aloof from a feverish journalistic pack on the hunt for sensation. Onora O'Neill was right to say, in her 2002 Reith Lectures, that too much journalism 'smears, sneers and jeers, names, shames and blames', pours out 'dementing amounts of trivia' and often 'teeters on the brink of defamation'. Her description of the results cannot be bettered. 'An erratically reliable or unassessable press may not matter for privileged people with other sources of information', she pointed out, *'but for most citizens it matters* [italics in the original] . . . If the media mis-lead, or if readers cannot assess their reporting, the wells of public discourse are poisoned.'[14] As she also implied, smearers, jeerers and defamers proliferate in social media and television studios as well as in the newsrooms of mass-circulation newspapers.

Accountability is fundamental to democracy of any sort, but genuine accountability is impossible unless those giving the account are prepared to admit mistakes and those to whom it is given are willing to listen without rushing to judgement. It is hard to do either of these things in the middle of a media feeding frenzy.

WHO GETS THE DUVET?

Well-poisoning by the media is part of a much wider story. The norms of representative democracy have rarely been challenged overtly. Even Oswald Mosley paid lip service to them in his days as a Member of Parliament, as did most British Communists. But that does not mean that they have always been observed in practice – still less that they are observed in the grossly unequal and hyper-individualistic Britain of the twenty-first century. Two interwoven themes run through their story. The first is very old: the mutual embrace of money and power. Money talks. (As noted in Chapter 1, Michael Walzer nicely called it 'the universal pander'.) It talked in ancient Rome, when Crassus bankrolled Caesar. It talked in medieval England when Italian bankers helped to finance the Hundred Years War with France and gave their name to Lombard Street. It talked shamelessly and raucously around the turn of the eighteenth and nineteenth centuries, when so-called 'nabobs' sought to convert fortunes made in India into rotten boroughs in England, and when the radicals fulminated against 'Old Corruption'. It also talks in modern democracies. The slow march from oligarchy to democracy and the accompanying growth of the public realm quieted its voice a little, but it never stopped talking. As I shall try to show in a moment, it talks more loudly in present-day Britain than it has done for more than a century.

The second theme is newer: the problematic relationship between capitalism and democracy. The assumption that they are natural bedfellows – the assumption that underpinned the West's approach to the ex-Communist world after the Soviet empire collapsed – is a classic example of hope triumphing over experience. Western policy makers wanted the former Soviet satellites in East/Central Europe and the successor states of the Soviet Union itself to embrace democratic rule *and* market economics, and thought the second would lead automatically to the first. The results were scarcely glittering. In the parts of East/Central Europe which had once belonged, in part or whole, to the Hapsburg or Hohenzollern empires, notably Poland,[15] Hungary and the Czech Republic, some of the building blocks of democracy – the rule of law, more-or-less autonomous civil institutions and reasonably free elections – had been in place before the First World War. There democratic rule did follow the collapse of Communism and the installation of market economies, though Hungarian democracy is currently under threat from the radical far right. But the successor states of the Soviet Union, which had been ruled by despotic Tsars before even more despotic Commissars arrived on the scene, are more kleptocratic than democratic: according to the global Corruption Perceptions Index, Russia and Ukraine, the two most populous of these states, are as corrupt as Zimbabwe and Sierra Leone.

It is true that democracy has taken root only in capitalist countries, where private property and market competition prevail. (The social democracies of Scandinavia count as capitalist in that sense.) But it is equally true that capitalist countries are not always democratic. Present-day China, present-day Russia, Pinochet's Chile and apartheid South Africa are all proofs of that. Democracy and capitalism *are* bedfellows of a sort, but they are very quarrelsome ones, constantly arguing about who should have the duvet. In truth, they are intrinsically in tension. The basic axioms of democracy are that citizens must be equal; that power must be accountable to those affected by it; and that all should have an equal right to contribute to the free deliberation and mutual education which are the soul of democratic dialogue. The hallmarks of the capitalist free market are almost the opposite. Rewards are bound to be unequal. There is no dialogue, there is only the demeaning chaff of public relations consultants and advertising firms. Above all, the very notion of *democratic* accountability, of accountability through participation and debate as opposed to market competition, is absent.

Capitalism in one form or another (as previous chapters have shown, there are several) dominates the modern world. For a generation after the Second World War it was on trial. The Soviet Union was not just a military threat to the capitalist West; it offered an ideological alternative incarnated in real institutions. Even in Europe, that alternative attracted significant support. (It attracted far more in the so-called 'Third World'.) Both in France and in Italy Communist parties won millions of votes as well as devoted and sometimes distinguished intellectual apostles. The taming of capitalism was, at least in part, a response to the Communist challenge. The implosion of the Soviet Union and the disappearance of the Communist regimes of East/Central Europe removed the challenge and allowed capitalism to slip its leash. Francis Fukuyama notoriously proclaimed 'the end of history', by which he meant that capitalism and democracy were not just bedfellows, but triumphant bedfellows, locked for ever in an unbreakable, unchallengeable and all-conquering embrace.

We know better today. Capitalism is certainly triumphant, but the democratic norms I have been discussing have not shared in the triumph. On the contrary, tension between capitalism and democracy has become increasingly acute as the market individualism of Hayek and the Chicago School has extended its sway and as inequality has grown. Since money is fungible, inequalities are bound to leak from the economy into the polity. A rich man has only one vote, but votes are by no means the only resources that matter in the struggle to shape opinion, to choose political leaders, and to determine policy. Tony Blair didn't scurry to pay court to Rupert Murdoch because he wanted Murdoch to vote for him in the polling station. (Since Murdoch is not a British citizen that would have been a vain enterprise.) He did so because he wanted the Murdoch media empire to support him and denigrate his enemies. More generally, the rising cost of elections and the increasing volatility of voters have altered the terms of trade between political leaders seeking money and commercial interests seeking influence, in favour of the latter.

Lobbyists have been a feature of British politics (and indeed of most politics outside savagely repressive totalitarian regimes) for as long as anyone can remember. But today the term 'lobbying' no longer captures a much more complex reality. It implies that big corporations lurk in an ante-chamber outside the decision makers' sanctum, bringing pressure to bear on the insiders. In fact, the global corporations of today are no longer confined to the lobby. In Colin Crouch's mordant formulation, they are 'right inside the room of political decision-making. They set standards, establish private regulatory systems, act as consultants to government, even have staff seconded to ministers' offices.'[16]

THE EXTREME CASE

As so often, the United States is an extreme case. The Nobel Prize-winning economist Joseph Stiglitz offers a chilling analysis. Though market forces 'help shape the degree of inequality', he argues, 'government policies help shape those market forces'.[17] The super-rich, the top 1.0 per cent as he calls them, have tilted the distribution of American incomes in their own favour through astonishingly successful rent-seeking ('extraction' in the language of Acemoglu and Robinson, whom I quoted in the last chapter). They have done so through their exorbitant influence on policy-making on almost every level. Regulatory bodies ranging from the Federal Communications Commission in telecoms, to the Securities and Exchange Commission in securities, to the Federal Reserve in many areas of banking have been captured by the interests they are supposed to regulate.

Sometimes, capture is blatant, as when the regulators come from the sector they are supposed to regulate, and to which they return when their regulatory role is over. Sometimes it is more discreet ('cognitive' as Stiglitz calls it) as when Alan Greenspan, head of the Federal Reserve from 1987 to 2006, and Timothy Geithner, head of the New York Federal Reserve from 2003 to 2009, shared the bankers' economic philosophy. The low rate of capital gains tax (15 per cent on long-term capital gains) biases the tax system in favour of the rich. The bottom 90 per cent of the population receive less than 10 per cent of all capital gains, while the top 10 per cent receive the rest. Thus, a tax break for capital gains is tantamount to a tax break for the rich, and above all for the ultra-rich. In 2008 the country's top 400 taxpayers posted a total of $61.5bn in capital gains; the tax break for their capital gains lowered American tax revenues by $12bn. Rent-seeking special-interest groups abound, in health care, energy, telecommunications and, most damagingly of all, in financial services. Altogether such groups spent \$3.2bn on lobbying Congressmen in 2011 alone. (3,100 lobbyists were employed by the health care sector and 2,100 by the energy and natural resources sector.)[18]

As though that were not enough, the rules governing voter registration discriminate against the poor. You can't vote if you don't register; and in many places you can't register without producing a government-issued photo ID – typically a driving licence or an identity card issued by the Department of Motor Vehicles. These take time and trouble to obtain and the poor have less time and trouble to spare than the rich. Altogether around a quarter of those eligible to vote – 51 million people – are not registered. The rising cost of election campaigns favours candidates acceptable to wealthy donors – the more so since the Supreme Court ruling in the 2010 case of *Citizens United* v. *Federal Election Commission* that approved effectively unlimited campaign spending by corporations. According to the Center for Responsive Politics, the presidential and congressional elections of 2012 are likely to have cost a record-breaking \$5.8bn; business interests have probably accounted for 77 per cent of all contributions.[19] Small wonder that, for Stiglitz, American democracy is 'in peril'.

BRITAIN FOLLOWS THE AMERICAN PATH

Britain has not gone as far as the United States, but she has taken essentially the same path. No implacable divinity authored the sad tale of bloated financial services, fetishized economic growth, a shrinking public realm, mounting inequality, soaring executive pay and dwindling public trust that I told in the last three chapters. The economistic explanations of Britain's present discontents that hold sway in business schools, middlebrow periodicals, right-leaning think-tanks and most of the political class do not stand up to serious scrutiny. One such explanation is that much-used but ill-defined portmanteau term 'globalization'; another is that information technology has necessarily raised the incomes of those with the skills needed to use it and lowered those of the unfortunates who lack the appropriate skills. But globalization is, by definition, global. It affects all the member-states of the European Union. Yet, as the last chapter showed, Britain is an outlier among the big economies of Europe both on poverty and on inequality, and as a consequence on the social ills associated with inequality. In France, inequality actually fell while it was rising in Britain.[20] The same applies to the effects of IT. Is it really the case that technological skills are much scarcer in Britain than in mainland Europe? If so, why should that be? And why have British governments done nothing to put things right? The explanation doesn't wash.

Political decisions, not ineluctable fate, are responsible for Britain's failure to emulate her continental neighbours. This applies with special force to the three most egregious features of her political economy: the overmighty financial sector, the proliferation of tax breaks for the rich and the wholesale appropriation of public assets by private interests. As Chapter 1 sought to show, the exceptional economic weight and political influence of Britain's financial sector go back to the end of the seventeenth century, but they have ebbed and flowed a good deal in the intervening 300 years. The question that matters is why they have flowed so inordinately in the last thirty years or so, and here too the answer lies in politics. Successive governments – starting with the Thatcher Government's 'Big Bang' – have deliberately privileged the financial sector. They were not *obliged* to do so. They did so of their own volition. No doubt their volition was affected, in some degree, by preconceptions inherited from the past, but these preconceptions had hovered in the air for decades without producing a comparable result. Thatcher was the most finance-friendly Conservative Prime Minister since the war. As noted in Chapter 1, when he was Chancellor of the Exchequer in the 1920s, Churchill had wanted finance to be less proud and industry more content; there is no reason to believe that he had abandoned his suspicion of the City as Prime Minister in the 1950s. Macmillan had nothing but contempt for it. By the same token, the Blair and Brown governments were easily the most finance-friendly in the Labour Party's history. To suggest that ancient preconceptions doomed them to be so is to mistake fatalism for analysis.

The same applies to the tax breaks that have fostered rent-seeking by the ultra-rich. Geoffrey Howe's cut in the top rate of income tax from 83 per cent to 60 per cent, and Nigel Lawson's cut from 60 to 40 per cent; Gordon Brown's cut in capital gains tax and 'limited touch' financial regulation; successive governments' refusal to clean up the manifold tax havens in British jurisdictions or to dismantle the privileges of the City; and the astonishingly favourable tax treatment of so-called 'non-doms' (British residents legally 'domiciled' in other countries) all flow or have flowed from political action or failures to act. A spectacular example of the results came with the publication of the *Sunday Times* Rich List for 2012. The total wealth of the 1,000 people on the list was £414bn, up by £315bn since 1997 and equivalent to around one third of Britain's GDP. Lord Ashcroft, Lord Paul, Viscount Rothermere and Lakshmi Mittal, among a host of others, live in Britain but, thanks to their non-dom status, pay no income tax or capital gains tax on their earnings from abroad. They all figure in the *Sunday Times* list; with an estimated fortune of £12.7bn in 2012 Lakshmi Mittal has consistently headed it. The most notorious beneficiary of the British state's tenderness to non-doms is Sir Philip Green, who avoided tax on dividends of £1.2bn from his Arcadia Group empire by crediting them to his Monaco-domiciled wife. An equally remarkable sign of tenderness was that he carried out a review of government spending for Cameron's coalition government soon after it was formed.

John Lanchester's summary is hard to better. 'The capital of the UK', he writes, 'has one of the world's largest concentrations of the super-rich, and the reason for that is that we have chosen to have them here, as a matter of deliberate government policy.' In effect, he adds, 'the UK has a gigantic sign hanging over it saying, "Rich people! Come and Live Here! You Won't Have to Pay Any Tax!"'[21] The privatizations and marketizations which have poured largesse into the hands of lawyers, management consultants, former nationalized industry heads, private health companies, former ministers, bus company CEOs, quango heads and companies involved in PFI schemes are even more obviously political in origin and execution.

DEMOCRATIC FORMS, OLIGARCHIC SUBSTANCE

The politics in question are democratic in form. Decisions are taken by ministers, accountable to Parliament. Political parties compete freely for the people's votes. MPs are elected by their constituents and may be thrown out by them. Vigorous debates take place in both Houses of Parliament. The Prime Minister of the day has to run the gauntlet of the gladiatorial combats known as Prime Minister's Questions. As Rupert Murdoch discovered to his cost, Commons committees are more powerful and more assertive than they used to be. But democratic forms conceal an increasingly oligarchic substance. Thanks to the emergence of a new style of governing, populist rather than pluralist, power is much more concentrated at the centre than it used to be – a phenomenon I shall examine in more depth later. For the moment, what matters is that this new governing style has made it easier for a corporate elite on the hunt for rents to insert itself into the political process and to use it for its own purposes.

Examples are legion. The most straightforward are to be found at the very heart of the democratic process: elections and political parties. Before governments can be formed, elections have to be won; and though British elections are much cheaper than American ones they still cost money. (Party spending in the 2010 election was £10m less than in 2005, but the total was still £31m.) Meanwhile, party membership has slumped. In 1964 the two big parties had around three million members altogether; by 2010 they had around 250,000. The combination of shrunken parties and costly elections has translated into swollen donations. In New Labour's salad days, Michael (eventually Lord) Levy, known as 'Lord Cashpoint' – Tony Blair's mendicant-emissary to the corporate sector – raised £7m for the blind trust that funded Blair's office as Opposition leader and nearly half of the £26m that Labour spent on its three-year election campaign to 1997. According to Democratic Audit, a mere 224 donations originating from fewer than sixty separate sources accounted for nearly 40 per cent of all the major parties' donation income between 2001 and mid-2010. In June 2012 the *Independent* reported that a quarter of donations to the Conservative Party since 2001 had come from people who figure on the *Sunday Times* Rich List. In the five years between Cameron's election as party leader and the 2010 general election, donations from City interests rose from a quarter to one half of all Conservative donations.[22] (It is fair to add that over the last eleven years 63 per cent of Labour funding has come from the trade unions. But that has not undone the triumph of the Juggernaut theory of wages that Keynes condemned.)

Not only do British candidates for parliament depend to varying degrees on corporate funding to finance their election campaigns, but far more British MPs and peers have connections with big private-sector corporations than is the case in most other democracies. A 2006 article by Mara Faccio in the *American Economic Review* tells a startling tale. She defines firms in which at least 10 per cent of voting stock is controlled by a minister or Member of Parliament, or in which a minister or Member of Parliament is a top officer, as 'politically connected'. On that basis there were 154 politically connected firms in the United Kingdom, compared to 31 in Japan (the runner-up), 24 in Italy and only 6 in the United States. Percentages tell a slightly different story. 7.17 per cent of all British firms were politically connected, a lower figure than in Russia or Japan, but much higher than the US figure of 0.08 per cent. When it came to the country's 'top fifty firms' the United Kingdom headed the list again. In Britain 46.0 per cent of such firms were politically connected, compared with 36.36 per cent in Russia and 6.00 per cent in the US.[23]

The authors of the 2012 Democratic Audit have aggregated Faccio's findings so as to compare Britain with four groups of other countries – EU-15 (the member states of the EU before its enlargement to take in East/Central Europe); the 'consensual democracies' of Central Europe, such as Germany, Austria and the Netherlands; the 'Nordic' democracies of Scandinavia; and 'Westminster democracies' such as Australia, Canada and Ireland as well as the United Kingdom itself. Once again the results are startling. Corporate power has a far smaller presence in all these comparator groups than in Britain. As stated above, 46 per cent of top firms in the United Kingdom are connected to a minister or Member of Parliament. The figure for the Westminster democracies as a group is 10.4 per cent, for the EU-15 7.1 per cent, for the consensual democracies 3.4 per cent and for the Nordics 2.5 per cent. After this, it comes as no surprise to learn that 124 members of the House of Lords (approximately 16 per cent of the total) have what the *Guardian* coyly calls 'paid links' with the financial-services sector. Most of them are Conservatives, but at least two are Labour.[24]

REVOLVING DOORS

More insidious than any of these is the lure of the so-called 'revolving door'. This plays a dual role in British government. Through it former public servants and politicians make their way into the corporate sector ('revolving out' in the jargon). Meanwhile, businessmen of varying degrees of eminence 'revolve in' to posts in the public service. Both powerfully reinforce the hold that private corporations exert on the machinery and policies of the state. Would-be revolvers-out have an obvious incentive to trim their sails to corporate-sector winds before the time for revolving arrives. The revolved-in have an equally strong incentive to stay on good terms with their former corporate paymasters against the day when they will return to private employment. As well, they cannot help importing the ethos of their private-sector pasts into their new roles. Indeed, part of the point of recruiting them in the first place is to encourage public servants to mimic the private sector.

The most prominent 'revolver-out' is Tony Blair, who fell happily into the outstretched arms of J. P. Morgan (reportedly for £500,000 a year) after leaving office. Tony Blair Associates is said to make £12m a year from advising firms and governments with which Blair dealt as Prime Minister. There are plenty of lesser examples. Altogether twenty-eight former ministers 'revolved out' between 2006 and 2008, and thirty-one in the twelve months before March 2011. Ministerial exports came chiefly from the Treasury and the health and defence departments. Seven former health ministers (Patricia Hewitt prominent among them) moved to posts or consultancies with private health care companies; not to be outdone six former ministers at the Ministry of Defence took up posts with defence contractors. Paul Flynn MP, of the Commons Public Administration Select Committee, commented appositely that, for their private-sector importers, this was 'a way of buying influence'.

Officialdom produced notable revolvers-out as well. One is Jonathan Powell, who became a senior managing director of the financial services firm Morgan Stanley when his role as Blair's chief of staff came to an end. Another is Vice-Admiral Tim Lawrence, who switched from running the Ministry of Defence's estates to a non-executive directorship of Capita, a £3bn outsourcing company which gets half its business from the government.[25] Military top brass were particularly eager to sell their services to the private sector. In a 'sting' by *Sunday Times* reporters in October 2012, a notable haul – including, among others, Lord Dannatt, former Chief of the General Staff, Admiral Sir Trevor Soar, the Royal Navy's former Commander-in-Chief Fleet, and Lieutenant-General Sir John Kiszely, former procurement chief at the Defence Department – were caught on camera claiming that they could set up multi-million-pound deals for firms anxious to do business with the British armed forces; Dannatt was offered what he called a 'reasonable' fee of £100,000 for two days' work a week. (It is fair to add that all of these have indignantly denied any wrong-doing.)[26]

Revolvers-in tend to be less well-known than revolvers-out, but in some ways they have had a greater impact on British government and British democracy. The very fact that they exist is proof of a subtle change, both in what the state does and, still more, in the way in which its servants understand it. As noted in Chapter 4, civil servants are now, willy-nilly, agents of a market state. The notions that the public interest – the interest of the entire society – is more than the sum of private interests and that the state's task is to pursue the public interest seem to have vanished from Whitehall as well as from the wider society. Revolvers-in carry the stigmata of the market state; collectively they prove that its invasion of the public realm has gone further than anyone would have thought possible thirty years ago. True, they do not seek personal enrichment, unlike many of the revolvers-out. They widen the gene pool of Whitehall, and bring a fresh perspective to its corridors. The trouble is that the perspective they bring is necessarily that of the private corporate sector; they are hired because governments are in thrall to the marketizers' slogan: 'private good; public bad'.

Some revolvers-in have been ennobled in order to make it possible for them to hold ministerial office. Under Gordon Brown, ten ministers were brought into government directly from outside; half of these came from the corporate sector. However, only a small minority of revolvers-in reach such dizzy heights. Far more prevalent – and a far better guide to the logic which has governed the reconstruction of the state in the last thirty years – are the revolvers-in who now inhabit the higher reaches of the civil service. In the five years up to 2010 30 per cent of the 'senior' civil service (defined as Deputy Director level and above) were externally recruited, most from the private sector. In the 'Top 200' group (Permanent Secretaries and Director General level) the proportion averaged more than 50 per cent a year.

Lower down the official tree are a series of 'departmental boards', typically composed of three or four senior civil servants and an equivalent number of 'non-executive directors', drawn overwhelmingly from the private sector. The Cameron government has commissioned Lord Browne of Browne Review (and BP) fame to recruit non-executive directors from the private sector into all departments. 'The non-executive board members', Browne has declared, 'will play a principal role in bringing a more business-like ethos to the very heart of government.'[27] Here are some of the results, as of early 2013. They are worth pondering. The lead non-executive in the Department of Energy and Climate Change was the CEO of the alcoholic-drinks group Diageo. In the Department of Transport the lead non-executive was the CEO of Centrica, the UK's largest energy supplier, which has extensive dealings with government. The three non-executives at the Department of Culture, Media and Sport were, or had been, board members of media companies. Two of the three non-executives at the Department of Education were major Conservative Party donors, one of whom runs a private equity firm that invests heavily in private schools.

Complementing departmental boards are consultancies, committees of inquiry and task forces, largely composed of 'outsiders'. Under the Blair Government, government spending on consultancies more than quadrupled. By 2005–6, central government was spending £1.8bn on them and other public bodies a total of £1bn. Task forces were also favourite devices: by 1999 there were 295 of them, predominantly recruited from producer interests. Later Andrew Lansley appointed a number of industry insiders to so-called 'responsibility deal' groups set up to examine pressing public-health issues such as obesity and alcoholism. The food group included representatives of McDonald's, Mars and Pepsico; the alcohol group was chaired by the chief executive of the Wine and Spirit Trade Association.

Present-day Britain is not a kleptocracy like Berlusconi's Italy or Putin's Russia. Nor are Britain's rent-seekers as blatant as their American equivalents. This is cold comfort, however. Thanks to party dependence on rich donors, to exceptionally close links between parliamentarians and big firms and, above all, to the revolving door, the corporate elite, what remains of the old public-service elite and the handful of politicians who manage to climb the greasy pole have merged into an informal constellation of power with shared values, assumptions and expectations. David Beetham calls it a 'power elite',[28] and it is hard to think of a better term. This power elite is not totally homogeneous or monolithic; its members do not always agree on all the issues they face. The important point is that they share an unquestioned set of beliefs that tell them they have a right to rule, along with a touching faith in the beneficence of untamed capitalism. At first sight they have something in common with the old elites I described in Chapter 2: elites nearly always think they are entitled to their positions. When they cease to do so, their days are numbered. The difference is that Beetham's 'power elite' takes the primacy of the market realm for granted whereas the old elites sought quite consciously to tame market forces in the interests of the public good. Another difference is that the old elites put their faith in persuasion and dialogue, whereas Beetham's power elite seeks to sweep away the obstacles to marketization by fiat from the central state.

THE POPULIST STYLE

At this point, the new, populist style of governing mentioned above comes back into the story. It is an easy style to recognize, but a difficult one to pin down. The eminent political scientist Richard Rose has called it 'managed populism',[29] but though careful management is certainly present Rose's term captures only the rational element in a complex reality which has as much to do with the emotions as with the intellect. With apologies to the great German sociologist and polymath Max Weber I shall call the new style charismatic populism. Weber distinguished between three different kinds of authority: traditional, 'rational-bureaucratic' and charismatic. Whereas traditional authority was bound by precedent and rational-bureaucratic by 'intellectually analysable rules', charismatic authority was unbounded. It repudiated the past and was inherently irrational. It was, in fact, 'a specifically revolutionary force'. While it lasted charismatic authority carried all before it by virtue of the 'devotion and trust' that the leader inspired in his followers, but these lasted only so long as the followers believed in his charismatic inspiration.[30]

Charismatic populism as I understand it does not rely on undiluted charismatic authority of the sort that is sometimes found in tight-knit cults like the People's Temple, whose members committed mass suicide in Jonestown, or among religious leaders like Jesus Christ or Buddha. However, it *does* depend on the devotion of a coterie of followers; it *does* repudiate the past; and it *is* revolutionary. It is also irrational, or at least supra-rational. It concentrates power in the hands of the charismatic leader, who becomes the vehicle and symbol of a messianic cause that promises salvation for believers and damnation for the unregenerate. As such, it is as remote from democratic norms as Beetham's power elite. Democratic norms depend on public reasoning, open debate and intellectual engagement. Emotion plays a part in the competition between opinions and the struggle to persuade, but it is a subordinate part. Charismatic populists, on the other hand, rely almost wholly on an emotional *rapport* with their audiences. In their own eyes (and those of their followers) they are outsiders confronting corrupt and self-seeking insiders. Instead of cold public reasoning they offer the warmth of apparent sincerity. Leaders become choreographers of collective emotion. They cut through the tedious ratiocination of rational-bureaucratic politics to speak to the heart; and they flourish in times of trouble when the head has lost its way.

Adolf Hitler, the most evil charismatic populist of the modern age (and perhaps of any age), came to power in the depths of the Great Depression, to which none of the conventional parties offered solutions, and in a nation burning with resentment of the humiliating Versailles settlement. Charles de Gaulle, the saviour of French honour in 1940 and of French democracy twenty years later, returned to power from his self-imposed exile in Colombey-les-Deux-Églises when the Algerian war had plunged the Fourth Republic into crisis and discredited the conventional politicians who had governed under it. Joe McCarthy, a more squalid example of the breed, won his mercifully brief spell in the limelight in the aftermath of what many Americans saw as the 'loss of China', in other words the Kuomintang's defeat at the hands of the Chinese Communists in 1949. All of these symbolized a cause of some kind; and each mobilized mass emotion in its service.

Against that background, the corporate infiltration of Britain's democratic process and the rise of David Beetham's 'power elite' fall into place. Charismatic *leadership* was not unknown in nineteenth- and early-twentieth-century Britain. There was a touch of it in Gladstone and more than a touch in Lloyd George. But Gladstone and Lloyd George were not charismatic *populists*. They were masters of the arts of rational-bureaucratic politics and symbolized no messianic cause. They sometimes tried to present themselves as outsiders, but the presentation was not very convincing. (Lloyd George's was more convincing than Gladstone's.) It was not until the late 1970s, in a Britain stricken by the crisis of 'stagflation' discussed in earlier chapters, that the stage was set for full-blown charismatic populism, and not until the 1980s that the originally rather conventional Margaret Thatcher turned herself into a charismatic populist *par excellence*.

She really *was* an outsider – partly by virtue of her gender, and partly by virtue of her contempt for what she saw as an effete establishment. She was also a revolutionary: as noted in Chapter 4, the most revolutionary British leader since Cromwell. She saw herself as the apostle and servant of a messianic cause: the regeneration of Britain through a state-imposed enterprise culture. She inspired passionate devotion among her followers and a strange mixture of fear and loathing among her opponents. She was a mistress of detail – impeccably briefed as well as impeccably dressed – but in true populist style she had an extraordinary capacity to cut through the detail to the emotional heart of her revelation. If she had not existed, the new power elite would have had to invent her. Indeed, if she had not existed the power elite might never have come into existence. Her cause was their cause. Over their assiduous rent-seeking she threw a veil of revolutionary purity. Her disdain for pluralist politics, for government by discussion, for intermediate institutions standing between the individual and the state and protecting the individual from the full rigour of the 'undistorted' market equalled theirs. I don't suggest that she was, in any direct or simple way, the agent of the power elite or of the untamed capitalism in which they put their faith, but her governments made Britain safe for both.

It remained so during the interregnum presided over by Thatcher's unfortunate successor, the notably un-charismatic John Major. More to the point, it also remained so under the second great charismatic-populist leader in modern British history, Tony Blair. As noted in Chapter 4, Blair was not a carbon copy of Thatcher. For one thing, he lacked a messianic cause, except insofar as the cause was his own person. Yet he had the same self-belief, the same unsleeping will, the same mesmeric capacity to inspire devotion, the same conviction that he had a direct line to a reified 'people' with whom he could communicate over the heads of Cabinet, party, Parliament and officialdom and the same disdain for open debate and unmediated dialogue. In the end he was brought down, just as Thatcher had been brought down, by a rather murky palace revolution in which the people, and even the party, played no part.

A POPULIST AGE

It is a complex story, with no neat, easily digested moral, but certain things are clear. It is not difficult to see why charismatic populism carried all before it for a total of twenty-one years out of the twenty-eight between 1979 and 2007. Ours is a populist age – instinctively hostile to the values of the old elites I discussed in Chapter 2 and suspicious of any suggestion that the voice of the people may not always be the voice of God. To be sure, it is also a hyper-individualistic age. But despite appearances to the contrary, populism and hyper-individualism go together. A mass of disaggregated individuals, in a society where the public realm has been demeaned and where public trust seems to be vanishing, is more likely to respond to a populist appeal than to any other. Populist languages make no demands on their listeners; they flatter the emotions; and they place the burdens of freedom on someone else's shoulders. When institutions are in disarray, when norms pull in different directions and when the disciplines of democracy have lost their hold, the easiest way to cut through the resulting contradictions is to appeal directly to the sovereign people, having first found out what they want to hear.

Quite apart from that, populists are equally suspicious of checks and balances – whether constitutional or customary – that impede the expression of the popular will, and chop up the power which emanates from the people into self-stultifying bits. They see no need to protect minorities from the tyranny of the majority. Minorities are either part of the whole, in which case they don't need protection, or self-excluded from it, in which case they don't deserve to be protected. Apparent differences of interest or value that cut across the body of the people, that divide the collective sovereign against itself, are products of devious manipulation or unyielding vested interests or both. For there is a strong paranoid streak in the populist mentality. Against the pure, virtuous people stand privileged elites and conspiratorial subversives. Tony Blair's 'forces of conservatism' were a perfect example of the first, and Margaret Thatcher's 'enemy within' of the second.

The implications for leadership are particularly striking. There is a large element of humbug in the populist leader's claim to speak to and for the inherently virtuous people. Even leaders who originally sprang from the ranks of the people no longer belong to the ranks once they start to lead. Their claim to a special, intuitive, supra-rational understanding of the people and of their true values and beliefs reflects that awkward truth. Humbug or not, however, the populist leaders' assumption that they embody the popular will, that they have a private line to that will, and that they can and should appeal to it directly without going through intermediaries becomes self-validating. Margaret Thatcher's 'conviction politics' and Tony Blair's 'sofa government' armoured them against opponents and – more importantly, perhaps – against the corrosion of self-doubt. Buoyed up by their belief in their power to divine the popular will, populist leaders offer certainty, security and glamour in place of the drab and confusing greys of the ordinary politician. While the magic lasts, the rewards are great. The German socialist Egon Wertheimer once described Ramsay MacDonald, in his day a heroic figure, as 'the focus for the mute hopes of a class'. Substitute 'people' for 'class' and that is the essence of populist leadership.

Of course, the magic can't last. Charisma wears out. Charismatic populism is not just inherently revolutionary, it is also inherently unstable. One reason is that the devotion that the populist leader inspires eventually backfires. Sycophants are to rulers what fleas are to dogs. Men and women of power are apt to inhabit halls of mirrors that reflect their own preconceptions and prejudices back to them. Power is addictive; and like other addictions it corrupts the addict. It encourages delusions of infallibility and fosters the bunker mentality. All rulers are tempted to stifle criticism and to surround themselves with yes-men or women, and charismatic populists almost always succumb to the temptation. The prime example in recent history is perhaps the decrepit Hitler manoeuvring phantom armies in the face of the advancing Russians during the battle for Berlin, but there are plenty of lesser ones – among them, Margaret Thatcher forging ahead with a poll tax that stank in the nostrils of Conservative voters and Tony Blair convincing himself that the UN Security Council would pass a resolution legalizing the Iraq War. Leaders need equivalents of the court jesters of the Middle Ages to remind them of their fallibility, but such people are hard to find today. (Harold Macmillan found one in the self-effacing John Wyndham, later Lord Egremont, but it is hard to think of any other recent examples.) There is an alternative: the alternative offered by the greatest practising political scientists of the modern world, the founding fathers of the American Republic. The American federalists saw that the way to preserve freedom in a world of power was to create checks and balances, so that power would countervail power. That, however, is a lesson that charismatic populists are, by definition, unwilling and perhaps unable to learn.

In the end, the case against charismatic populism is moral, not practical. It has to do with the nature of and case for democracy and,

on a deeper level, with the nature of and case for the open society.[31]
The democratic norms discussed in this chapter stem from the
belief that it is better – morally better, not just pleasanter or more
expedient – to be a free citizen, bearing the burdens of freedom, than
a slave. The burdens are heavy: fortitude, self-discipline, a willingness
to make hard choices in the public interest and to accept responsibility for them. These are among the preconditions of the open society I
described briefly in Chapter 2. They imply a deliberative, reflective
politics of power-sharing and mutual education. Absolute popular
sovereignty is as alien to such a politics as the absolute sovereignty of
the global marketplace, of a totalitarian party, or even of an elected
parliament, such as the British one.[32]

7

Who Do We Think We Are?

No man comes into the world with a saddle on his back, neither any booted and spurred to ride him.

> Richard Rumbold, speech from the
> scaffold before his execution, 1685

In the deserts of the heart
Let the healing fountain start.

> W. H. Auden,
> *In Memory of W. B. Yeats, 1939*

I pondered all these things, and how men fight and lose the battle, and the thing that they fought for comes about in spite of their defeat, and when it comes turns out not to be what they meant, and other men have to fight for what they meant under another name.

> William Morris, *A Dream of John Ball*, 1888

If William Morris were to return from the dead and look around him, he would find ample grounds for the mixture of wry stoicism and stubborn optimism that he put into the mouth of the heretical hedge priest and incorrigible rebel John Ball. As the last six chapters showed, present-day Britain seems trapped in a combination of mutually reinforcing ills. She is reeling from the effects of the crash of 2007–8, but despite talk of 'hard economic times' and 'difficult choices' the culture and institutions that procured the crash are still riding high. Most of the political class are still mesmerized by the fetish of everlasting economic growth; hardly any have challenged the market fundamentalist moral economy from which the growth fetish stems. The attrition of the public realm which has continued remorselessly under governments of all hues for thirty years shows no sign of slowing down. In health care, universities and schools marketization has speeded up, turning yet more public goods into commodities and yet more public servants into harassed salespeople.

Britain is one of the least egalitarian societies in Europe with one of the highest levels of poverty; partly because of this, the level of public trust has fallen precipitately. In form, Britain is still a democracy, but in fact the policy-making process is dominated by an oligarchic elite of rent-seekers. Legitimizing and disguising their spoliation is a strange, new Holy Trinity: a trinity of Choice, Freedom and the Individual, the three great mantras of the resurgent capitalism of our time.

These ills feed off each other. They form a system or, in medical language, a syndrome. The culture of untamed capitalism strikes at the heart of the public realm; the market realm's invasion of the public realm has helped to procure rising levels of inequality, and falling levels of public trust. Declining trust undermines the norms and culture of democracy and makes it easier for the oligarchic elite to extract rents from the rest of us. Holding the system together is the culture of hedonistic individualism described in Chapter 2. The result is that we no longer have a common language in which to reflect on our predicament and hammer out a solution. The air is loud with anger, but the angry and those they are angry with talk past each other.

Yet a gleam of light pierces the gloom. The trap is of our own making. We, not some mysterious and evil 'other', brought us to our present pass. The culture of hedonistic individualism is our culture; it shapes us, but we shaped it. We toppled the old elites that stood in its way, and we turned instead to the coarse new elites of money and celebrity that reflect and fortify it. We, and not just the bankers, were the authors of the wildly over-leveraged economy that crashed in 2007–8. If we no longer speak the language of the common good, it is because we have forgotten how to, not because an alien despot censors our conversations. If we get carried away by populist media campaigns, or sneer at 'scroungers' and 'shirkers', or gawp at flashy 'celebs', it is because we choose to do so; no one forces us. Since we built the trap we should, at least in principle, be able to spring it.

The question is, how? The first essential is to recognize that it is a *British* trap. Of course, it has parallels in other countries, whose experiences can throw light on ours. (Rent-seeking by the richest 1.0 per cent in the United States is a good example.) Equally, we have much to learn from the wisdom taught and learned during the long history of the civilization of which our culture is part. For centuries, the nations of the British archipelago have been part of what Edward Gibbon called the 'great republic' of Europe. The legacies of ancient Athens and republican Rome can still be detected in our political culture. Those of ancient Jerusalem, medieval Christendom and early modern Europe still colour our moral imaginations. The teachings of the Hebrew prophets and of Aristotle, Augustine and Aquinas, to mention only a few, are part of our inheritance. We won't rediscover the language of the common good or resolve the crisis of the moral economy that broke in 2007–8 if we close our minds to their legacy – or to that of the Muslim scholars whose commentaries on Aristotle left an enduring impression on Christian thought.

That said, we must not allow ourselves to be diverted from the specificities of our own, peculiar predicament. As the last few chapters have shown, our ills are *exceptional*. Britain is an outlier in Western Europe on inequality, on poverty, on the social problems they bring with them and, not least, on the interpenetration of political and corporate elites. On a deeper level, we have lost our bearings as a people. We no longer know who we are or where we belong. We are in the European Union, but we seem unwilling to be of it. We are sleepwalking towards a market society that none of us has voted for. We are shocked by the level of inequality in our society, but we can't summon up the political will to reduce it. The narratives that structured the early post-war period have lost their purchase, but no new narratives have filled the resulting vacuum. Our ills are intangible, even more than tangible. They are those of a disorientated people adrift in a bewildering moral and emotional sea. The routines of conventional party politics and policy-making offer no solution: they are part of the problem. To resolve our predicament we must first dig into the buried riches of our culture.

For the trap that pinions us is cultural. It has to do with the way we live our lives and the deep-seated habits of the heart that shape our choices, with what eighteenth-century thinkers like Edmund Burke and Adam Smith called 'manners' or 'sentiments'. As I tried to show in Chapter 2, cultural changes did far more than technological or economic ones to topple the elites of mid-century and elevate the successor elites that now dominate our public culture. These changes amounted to a revolution of sentiment. It is time for another revolution, comparable in scale but different in direction.

EQUAL AND OPPOSITE DANGERS

Now, this is treacherous terrain, where two equal and opposite dangers lie in wait. The first is cultural determinism: the assumption that cultures and the traditions associated with them are timeless and unchangeable. For example, a trope of New Right rhetoric in the 1970s and 1980s was that English culture had been individualistic and enterprising for centuries, and that the alleged attempts of post-war governments to halt the 'forward march of *embourgeoisement*' which had made it so were not just deplorable, but in some sense against nature.[1] The second danger is a form of cultural presentism whose exponents scoff at tradition and talk as if cultures can be made and re-made at will. Blair's early talk of Britain as a 'young country' that I mentioned in Chapter 3 is a case in point.

The truth is more complicated. Cultures bind their members together and survive through time; attempts to force them to change by mechanistic social engineering are apt to come to a sticky end, as Communists seeking to create a new Soviet man and Zionists hoping to construct a new Jewish identity discovered to their cost. But cultures are neither monolithic nor immutable. (If they were, the slow rise and subsequent fall of the culture of mid-century Britain could not have taken place.) They are sites of conflict that develop and change through the give and take of sometimes passionate dispute:

the still sadly incomplete, but steadily advancing, feminization of Britain's public culture is a good example. Different members of the same culture often understand it in different ways and cherish different hopes for its future. They are rather like the members of an old, but quarrelsome family, who have certain traits in common – a way of tossing the head here, a set of the chin there – but feud endlessly about their inheritance.[2]

Much the same is true of traditions. To survive, they have to adapt and change, in response to new circumstances and challenges from other traditions; in Alasdair MacIntyre's language, they have to resolve the 'epistemological crises' that such challenges provoke. To do so the challenged tradition has to develop new concepts and practices that meet the challenge while remaining true to its history. A tradition that lacks the resources to do this will die out.[3] That is why there are no Druids in present-day Britain and no worshippers of Jove or Zeus in present-day Italy or Greece. On the other hand, Christianity has survived for 2,000 years because it has shown an astonishing capacity to adapt and develop, from obscure Jewish cult to the world's biggest faith, through innumerable schisms and sometimes violent internecine wars. Within Christianity, the Roman Catholic tradition survived the Protestant Reformation, which might well have overwhelmed it, by drawing on ideological and moral reserves that were barely in evidence when Luther posted his theses on the church door in Wittenberg. But though the Church that survived was still the Catholic Church, it was a very different creature from the one the reformers had challenged. With beautiful economy, Orwell made essentially that point in the early days of the Second World War.

> What can the England of 1940 have in common with the England of
> 1840? But then, what have you in common with the child of five whose
> photograph your mother keeps on the mantelpiece? Nothing, except
> that you happen to be the same person.[4]

This chapter looks at the trap described above through that prism. I shall argue that the road to freedom runs through emotional engagement with our cultural inheritance and open-ended debate about the implications, not through partisan battles or ideological trench warfare. There could scarcely be a better time to take it. As noted in

Chapter 3, we have not yet had an equivalent to Franklin Roosevelt's electrifying First Inaugural, but the time is over-ripe for a comparable break with the recent past. Mammon has been shown up as a false god. The irrationally rationalistic economics of the last thirty years is patently broken-backed. The newly untamed capitalism of the last thirty years is still engulfed in a crisis reminiscent of the crisis that engulfed the tamed capitalism of a generation ago. Public unease hangs over the increasingly threadbare market fundamentalist moral economy of the last thirty years like a pall of smog.

Like smog, however, it is unfocussed. We can't go back to the highly structured society of fifty years ago. (Even if we could, most of us wouldn't want to.) The trouble is that we don't yet know what to do instead. The air is loud with the noise of protests against the 'collateral damage'[5] that the capitalist renaissance of our time has brought with it. The protesters are mostly young, idealistic, iconoclastic, street-wise and internet-savvy; often they are inspiring. The Occupy London protest spoke for most of them when it denounced the existing system as 'unsustainable', 'undemocratic' and 'unjust'. But, though the protests have posed the right questions, they have not yet found convincing answers. To fill that gap, we need a wide-ranging national conversation, across the boundaries of party, doctrine and tradition, about the economic, political and moral crisis that has engulfed us: a twenty-first-century equivalent of the nineteenth-century debate on 'the Condition of England Question' described in Chapter 2.

Such a conversation would have to draw on the three main traditions of our political culture – conservative, liberal and socialist or social-democratic. But it should go wider than them. Religious traditions have as much to say to a troubled people as do political ones. So do a wide range of voluntary bodies; the protest movements I mentioned a moment ago; and, most of all, the burgeoning green movement and its insistent demand for a radical transformation of the moral economy. None of these has a monopoly of the truth: all of them have valuable insights. The conversation should not be an end in itself. The ultimate objective is change, not talk. But there can be no worthwhile change without a new public philosophy; and the last, best hope for discovering such a philosophy lies in talking together and learning from each other.

THE VIGOROUS VIRTUES

It won't be easy. An incoherent, but passionately held *moral* vision has underpinned the British version of untamed capitalism and it still permeates the common sense of the political class, the corporate elite and most of the commentariat. It derives, in part, from the teachings of Friedrich Hayek and his followers discussed in Chapter 2, but it is less cerebral, more concrete and more rooted than they are. Hayek and his followers were for freedom in the abstract; they had little to say about its emotional meaning for individual people or particular countries and cultures. They insisted that individuals should be free to live their economic lives as they wished, but they offered no picture of the individuals they were thinking of or of the lives they could be expected to lead. Apart from Hayek's wistful yearning for the lost age of the 'good husbandman and provider', they did not explain how the freedom they extolled might be incarnated in the way of life of any actual or possible society in the real world. The vision I have in mind is subtly different. It is a distillation of a narrative or set of narratives peculiar to Britain. It is designed to tell the British who they are and who they ought to be, not only or even mainly in economics but in every sphere of life.

For its devotees, the unhindered pursuit of individual self-interest in free, competitive markets is morally right as well as efficient. Only if individuals are free to pursue their interests as they wish, in a society governed by the rule of law, will they be moral beings; in Mrs Thatcher's striking phrase, collectivist interference turns them into 'moral cripples'.[6] For Shirley Letwin, its most acute interpreter, the heart and soul of this vision are the 'vigorous virtues': the virtues of 'upright, self-sufficient, energetic, independent-minded' people who are 'loyal to friends and robust against enemies'. For Letwin such people are creatures of flesh and blood, not disembodied abstractions; the virtues they exemplify are made manifest in real lives and we recognize them when we see them. Letwin concedes that they are not the only virtues. There are also 'softer' virtues, including kindness, humility, gentleness and sympathy among others, but for her the vigorous virtues should be given priority over the softer ones. Otherwise self-sufficient vigour may be crowded out by kindly gentleness.[7]

This vision harks back to the entrepreneurial ideal of the abstinent, self-reliant owner-managers of Industrial Revolution Britain, who invested their own savings, hired their own labour, ran their own businesses and bore their own risks. In their own eyes, they were the heroes of the economic battlefield, paragons of the supreme virtue of self-help. In a couple of sentences, Samuel Smiles, the most famous laureate of that virtue, summed up the gist: 'The spirit of self-help', he wrote, 'constitutes the true source of national vigour and strength. Help from without is often enfeebling in its effects, but help from within invariably invigorates.'[8]

It goes without saying that today's economic landscape bears no resemblance to the landscape posited by the entrepreneurial ideal of 150 years ago. Giant firms like BP and GlaxoSmithKline that dispose of immense market power and often penetrate the institutions of the state have virtually nothing in common with the owner-managed undertakings of Industrial Revolution Britain. Equally, the CEOs of today's big firms, with their inordinate remuneration packages, and their retinues of accountants, lawyers, public relations consultants and personal assistants live lives more akin to those of the hereditary aristocrats of the eighteenth century than to those of the self-made men of Samuel Smiles' imagining. But that does not detract from the emotional power of the moral vision that they pray in aid and that inspired Thatcher and her successors.

It tells the ultra-rich that they are entitled to their riches, and assures the aspirant middle and working classes that if they obey its precepts, they too will be rich, or at least richer. That is not the chief source of its authority, however. To understand its enduring appeal, we must revisit Letwin's vigorous virtues. The crucial point is that most of them *are* virtues. Indeed, they have something in common with the republican virtues that Milton celebrated and the virtues of solidarity and mutual help that sustained the early labour movement. As that implies, they are not confined to the rich and successful; they are found and respected in council estates as much as in comfortable suburbs. With brilliant intuition and compelling rhetorical skill, Thatcher spotted that they are essentially classless, and managed to harness them to her cause and the cause of Chicagoan economics. By a curious irony, however, her achievement was a dazzling conjuring trick, with which her hand deceived a multitude of eyes. For in truth, the vigorous virtues have no connection with Chicagoan economics. Their most dangerous enemy is the febrile, unmastered market, not the coercive state. The corrosive populism of the mass media, the restless lurchings of the money markets, the tax avoidance of giant firms and the conspicuous consumption of the ultra-rich have done more to undermine them than any number of itchy fingers in Whitehall.

That irony has been a central theme of British history for more than a generation. Margaret Thatcher sought to return to the sturdy, Methodist values she thought she had learned in her father's corner shop in interwar Grantham. Though not a Methodist, Tony Blair followed essentially the same path. The end result was bitterly disappointing. There was plenty of vigour around, but not much virtue. The Thatcher and Blair regimes presided over unsustainable booms, soaring household debt and the apparently irresistible rise of 'casino banking'. It was the age of 'Loadsamoney', a fictitious character invented by the comedian Harry Enfield and subsequently taken up by the *Sun*, and of city dealers whose raucous bawling reminded a visitor from the Midlands of the 'feeding frenzies of sharks'.[9] Symptomatic of the time were the 'Flaming Ferraris', a group of louche and braggart City traders, with more money than sense, whose favourite tipple was the 'Flaming Ferrari', a cocktail of rum and Grand Marnier. Their most famous exploit was to arrange for photographers to be on hand when they arrived, in grand style, at Nobu, a fancy Japanese restaurant in Park Lane. (The stunt backfired. Credit Suisse, for whom the Flaming Ferraris worked, was not amused; the ringleader, James Archer, Jeffrey Archer's son, was sacked the following year.)

Means and ends were in conflict, both under Thatcher and under Blair. The 'great engine of the market',[10] in which they both put their faith, turned out to be the enemy of the values they stood for. The Holy Trinity of Choice, Freedom and the Individual, which had been sacred for both of them, turned traitor. There was nothing odd or surprising about the contradiction between means and ends. As Marx and Engels pointed out, markets are inherently subversive: that was what they meant when they said, early in *The Communist Manifesto*, that in bourgeois societies 'All that is solid melts into air.' What consumers want and are prepared to pay for, suppliers will supply. That is the lesson of the drug trade, of people-trafficking, of Murdoch's media empire, of internet gambling, of prostitution and of gas-guzzling four-by-fours.

But Thatcher and Blair could not bring themselves to understand that; had they done so they would have had to jettison the world-view which had become part of them. Instead they took refuge in cognitive dissonance. They did all they could to foster the turbulent, buccaneering, casino capitalism[11] of the late twentieth century and the market fundamentalist moral economy that accompanied it, while calling, in Blair's case, for a timeless (and characterless) 'society of respect'[12] and in Thatcher's for a return to the 'Victorian values' instilled in her during her Grantham childhood, when

> You were taught to work jolly hard, you were taught to improve yourself, you were taught self-reliance, you were taught to live within your income, you were taught that cleanliness was next to godliness. You were taught self-respect, you were taught always to give a hand to your neighbour, you were taught tremendous pride in your country, you were taught to be a good member of your community.[13]

That history is now repeating itself. David Cameron came to power promising to 'fix' what he called 'broken Britain': in effect a Britain from which the vigorous virtues had disappeared. Yet, despite its treacherous proclivities, the Trinity of Choice, Freedom and the Individual is the lodestar of the Cameron–Clegg government, just as it was for the governments of Thatcher, Major, Blair and Brown. Much more important, it is still entrenched in the public culture. It is buttressed by a widely held, but sadly diminished version of liberalism, which holds that it is illegitimate for the whole society, as opposed to separate individuals, to value some ways of life more than others. One striking result is that the power elite pray the Holy Trinity in aid without serious challenge; another is that no major opposition party has assaulted it head-on.

The common sense of the age holds that this is as it should be. Surely everyone is for choice? Surely freedom is a good thing? Surely individuals are entitled to live their lives as they wish? To all these questions, there is a simple answer: 'Yes, but'. We do not make our choices in a cultural vacuum. We can't; we don't inhabit a cultural vacuum. The choosing self is enmeshed in and shaped by a complex web of relationships, traditions and sometimes shifting values. The diminished liberal notion that society should be neutral as between different ways of life and play no part in the choices they entail is incoherent in principle and unfeasible in practice. Moreover, it flies in the face of historical experience. The battles over the extensions of the suffrage in the nineteenth century were fought between champions of different conceptions of a worthy life, and different pictures of the people who could be expected to live it. Gladstone made his extraordinary journey from high Tory to Liberal messiah because he came to believe that the masses were more virtuous than the classes. Early socialists like William Morris and Keir Hardie challenged the injustices of their society in the name of a different and better way of life and not just of a different distribution of income. Shirley Letwin's vigorous virtues, Margaret Thatcher's Victorian values and Tony Blair's society of respect were all salvoes in a battle over social ethics and not just over private choices.

A worthwhile national conversation would start from the premise that our choices are not ours alone: that they are bound to impact on others, indirectly even if not directly; and that others will certainly influence them. Amartya Sen puts it well: 'When someone thinks and chooses and does something, it is for sure that person – and not someone else – who is doing these things. But it would be hard to understand why and how he or she undertakes these activities without some comprehension of his or her societal relations.'[14] A closely related premise is that choices are not all morally equal: that some are *better*, and not just more expedient, than others. The choices that created our current predicament were freely made, but bad. Money worship is certainly disgusting, as Keynes thought, but that is not all it is. It is wrong, and the values it has fostered are wrong too. To throw those values over, we shall have to make better choices and to do that we shall have to recover the lost language of the common good.

The same is true of freedom and the individual. Freedom as a source of human flourishing is one thing; freedom to ignore the common good and exploit or seek to dominate others is quite another. The individual, yes: but as a complex being, rooted in shared memories and lived traditions, not as the bloodless, egocentric and fanciful abstraction, detached from community and history, that today's Chicagoan economists have inherited from nineteenth-century utilitarianism.

INTIMATIONS OF A CHALLENGE

Intimations of a challenge to the Holy Trinity are already present in a growing variety of campaigning groups, social movements, co-operative societies, NGOs and trade unions as well as in some of the protests I mentioned a moment ago. Only a few examples can be discussed here. Women's Institutes have campaigned to save honeybees and for action on climate change. The co-operative movement has campaigned for debt cancellation in developing countries. Occupy London's most spectacular manifestation was the camp outside St Paul's in early 2012. UK Uncut has organized 'days of action' against firms like Vodafone, Starbucks and Barclays, accused of avoiding tax. Liberty and Unlock Democracy focus on human and political rights.

The charity Citizens UK – a network of faith communities, schools, universities, trade unions and community groups – has inspired campaigns for a 'living wage' across the country. Its London arm, London Citizens, started in a mosque in the East End in 1994; during the next two years forty-eight local organizations came together to campaign on local issues, starting with the rising cost of funerals and a smelly factory processing lard. The Living Wage campaign started six years later. The trade union demonstrations against the Coalition's spending cuts in March 2011 and October 2012 come into the same category. A more remarkable example is 38 Degrees, an internet campaigning community with more than a million members, launched in May 2009. It has a staff of nine people, in addition to the dynamic Executive Director, David Babbs. 38 Degrees has no party affiliation; in the 2010 general election members split three ways, with the Liberal Democrats slightly in the lead over Labour and the Conservatives a good third. Its members might be called 'Danny Boyle's people': they were enthused by the London Olympics Opening Ceremony and words like 'society', 'people', 'equal' and 'fair' strike more sparks with them than 'government' or 'state'. They have campaigned against the sale of public woodlands to private purchasers; in favour of the EU directive to combat human trafficking; against Donald Trump's planned compulsory purchase orders on his Menie estate in Aberdeenshire; and in favour of the *Which*-backed energy 'Big Switch' initiative that led 30,000 consumers to turn to Co-operative Energy from more expensive providers.

Another example is Compass, a non-party campaigning and pressure group of the 'democratic left'.[15] Compass was born out of rank-and-file Labour disillusion with the New Labour leadership; though it had supporters outside the Labour Party, full Compass membership was at first confined to Labour Party members. Since 2010, however, it has been open to members of other parties and of none. The combined members and supporters list now numbers more than 50,000. Compass is more obviously political than the Living Wage campaign and 38 Degrees, but its activities are bound together by an overarching theme that goes beyond politics: the 'Good Society'. The High Pay Commission, whose findings I mentioned in Chapter 3, was a Compass initiative. In addition, it has set up a Good Banking Forum; examined issues like media ownership and the role of the financial sector; and published reports on issues such as debt and the lessons Britain can learn from Germany's economic performance. However, the simple notion of a 'Good Society' has a wider significance than the activities conducted in its name. In two words it encapsulates a way of talking and thinking about the public realm that transcends the instrumental utilitarianism of contemporary political and economic debate. Simply put, it implies that human beings must be seen as ends in themselves, not as means to an end defined by governments, firms, bond markets or media moguls.

In a different way, the same applies to the Green movement. Motivating organizations such as Greenpeace, Friends of the Earth, the World Development Movement, the World Wildlife Fund and the Green Party itself is a concern for the future of the human species, and not just for particular nations and cultures. On a deeper level, they are also inspired by a concern for the sacredness of life as such, as Rowan Williams nicely puts it, 'for human life's involvement with all other life, vegetable and animal – the variegated life of the rain forest as well as the multiple species of pollinating bees'.[16]

The problem is that, in a culture suffused with instrumental utilitarianism, it is hard to make such concerns bite. The charismatic barrister Polly Higgins has discovered – or rather rediscovered – the most promising answer: an international law criminalizing 'ecocide'. For her, the threat of environmental degradation can be overcome only through laws making environmental sustainability an overriding objective.[17] For practical purposes ecocide amounts to the destruction of natural ecosystems in a given territory on such a scale as to jeopardize the continued peaceful existence of the territory's population. The term came into prominence in 1998, when the so-called Rome Statute set up the International Criminal Court. The Statute specified four crimes against peace: genocide, crimes against humanity, war crimes and the crime of aggression. A widely supported attempt to include ecocide in the list was foiled at the last moment by France, Britain, the Netherlands and the United States.

Higgins sees ecocide as the 'missing fifth crime against peace'. Her aim is to ensure that when the Rome Statute is reviewed in 2014, it will be amended to add ecocide to the four crimes against peace agreed in 1998. To that end she and her colleagues at Eradicating Ecocide have advised governments, lobbied ambassadors, addressed international conferences, launched an EU Citizens' Initiative to put an ecocide law before the European Parliament, initiated an 'Ecocide Project' at London University's Human Rights Consortium and organized a mock trial for ecocide at the Supreme Court of the United Kingdom.

These intimations are just that: intimations. Their impact and significance must not be exaggerated. They do not, in themselves, amount to a national conversation, still less to a revolution of sentiment. Yet they are straws in a refreshing wind. The campaigners involved in them have a captivating élan – a sense that history is with them – which no conventional party can equal. Above all, they show that though the language of the common good barely figures in political discourse any longer, the notion itself is still very much alive.

EDMUND BURKE AND THE ETHIC OF STEWARDSHIP

Here the traditions I mentioned a moment ago move centre-stage. They are all much richer and more subtle than they seem to an amnesiac age, and they are all repositories of wisdom that twenty-first-century Britain sorely needs to tap. I begin with the conservative, liberal and socialist traditions that have left an enduring impress on our political languages and identities. I shall argue that, despite the obvious differences between them, they overlap in unexpected and enriching ways, and that the revolution of sentiment I call for in this chapter will have to draw on all of them. They are all fluid and heterogeneous; none can be summarized in a few sentences. The dry-as-dust procedures of academic political theory cannot do justice to them. They have emerged from the give-and-take of political debate in response to the flux of unpredictable events, and they are best approached by way of the debaters who did most to shape them.

I shall start with the conservative tradition, by way of the tormented genius of Edmund Burke; and I shall try to show that it is both more diverse and, in twenty-first-century terms, far more iconoclastic than most present-day Conservatives imagine. Burke has been called 'the father of conservatism' and thoughtful conservatives have looked back to him for more than 200 years, but his legacy is much richer than those simple statements imply. His admirers included Gladstone, the Liberal politician and writer John Morley, and, more remarkably, the New Left thinker Raymond Williams. He was a deadly parliamentary gladiator, and a good hater, yet his politics were suffused with generosity of spirit. He was a man for all seasons – notably including the strange and stormy season through which Britain is now living.

Burke believed in property, hierarchy and tradition and defended them with passion and occasional savagery, but with equal passion he insisted that 'in a contest of blood ... I would take my fate with the poor and low and feeble'.[18] He castigated George III and the so-called 'King's Friends' for seeking to extend the power of the Crown at the expense of the Commons, and savaged Lord North's Government for the pettifogging arrogance of its behaviour towards the rebellious American colonists. He persuaded the House of Commons to impeach Warren Hastings, the East India Company's Governor-General of Bengal, on behalf of powerless native victims of the Company's extortion, cruelty, torture and judicial murder; and devoted the best years of his life to a decade-long crusade to ensure that Hastings was found guilty. He fought for a people he had not met, in a continent thousands of miles away; though his crusade failed, it was one of the finest episodes in British parliamentary history.

Burke's anguished fellow feeling with the victims of arbitrary power sprang from the deepest recesses of his nature; it also reflected his complex personal history. He was born in Dublin in 1729, when Ireland was effectively a colony. The majority population, the Catholic Irish, were held down, in the last resort by force, but more immediately by laws that consigned them to social and political inferiority. Catholics could not bear arms, then an essential attribute of gentility; they were not allowed to vote in elections to the Irish Parliament; and they could not practise law. Towards the end of his life, Burke described this legal code with a ferocious irony, reminiscent of Swift. It was, he wrote, 'a machine of wise and elaborate contrivance, and as well fitted for the oppression, impoverishment, and degradation of a people, and the debasement, in them, of human nature itself, as ever proceeded from the perverted ingenuity of man'.[19]

When Burke wrote that he was in his early sixties, an old man by eighteenth-century standards. Yet the pain of carefully contrived degradation still throbbed. For though Burke's father was an attorney, and as such a Protestant, his mother was a Catholic, and his sister was brought up as a Catholic. Burke himself was baptized into the Anglican Church of Ireland, but he spent much of his childhood with his mother's Catholic relatives. In a luminous phrase of Conor Cruise O'Brien's he inhabited 'a zone of insecurity'[20] between two antagonistic social worlds, one of the conquerors and the other of the conquered. He made his career in London, but Ireland was in his blood. Oratorical brilliance, obsessive pertinacity and exceptional political imagination carried him into the governing class, but he never penetrated to its heart. He was always a marginal outsider looking in, not an insider looking out.

Marginality had a high price, psychically and politically, but it helps to account for his extraordinary empathy with the cultures of British subjects in North America and India. The 'temper and character' of the American colonists, he declared in a famous speech on conciliation with America, were suffused with 'a fierce spirit of liberty'.[21] Attempts to govern them in defiance of their particular culture were doomed to fail; insofar as they succeeded they would jeopardize freedom in Britain as well. India was closer to his heart than America. In a magnificent Commons speech – his greatest, and one of the greatest ever made in the House of Commons – he reminded his fellow MPs that Britain's Indian subjects had been 'cultivated by all the arts of polished life, whilst we were yet in the woods'. In the territories governed by the East India Company, he went on,

> is to be found an ancient and venerable priesthood, the depository of their laws, learning and history, the guides of the people whilst living, and their consolation in death; a nobility of great antiquity and renown; a multitude of cities, not exceeded in population and trade by those of the first class in Europe; merchants and bankers, individual houses of which have once vied in capital with the Bank of England ... millions of ingenious manufacturers and mechanics; millions of the most diligent, and not the least intelligent, tillers of the earth. Here are to be found almost all the religions professed by men, the Braminical, the Musselmen, the Eastern and the Western Christians.[22]

The accents of the Irish colonial, brought up in Conor Cruise O'Brien's 'zone of insecurity' between conquerors and conquered, are impossible to miss.

In all this he was far ahead of his time: a prophet of cultural pluralism *avant la lettre*. Respect for cultural difference is as much a part of his legacy as the revulsion from the abuse of power that ran through his crusade against Warren Hastings and inspired his ferocious opposition to the mob rule spawned by the French Revolution. With it went a corresponding respect for the human need for continuity and belonging, and a deep suspicion of the asocial individualism that he detected in the *philosophes*, who prefigured the revolution. He was for the 'splendid flame of Liberty', he wrote in its early stages, but not for 'solitary, unconnected, individual, selfish Liberty. As if every Man was to regulate the whole of his Conduct by his own will. The Liberty I mean is social freedom.'[23]

Social freedom ran athwart the then fashionable notion of the social contract. For Burke, that notion as normally understood was impious. It implied that political communities could be made and unmade at whim. Concede that, and there would be nothing to link one generation with another. 'Men would be little better than the flies of summer.' Society was 'indeed a contract', he conceded in a passage that resonates as powerfully in the twenty-first century as it did in the eighteenth, but it was a contract of a special kind.

> Subordinate contracts of mere occasional interest may be dissolved at pleasure – but the state ought not to be considered as nothing better than a partnership agreement in a trade of pepper and coffee, callico or tobacco ... It is a partnership in all science, a partnership in all art; a partnership in every virtue and in all perfection. As the ends of such a partnership cannot be obtained in many generations, it becomes a partnership not only between those who are living, but between those who are living, those who are dead, and those who are to be born. Each contract of each particular state is but a clause in the great primaeval contract of eternal society.[24]

Individuals were tenants, not freeholders, of the political communities into which they had been born, by which they had been shaped and into which their descendants would be born in turn. From that insight sprang an ethic of stewardship, closer to today's Greens than to any conventional political party, and utterly at variance with the Trinity of Choice, Freedom and the Individual.

JOHN STUART MILL: COMPLEX ICON

The liberal tradition is less rounded and, in an odd way, less rooted. It boasts two towering political leaders – Gladstone and Lloyd George – but though they easily outranked Burke in executive achievement, neither of them speaks to the twenty-first century as he does. The standard bearer of the liberal tradition with most to say to our time is John Stuart Mill, whom we met in Chapter 2. He has been an icon for British liberals, both with a big and a small 'L', for more than 150 years; not long ago, the Liberal Democrats voted him the greatest liberal in British history. As befits that status, his legacy appears at first sight to have nothing in common with Burke's. Like many icons, however, he was a richly complex figure, and there is more than a touch of Burke in his sometimes contorted message.

His exemplary life compels affection as well as admiration. His terrifying education, at the hands of a rigid and dogmatic father who seems to have had no sense of humour and no empathy for others, is legendary. He learned the Greek alphabet at three; read Plato (in Greek) at seven; learned Latin at eight; and read Aristotle on logic at eleven. Despite this grim upbringing, he was astonishingly productive. His day job as a high official in the East India Company's London headquarters would have been enough for most people, but thick, closely argued volumes poured from his pen. His *System of Logic* and *Principles of Political Economy* both ran to seven editions in his lifetime. He wrote several shorter books as well as a stream of essays and reviews in the leading intellectual journals of the time. He was a Member of Parliament for three years and proposed an amendment to the 1867 Reform Bill which would have given the vote to women fifty years before they actually won it. He was a scourge of the brutal Governor Eyre of Jamaica and an unyielding opponent of the notorious Contagious Diseases Act that empowered the police to arrest women suspected of being prostitutes in garrison towns and to subject them to forcible and humiliating medical examination. He championed Irish land reform, the 1848 revolution in France and the unionist cause in the American Civil War.

If that were all, only specialists in Victorian intellectual history would remember him. His iconic status rests on a short tract simply entitled *On Liberty*. It propounds two messages, which are easily muddled up. The first, conveyed in a tone of passionate indignation, is negative. The second, suffused with exhilarating optimism, is positive. In the first message, Mill's wrath is directed against society, not against the state: against 'prevailing opinion', not against 'the magistrate'. The enemies are unthinking conformity; fear of eccentricity; the narrow and complacent pieties of the Victorian middle class that Dickens caricatured in novel after novel. At times, Mill got carried away by his own indignant rhetoric. Sometimes he gives the impression that individuals have an absolute right to live their lives as they wish, insulated in some strange way from the society that formed them and in which they live, provided only that they do no harm to others. (Admittedly a mammoth proviso.) That sounds rather like the 'solitary, unconnected' liberty against which Burke trained his heaviest guns; if it were taken seriously, it would imply a society of rootless atoms, with no place for the human need for continuity and belonging.

The second message is radically different. It recalls Milton's attack on censorship in *Areopagitica*,[25] and his glowing picture of revolutionary London as the 'mansion house of liberty' where vigorous public debate armed the people against the enemies of freedom. Like Milton, Mill had no time for cloistered virtue. Truth could be established only in open and continuous contest with error. In one of the most famous passages in *On Liberty* he insisted that all attempts to control the expression of opinion are, by definition, illegitimate.

> The best government has no more title to it than the worst. It is as noxious, or more noxious, when exercised in accordance with public opinion than when in opposition to it. If all mankind minus one, were of one opinion, and only one person were of the contrary opinion, mankind would be no more justified in silencing that one person, than he, if he had the power, would be justified in silencing mankind . . . [T]he peculiar evil of silencing the expression of an opinion is that it is robbing the human race; posterity as well as the existing generation; those who dissent from the opinion, still more than those who hold it. If the opinion is right, they are deprived of the opportunity of exchanging error for truth: if wrong, they lose, what is almost as great a benefit, the clearer perception and livelier impression of truth, produced by its collision with error.[26]

Mill was not an individualist in the sense used in this book. Both the market and the moral individualism described in Chapter 2 would have seemed to him perverse and dangerous. He was himself a bureaucrat by profession; Hayek's strictures on 'functionaries'[27] would have exasperated him. Like the rest of the Victorian clerisy of which he was an ornament, he took it for granted that there was something sordid and demeaning about money-grubbing in the marketplace. Though he thought the laws of political economy were timeless and unchangeable, he was shocked by the buccaneering capitalism of the nineteenth century. Today's moral individualism would have shocked him even more. He would have had no truck with the notion that all individual choices were equally worthy: that the individual was the solitary captain of her own soul, entitled to steer it in whatever direction she wished. As I shall show in a moment, he insisted again and again that some choices were better than others, and, at least by implication, that some individuals were inferior to others.

But though Mill was not an individual*ist*, respect for individual*ity* – for him the quality that made human beings 'noble' – lay at the core of his world-view. And individuality stemmed from exertion. A striking passage in *On Liberty* explains why.

> The mental and moral, like the muscular powers, are improved only by being used . . .
>
> It really is of importance, not only what men do, but also what manner of men they are who do it. Among the works of man, which human life is rightly employed in perfecting and beautifying, the first in importance surely is man himself. Supposing it were possible to get houses built, corn grown, battles fought, causes tried and even churches built and prayers said, by machinery – automatons in human form – it would be a considerable loss to exchange for these automatons even the men and women who at present inhabit the more civilised parts of the world, and who assuredly are but starved specimens of what nature can and will produce. Human nature is not a machine to be built after a model and set to do exactly the work prescribed for it, but a tree, which requires to grow and develope [*sic*] itself on all sides, according to the tendency of the inward forces which make it a living thing.[28]

Growth would not come from solitary ratiocination. Only human interaction could strengthen the mental and moral powers in the way that was needed. Human beings owed each other 'help to distinguish the better from the worse, and encouragement to choose the former and avoid the latter'. They should continually stimulate each other 'to increased exercise of their higher faculties'.[29] Society was no longer an enemy. It was the soil that nurtured the tree of individuality. In the resounding final paragraph, Mill had the state in his sights, not society.

> The worth of a State, in the long run, is the worth of the individuals composing it; and a State which postpones the interests of *their* mental expansion and elevation, to a little more of administrative skill, or that semblance of it which practice gives, in the details of business; a State which dwarfs its men, in order that they may be more docile instruments

in its hands even for beneficial purposes – will find that with small men no great thing can really be accomplished.[30]

It would be absurd to suggest that Mill was a Burkean conservative in disguise, but there is more in common between his vision of socially fostered individuality and Burke's social freedom than appears at first sight.

The great question was how to ensure that individuals were indeed worthy, that they *could* accomplish great things. Mill did not answer it in *On Liberty*, but tantalizing hints are scattered through some of his other writings. In an early essay on 'The Spirit of the Age', Mill argued that the key to moral growth and social improvement lay in what he called 'discussion'. Discussion had 'penetrated deeper into society; and if no greater numbers than before have attained the higher degrees of intelligence, fewer grovel in that state of abject stupidity, which can only co-exist with utter apathy and sluggishness'.[31] In similar vein a decade later Mill published a substantial review of de Tocqueville's *Democracy in America*. 'Life is a problem, not a theorem . . .', he wrote, 'action can only be learned in action. A child learns its name only by a succession of trials; and is a man to be taught to use his mind and guide his conduct by mere precept?'[32]

Actions were not all equally valuable, however. 'Private money-getting' made its practitioners 'indifferent to the public, to the more generous objects and the nobler interests'. But by participating actively in local government, the individual citizen would come to feel 'that besides the interests which separate him from his fellow-citizens, he has interests which connect him with them; that not only the common weal is his weal, but that it partly depends on his exertions'.[33] In the *Principles of Political Economy* he rammed the point home. 'The business of life', he wrote, 'is an essential part of the practical education of a people.' A people who lacked the habit of 'spontaneous action for a collective interest' would be governed 'as sheep by their shepherd'.[34] So far from being enemies or rivals individual freedom and collective action were interdependent. Laissez-faire at the centre should therefore go hand in hand with active self-government in the localities.

'Worth', 'noble', the 'common weal', the 'better' versus the 'worse' and, above all, 'growth': these are Mill's key words. They capture the essence of his legacy. The metaphor of the tree is particularly arresting. For Mill, human life was dynamic, not static. On a level deeper than that of argument, he tells us to nurture the better angels of our nature through arduous practice in the public sphere.

R. H. TAWNEY AND
THE CULTURE OF DEMOCRACY

The socialist tradition is best approached through the economic historian and cultural critic R. H. Tawney. Burke was an outsider who wanted to be an insider; Tawney was an insider who would have liked to be an outsider. By upbringing and education he belonged to the professional service class, by vocation to the clerisy. He was part English gentleman, part adept committee member and part Old Testament prophet. He was educated at Rugby School and Balliol College, Oxford, then in the full flush of Hegelian idealism. Before the First World War he lectured for the Workers' Educational Association (WEA); his classes, he told me when I interviewed him some fifty years ago, taught him more than he taught them. He enlisted as a private in the Manchester Regiment in November 1914, refused a commission and rose to be a sergeant. He was grievously wounded on the first day of the battle of the Somme, and narrowly escaped death.

After the war he spent virtually his entire working life at the London School of Economics. He published at least one masterpiece of cultural and economic history, *Religion and the Rise of Capitalism*, and two seminal social-democratic texts, *The Acquisitive Society* and *Equality*, as well as innumerable articles and several other books. He sat on a wide range of committees and served as president of the WEA for fifteen years. He was defiantly shabby and gloriously untidy. He padded about his flat in Mecklenburgh Square in carpet slippers and his old sergeant's tunic; scraps of 'half eaten food sat among piles of books' and a mouse would sometimes 'hop over the one to get at the other'. He died during the hard winter of 1962–3. At his memorial service, Hugh Gaitskell called him 'the best man I have ever known'.[35]

Tawney has been called a 'prophet of equality', an 'ethical socialist' and a 'Christian socialist'. He called himself a 'displaced peasant'. His greatest book, *The Acquisitive Society*, was published in 1921, when he was forty. It was written with captivating *brio*. It is at one and the same time a savage assault on the functionless property of the shareholder, a mordant critique of the public doctrine that underpinned it and a call for a new doctrine, centred on an ideal of function and service, ultimately based on Christian ethics. Tawney's loathing for the 'fetish' of industrialism – as he saw it, the British equivalent of the Prussian fetish of militarism – harked back to Blake, William Morris and Ruskin. 'Men may use what mechanical instruments they please and be none the worse for their use,' he wrote. 'What kills their souls is when they allow their instruments to use *them*.'[36]

At the heart of Tawney's analysis of the acquisitive society lay two simple propositions: economic and social lives are inextricably entangled; and both are governed by the same broad set of principles. For him, the principles governing economic and social life in interwar Britain were perverted. In days gone by, they had inspired attacks on aristocratic privilege, now they were prayed in aid to justify the privileges of property. As such, they legitimized an Acquisitive Society in which each new generation was 'shovelled like raw material into an economic mill to be pounded and ground and kneaded into ... malleable human pulp'.[37] Property was divorced from function, and rights from duties. The result was a 'class of pensioners upon industry, who levy toll upon its product, but contribute nothing to its increase'. Outwardly, the pensioners led delightful lives: 'London in June, when London is pleasant, the moors in August, and pheasants in October, Cannes in December and hunting in February and March.'[38] Inwardly even the pensioners sensed that something was wrong. They were 'like the spirits in the Inferno ... punished by the attainment of their desires'.[39]

Tawney's alternative was a 'Functional Society', permeated by an ethic of equity and service. Property rights would survive if they went hand in hand with the performance of service and abolished if they did not. Producers would answer to the community instead of being subject to shareholders whose interest was gain rather than service. However, the heart of his message lay elsewhere. The great 'affliction' of contemporary society was not that industry's product was badly distributed. It was that industry held 'a position of exclusive predominance among human interests'. Like 'a hypochondriac who is so absorbed in the processes of his own digestion that he goes to his grave before he has begun to live, industrialized communities neglect the very objects for which it is worth while to acquire riches in their feverish preoccupation with the means by which riches can be acquired.'[40]

Tawney remained true to his socialist convictions through all the travails of the interwar years, but as time went on a more sombre tone appeared in his writings. In some industries, though not all, he thought outright nationalization was the best alternative to functionless property, but he came to believe that there was a larger question. What mattered was not 'merely whether the State owns and controls the means of production. It is also who owns and controls the State.'[41] In Britain ordinary citizens did not. In her transition to political democracy, Tawney wrote in a resonant passage that contains the gist of his vision of democratic citizenship, Britain had undergone 'no inner conversion'.

> She accepted it as a convenience, like an improved system of telephones; she did not dedicate herself to it as the expression of a moral ideal of comradeship and equality, the avowal of which would leave nothing the same. She changed her political garments, but not her heart. She carried into the democratic era, not only the institutions, but the social habits and mentality of the oldest and toughest plutocracy in the world . . . She went to the ballot box touching her hat.[42]

The great question was how to bring the heart into line with the garments; and this was a cultural and moral question far more than an economic or political one. Like Tom Paine in the 1790s, and the working-class Chartist movement in the 1830s and 1840s, Tawney dreamed of a democracy of free and equal citizens, bowing their knees to no one. He did not know how to achieve it, but he was sure of one thing. Britain would not be a true democracy so long as her people were trapped in a vicious circle of subordination and submissiveness. To break through that circle, Tawney believed, the culture of the British state, with its petty snobberies and subservient flunkeyism, had to be demystified; and some of his most resonant writing was designed to do just that.

At times, he attacked the culture of flunkeyism head-on. At other times he tried to subvert it with mocking irony. In a famous letter to the *New Statesman*, protesting against the Labour chief whip's acceptance of a knighthood, he did both. Had Labour jettisoned its belief in social equality, he asked.

> Or does it suppose that it will convert the public to a belief in Equality if it does not, in its heart, believe in it itself? And does it expect to persuade them of the genuineness of its convictions, if prominent members of the Party sit up, like poodles in a drawing-room, wag their tails when patted, and lick their lips at the social sugar-plums tossed them by their masters? . . . It has declared that it is committed to an uncompromising struggle with the plutocracy and all its works. Then why stick in its hair the very feathers which the plutocracy, in its more imbecile moments, loves to wear in its own? . . . The truth is, that the whole business of political honours stinks – stinks of snobbery, of the money for which, unless rumour is wholly misleading, a good many of them are sold, of the servile respect for wealth and social position which remains even today the characteristic and contemptible vice of large numbers of our fellow-countrymen.[43]

Milton, Paine and the Chartist leader Bronterre O'Brien would have cheered. But they might have wondered why the culture of flunkeyism had lasted for so long.

INTOLERANT TOLERANCE

As I suggested earlier we have at least as much to learn from religious traditions as from political ones. Some may jib at that suggestion. Though it is not overtly or explicitly hostile to religion as such, the diminished liberalism of our time has drastically narrowed the cultural space accessible to religious beliefs. It has bred a strange, intolerant tolerance which holds that religion is fine, so long as it is a purely private preference, like a taste for spicy food or designer stubble, and that believers have no right to intrude their faith into public debate.

The intolerantly tolerant are a strange breed. (Two prominent examples are Richard Dawkins and the late Christopher Hitchens.)

They think of themselves as gallant champions of free expression and scientific enlightenment, fighting for the light against the massed forces of clerical darkness: latter-day equivalents of Voltaire. To listen to them, you would think they risked incarceration in the Bastille, or at the very least prosecution for blasphemy. In truth, the forces of clerical darkness, insofar as they exist at all, are now a tiny and powerless minority in almost all European countries (though, to be fair, not in the United States or parts of the Muslim world). So why do the intolerantly tolerant protest so much? Having won the battle against clerical intolerance, why are they so anxious to trample on the dead? The answer, I suspect, is twofold. They are the children of the moral individualism I described in Chapter 2. They believe that the individual should be absolutely sovereign and they are outraged by any suggestion to the contrary. As well, they are classic examples of the collective amnesia described in Chapter 3. The notion that the wisdom of the past can illuminate the ethical dilemmas of the present seems to them absurd and dangerous. For them, there is no such wisdom. The past was steeped in ignorance and error. Its teachings belong in the dustbin of history.

Intolerant tolerance is based on a profound misunderstanding of almost all organized religions, and indeed of the human self. The very notion of a private religion is an oxymoron. Religion is public, by definition. It is public in the obvious sense that its rituals and ceremonies take place in public, and also in the more important sense that believers are supposed to bear witness and that bearing witness is a public act. For Islam, 'the transcendent is made manifest in every aspect of daily experience'.[44] The weekly ritual of the Jewish Sabbath centres on the family, but it is public as well as familial, as any visitor to Israel (or, for that matter, to Stoke Newington) will soon discover. Famously, Christians are not supposed to hide their light under a bushel. They are supposed to confront the evanescent powers and principalities of this world in the name of timeless and, in the profoundest sense, unworldly truths. In the Roman Empire, early Christians risked martyrdom and were sometimes martyred because they refused to accept the divinity of the emperor. In Nazi Germany, the theologian and pastor Dietrich Bonhoeffer was hanged by the Gestapo for raising money to help Jews to escape from the Reich. The Martyrs'

Memorial in central Oxford commemorates Nicholas Ridley, Hugh Latimer and Thomas Cranmer, who were burned at the stake under Queen Mary for refusing to abjure their heresy. (Needless to say, there were Catholic martyrs under Protestant rulers.)

Even in unbelievers like me, the magical words of the Magnificat, as translated in the English *Book of Common Prayer*, make the heart sing.

> He hath put down the mighty from their seat: and hath
> Exalted the humble and meek.
> He hath filled the hungry with good things: and the rich he
> Hath sent empty away.

The incarnate God-the-Son of Christianity, we should never forget, was born in a stable, grew up in the family of a humble craftsman and was sentenced to a terrible death for sedition. All too often, the churches *have* forgotten. Sometimes they have kowtowed to the powers of this world, sometimes they have sat inertly alongside them. All too often, they have sought worldly power for themselves. That does not affect the central point, however. As everyone knows, Christ told his followers to render unto Caesar the things that are Caesar's and unto God the things that are God's. However, the things that are God's are necessarily political. Rowan Williams puts it well.

> The Christian Church began as a reconstructed version of the notion of God's people – a community called by God to make God known to the world in and through the forms of law-governed common life – the 'law' being, in the Christian case, the model of action and suffering revealed in Jesus Christ. It claimed to make real a pattern of common life lived in the fullest possible accord with the nature and will of God – a life in which each member's flourishing depended closely and strictly on the flourishing of every other ... So Christian identity is irreducibly political in the sense that it defines a *politeia*, a kind of citizenship.[45]

Mutatis mutandis, the same applies to Judaism and Islam. To say that religion should be confined to the private sphere is to say that it should cease to be religion.

A tangible example may help to pin the point down. All three of the Abrahamic religions profess teachings that are intrinsically at odds with the materialistic economism of our time – for example, the medieval Christian doctrine of the just price, the Islamic prohibition of *riba* and the Book of Deuteronomy's complex provisions for redistributing resources from the rich and powerful to the marginal and dispossessed. To suggest that it is somehow improper for religious people to make a *religious* case against inequality or in favour of higher taxes on the rich is to exclude potentially resonant voices from the public sphere in a way that makes nonsense of the liberal professions of the excluders.

It is also to impoverish the public sphere itself. Believers should not be privileged in any way. They should take their chance in the give-and-take of public debate along with everyone else. But the traditions for which they speak (including the Muslim tradition) have been part of the warp and woof of European history for 1,400 years; today Islam is Britain's second faith, and it may well be that practising Muslims now outnumber practising Christians. The Church of England has spoken to and for the English people (though not to and for the Scots or Welsh) since the time of Elizabeth I. Sometimes it has spoken feebly and complacently, as in the eighteenth century. At other times its voice has been courageous and defiant, as in the last thirty years. *Faith in the City*, issued by a Church of England Commission in 1985 and mentioned in Chapter 4, excoriated the Thatcher Government's 'crude exaltation' of 'individual self interest'. What was true of the Church of England south of the Border was even more true of the religious traditions north of it. Not the least of the reasons for the electoral catastrophe suffered by the Scottish Conservative Party in the 1980s was that Thatcher's clamant market individualism outraged a people whose political culture was suffused by the twin legacies of Catholicism and Calvinism.

To refuse on principle to pay attention to these traditions is to deny ourselves the chance to mine some of the richest seams of our increasingly variegated culture. We need not use religious language to mine them. In a polemic against the narrowly economistic approach to higher education exemplified (among other places) in the Browne review described in Chapter 4, Martha Nussbaum, convert to Judaism and Professor of Law and Ethics at Chicago University, inveighs against the modern world's failure to remember how to 'approach another person as a soul, rather than as a mere useful instrument'.

Her religious commitment shines through that passage, but she adds that the word 'soul' is neither here nor there. What matter are the qualities it implies: 'the faculties of thought and imagination that make us human and make our relationships rich human relationships, rather than relationships of mere use and manipulation'. Without such relationships, she adds, democracy is impossible.[46]

The utilitarian instrumentalism that Nussbaum excoriates can be resisted on non-religious grounds as well as on religious ones: Kant's claim that everyone has an intrinsic value provides one of them. But Kantian philosophy is cold where religion is warm. It speaks to the head, where religion speaks to the heart. And only the heart can make a revolution of sentiment.

THE DECENT SOCIETY

Avishai Margalit's notion of a 'decent society', discussed briefly in Chapter 5, serves as a coda. The notion of a 'just society' has preoccupied philosophers for millennia. In the guise of a 'fair society', it has been a recurrent theme in British political debate. In *The Decent Society*, Margalit forsakes that well-trodden path for a more original and, I believe, a more challenging one. The 'decent society' may or may not be just; that, he implies, is a question for another day. What matters here and now is that a 'decent society' is one whose institutions do not humiliate its members. This is a much more demanding test than appears at first sight. 'Humiliation', Margalit writes, 'is any sort of behaviour or condition that constitutes a sound reason for a person to consider his or her self-respect injured.'[47] Self-respect translates into honour, and honour into dignity, so an indecent society is one whose institutions dishonour its members and deny them human dignity. These are forms of mental cruelty; and the scars left by mental cruelty are often slower to heal than those caused by physical injury. (Burke's memories of the indignities imposed by the Irish penal laws spring to mind.)

On a deeper level, humiliators treat the humiliated as non-human, as though they don't belong to the family of man. It follows that second-class citizenship, like that of Israeli Arabs today or of Blacks in the American South when segregation was in force, is *ipso facto* humiliating: second-class citizens are treated, by definition, as though they are not fully human. They are excluded, not from the human family it is true, but from full membership of their own society. To be a second-class citizen is to be a second-class human being. Second-class citizens are denied respect, and respect is the key to self-realization.

Margalit's language is careful, precise and rather colourless; he writes as an academic philosopher for an academic audience. But the implications of his argument are profound. States may and sometimes do humiliate their citizens (or subjects): the Israeli Arabs and Southern Blacks that Margalit mentions are only two of a long list of examples that also includes the Catholic minority in Northern Ireland before the Civil Rights marches of the 1960s, the Jewish inhabitants of the Russian Pale in Tsarist times and the Japanese-born minority in California during the Second World War. But in modern capitalist societies, poverty, homelessness, exploitation and degrading working conditions are the chief sources of humiliation; and these are rarely the products of deliberate state policy. The market state described in earlier chapters has done nothing to mitigate them, but except indirectly it has not caused them. They are inflicted by market institutions, whose coercive power may well be as great as that of the institutions of the state.

Looked at through the prism of Margalit's account, the story I have tried to tell in earlier chapters takes on a new meaning. In Margalit's language, the slow taming of capitalism in the first half of the last century made British society more decent. Capitalism's helter-skelter untaming in the last thirty years has made it blatantly indecent.

TOWARDS A NEW PUBLIC PHILOSOPHY

The insights discussed above are not carved on tablets of stone, to be approached with reverential awe, but they do point the way towards a new and richer public philosophy. It will be a philosophy for a disillusioned people, battered by a crisis they did not cause and alienated from their leaders. It will not be a blueprint for a future government, but a philosophy of dialogue, open-ended and indeterminate. Another way of saying the same thing is that it will be a philosophy of mutual education, through which we learn, in Martha Nussbaum's haunting language, to approach each other as 'souls' and not as 'useful instruments'. It follows that we cannot lay down, in advance, precisely where the dialogue should take us; if we could, it would not be a dialogue. For the moment, at least, the direction is what matters, not the end point: the 'movement', as the revisionist German Social Democrat Eduard Bernstein once put it, not the 'goal'. The starting point is clear: the bitter, but liberating realization that we British have followed a calamitous course since the untaming of capitalism began in the 1980s, and that a change of direction is imperative. Beyond that, all I can do – all anyone can do – is to propose certain interconnected guiding principles.

Pride of place goes to the ethic of stewardship and the vision of the human self and human history implicit in Edmund's Burke's critique of the eighteenth-century notion of a social contract. Burke's insistence that human communities include not just the living, but also the dead and the unborn, poses a radical challenge to the parched economism and unhistorical individualism that still suffuse public debate. The human self becomes part of a rich and enduring tapestry of selves; individuals have obligations to future generations that transcend their immediate self-interest and even the interests of their children and grandchildren. Not only is there such a thing as society; society (not just this particular society, but the wider society of the human family) extends far into the future, and also into the past. The question is no longer, 'What's in it for me?' It is 'How can I best honour the generations that have gone before me and discharge my duty to distant generations that I will never know?'

The implications for environmental debate are particularly striking. Individuals are not merely tenants rather than freeholders of the societies into which they are born; by extension they are tenants rather than freeholders of the earth. The Green movement's commitment to sustainability becomes an ethical imperative as well as, indeed more than, a utilitarian one. The notion of 'mother earth' and the related notion of the sacredness of life cease to be romantic slogans. Instead they help to define the parameters of public debate and eventual action. Painful intellectual contortions designed to reconcile the real imperative of sustainability with the imaginary imperative of economic growth become redundant. Growth is no longer an imperative. It can be expected to continue: technological and economic changes will make sure of that. But it becomes a by-product of policies designed to achieve other objectives. The imperative is sustainability.

That leads on to the second guiding principle. It can be summed up in three words: to master capitalism. To grasp their meaning I shall look again at the political and religious traditions that I discussed more fully above. Though industrial capitalism was barely in its infancy when Burke died, his ethic of stewardship and contempt for mean-minded 'sophists, calculators and economists'[48] contest the thinking behind the onward march of masterless capitalism with compelling force. The same is true of Tawney's attack on the 'fetish' of industrialism, of Margalit's notion of the decent society and of the challenge that all the Abrahamic religions pose to the narrow economism that lies at the heart of our present discontents. Tawney's critique of the culture of acquisition stemmed from a passionate belief that it was both demeaning and corrupting to scrabble for the bauble of material gain in a psychic desert: to elevate what should have been means into all-conquering ends. That was what he meant when he compared industrial civilization to a hypochondriac who dies without ever having lived. Catholic social teaching, Archbishop Temple's insistence that if laissez-faire economics were true then Christ was wrong and the Islamic tradition's anathemas against usury spring from the same emotional roots. Margalit goes further. As noted above, the decent society, as he defines it, is incompatible with today's untamed capitalism and the proliferating humiliations that are its hallmarks. All these point to the same conclusion: a decent society in which the culture of acquisition has been laid to rest and an ethic of stewardship holds sway is impossible without a decent capitalism.

This too is dangerous territory. Churchill is supposed to have said that democracy is the worst form of government, except for all the others. The same is true of capitalism. Attempts to abolish it have invariably ended in tears, sometimes very bitter ones. But, like democracy, it is a coat of many colours. Marx and Engels were right about the revolutionary voracity of untamed capitalism, and the new public philosophy I am calling for must take full cognizance of their insight. However, they were wrong in thinking that it is bound to roam in the wild until its inherent contradictions destroy it altogether. The masterless capitalism of today is not the only variety the world has known; indeed British capitalism is by no means the only variety that Europe knows today, as we saw in Chapter 5. The old elites tamed the capitalism of the nineteenth century in the name of an overriding public morality. In the last thirty years their achievement has been undone. It is time to repeat it, in a different idiom. We can't follow mechanically in their footsteps, but it is a counsel of despair to assume that we can't emulate their imagination and creativity. The obstacles are manifold: the doomed pursuit of everlasting economic growth, the strange survival of the eighteenth-century doctrine of unconditional property rights, over-blown financial services, growing inequality, the interpenetration of corporate and state elites, and the attrition of the public realm, among others.

None of these is bound to last, however. No iron law decrees that growth should continue to have pride of place among policy objectives; that we cannot move towards the stakeholder capitalism that the Dahrendorf Commission recommended, as noted in Chapter 5; that it is out of the question for Britain to introduce a financial-services tax to curb speculation; that Britain's ring of secrecy jurisdictions should remain in being; that the revolving door should continue to revolve; or that the public realm must be left open to incursions from the market realm. Polly Higgins's proposed law to criminalize ecocide; a change in company law to oblige private firms to take proper account of stakeholder interests; a return to the founding principles of the National Health Service; the suppression of the tax havens in British jurisdictions; substantial state investment (and state-fostered private investment) to promote green technologies; and stringent rules to stop retired politicians and public servants from finding lucrative perches in the private sector would all help to tilt the balance of the economy in a new and better direction. It would be difficult to change course; powerful vested interests stand in the way, and they would fight to retain their privileges. But the post-war generation overcame comparable difficulties. The greatest obstacles to a decent capitalism are in our minds. For a nation to be free, wrote Thomas Paine just over 200 years ago, 'it is sufficient that she wills it'.[49] The same applies to decent capitalism.

The third guiding principle is more complicated and in some ways less comfortable. Decent capitalism is not the only prerequisite of a decent society; so too are decent elites and a decent democracy. The two go together. We have no hope of rebuilding the battered public realm, or of protecting it from the inevitable imperialism of the market realm, unless we acknowledge that protection can come only from elites. The great insight of the founding fathers of the American Republic – that only power can check power – is as valid in the early twenty-first century as it was in the late eighteenth. The old elites (the working-class elite prominent among them) built the public realm in the first place, and acted as its guardians thereafter. Their fall opened the door to the privatizations and marketizations that have diminished and corrupted it.

They were far from perfect, as I tried to show in Chapter 2; apart from the working-class elite, they were recruited from a very narrow social base and they were all suffused with unthinking sexism and sometimes with racism. As time went on, their imaginative arteries started to harden. They became increasingly remote from the society around them, and increasingly complacent about its flaws. These imperfections helped to erode their legitimacy. Yet before they fell, they had the root of the matter in them. They knew that the public interest is more than the sum of private interests: that what individuals want is not always what they need; and that the voice of the people is not invariably the voice of God. None of this is true of the 'power elite' described by David Beetham.[50] The new public philosophy I am arguing for would reject the unthinking anti-elitism which has fostered (and been fostered by) the culture of hedonistic individualism described in Chapter 2. It would stand for open, tolerant, responsive and accountable elites, from diverse communities and backgrounds, imbued with an ethic of civic duty and public service.

Decent democracy is equally fundamental to a decent society. As I tried to show in the last chapter, the sad simulacrum of democracy we know today fosters rent-seeking by the ultra-rich, making inequality more glaring and its associated humiliations more painful. The charismatic populism which is of its essence makes democratic dialogue virtually impossible. But, though these ills are more acute than at any time since Britain belatedly acquired a democratic suffrage in 1928,[51] they did not descend on the body politic like thunderbolts from a previously clear sky. Tawney was right in saying that when formal democracy came to Britain she changed only her political garments and not her heart. That insight has resounded through the last eighty years of British history like a tolling bell. For a brilliant moment during and immediately after the Second World War it looked as though a change of heart might be on the way, but the moment did not last. Tawney's answer was a change of mentality, but as John Stuart Mill saw more clearly than any of the other thinkers discussed above, mentality and practice go together. (Aristotle made essentially the same point.)

As Mill insisted, we learn by doing; we absorb the disciplines of self-government by governing ourselves; we enlarge our horizons to embrace the common good by taking part in collective action, first and foremost on the local level. The answer to charismatic populism and the attrition of the public realm which it reflects and fosters is, in short, a richer, deeper version of democracy. Our search for it should begin with Amartya Sen's conception of democracy as public reasoning – a notion that harks back to the young Mill's belief in 'discussion'. Sen shows first that democracy in his sense is not a 'Western' invention, exported from Europe and North America to benighted Asians and Africans.

Public deliberation took place in Indian 'Buddhist councils', beginning in the sixth century BCE; the Emperor Ashoka codified procedural rules to regulate such deliberations. In 604 CE, the Buddhist Prince of Japan, Shotoku, promulgated a constitution insisting that decisions on important matters 'should not be taken by one person alone. They should be discussed with many'; differences of opinion, it added, were inevitable: 'all men have hearts, and each heart has its own leanings'. For 'several centuries', the ancient Iranian city of Susa 'had an elected council, a popular assembly and magistrates who were elected by the assembly'. Many centuries later, the young Nelson Mandela was profoundly influenced by the open debates, in which labourers took part alongside chiefs, that were held in the regent's house in Mqhekezweni in the Transkei. In short, the dream of participatory governance has had a powerful hold on human imaginations and aspirations across centuries, cultures and continents.

Too often, Sen argues, democracy is defined in the narrow, legalistic language of political institutions – above all in that of free elections. These matter, of course; but they are by no means the only things that matter. Without free speech, access to information, civil rights and freedom to dissent, democratic forms can be used to disguise totalitarian realities and frequently have been. Many dictators, Sen points out, 'have achieved gigantic electoral victories even without any overt coercion in the process of voting, mainly through suppressing public discussion and freedom of information and through generating a climate of fear and anxiety'. In themselves, formally democratic institutions do not guarantee a democratic reality.

> The success of democracy is not merely a matter of having the most perfect institutional structure that we can think of. It depends inescapably on our actual behaviour patterns and the working of political and social interactions. There is no chance of resting the matter in the 'safe' hands of purely institutional virtuosity. The working of democratic institutions, like that of all other institutions, depends on the activities of human agents in utilizing opportunities for reasonable realization.[52]

Manifestly, Sen's vision of democracy as public reasoning is far removed from the bleak realities of twenty-first-century Britain. To mention only a few examples, the media's race for the bottom; the ideology of marketization that I described in Chapter 4; the 'religion of inequality' that Tawney excoriated; and, above all, the populist political style described in the previous chapter are all incompatible with it. But it would be wrong to despair. Internet campaigning groups like 38 Degrees and Avaaz; the internet journal Open Democracy; Citizens UK; and the Occupy movement all engage in public reasoning of a kind. It is a limited kind, no doubt; communication between separate individuals glued to their computer screens or even brief encounters between protestors and their audiences are a poor substitute for the debates in the regent's house that so impressed the young Mandela. But with all their deficiencies, protest movements like these show that the ancient dream of participatory governance lives on in twenty-first-century Britain.

The most formidable obstacles to a democracy of public reasoning and social learning are within us. Such a democracy needs open, welcoming spaces for civic engagement, where uninhibited public reasoning can take place: that is the lesson that the young Mandela learned from the debates in the regent's house in the Transkei. Sen is right to warn that institutional virtuosity will not, by itself, create the spaces without which his vision of democracy as public reasoning will be little more than a utopian dream. But it does not follow that no institutional changes are needed. The creation of devolved administrations and legislatures in Scotland and Wales has procured far-reaching changes in the political cultures of both nations and tapped civic energies that were barely in evidence a generation ago. England has so far lagged behind; the long arm and clenched fist of the market state have seen to that. But the market state is a human artefact, not a force of nature. Its depredations can perfectly well be reversed. The first essential is to rescue local government from its status as the humiliated Cinderella of English governance and to furnish it with constitutionally entrenched protections from incursions by the central state. Further instalments might include citizens' assemblies chosen by lot, on the model of the assemblies set up to recommend changes in the electoral systems of two Canadian provinces, and local and parish councils also chosen by lot.[53] These changes are perfectly feasible; they could be made almost without delay. A constitutional convention to decide how the nations of the United Kingdom should relate to each other would take longer to arrange, but it need not take much longer. On a much deeper level, it would take a great deal longer to overcome the ideology that underpins the market state or the religion of inequality that it has fostered. What is needed in all these cases is the will.

Part of the point of the national conversation I am calling for is to generate that will. We won't learn how to walk the walk unless we first learn together to talk the talk. That is not feasible without a common language, and as I suggested at the start of this chapter the culture of hedonistic individualism – whether market or moral – has no place for one. Hedonistic individualists inhabit separate cultural enclaves, each with its own language: that is why the destructive appeals of charismatic populists have made so much headway. The great questions, then, are whether we can discover (or rediscover) a common language, and begin to fashion a new public philosophy and moral economy. To do so we shall have to answer the primordial question that faces all political communities, implicitly if not explicitly: who are we?

At bottom, this is a moral question. It can't be answered in the debased discourses of utilitarian individualism and its diminished liberal twin. Somehow we shall have to find a richer discourse, drawn largely (but not exclusively) from the religious traditions I discussed above. That doesn't imply that only religious people will be able to take part in it. On the contrary: I write as an unbeliever myself. What it does imply is that we shall have to learn how to make claims, debate choices, conduct arguments and reach agreements in terms premised on the assumption that the common good comes before individual appetites. Above all, it implies that there are limits to what we can rightly do: that the astonishingly enhanced power over nature that applied science has given us does not justify us in using it just as we please.

The magnificent third line of the Welsh hymn 'Cwm Rhondda' – 'I am weak, but Thou art mighty' – encapsulates the new philosophy that the times demand. Puffed up by indecent pride in our scientific knowledge and technical achievements, we have come to believe that we are mighty. In reality, we are inescapably weak. We face formidable challenges, but given determination and courage we can meet them. We can break with the arid fancies of Chicagoan economics. We can begin to master markets instead of allowing them to master us. We can start to rebuild the battered public realm, and halt the drift towards a market society. We can put the ethic of stewardship ahead of profit, empathetic understanding ahead of command and control, and sustainability ahead of growth. But there will be new challenges, and we shall have to meet them in new ways. It will never be time to rest on our laurels.

Sceptics may wonder if such a philosophy can fly in the harsh world of the twenty-first century. The answer is straightforward. We can't go on as we are.

Acknowledgements

Writing this book has been a voyage of discovery. During the voyage I accumulated a formidable range of debts. At an early stage Neal Lawson, chair of the non-party, left-of-centre pressure group Compass, invited me to give the Compass Annual Lecture for 2011. The lecture, entitled 'Towards a Realignment of the Mind', contained the germ of the present book. I give warm thanks to Neal, and also to the lively and thought-provoking questioners who quizzed me after the lecture. I owe a debt of gratitude to the environmental campaigner Polly Higgins, who spared time from a busy life to share her thoughts on 'ecocide' with me. I should also acknowledge my debts to the superb online edition of the *Oxford Dictionary of National Biography* and to the unfailing courtesy and skill of the staff of Oxford University's Bodleian libraries.

The endnotes give a full picture of the books and other works I have consulted, but some of these have had a bigger influence on my journey than others. Robert Skidelsky, a friend and occasional sparring partner for more than fifty years, has taught me almost everything I know about Keynes, as well as helping me to understand the curious career of the moral individualism that helped to undermine the Keynesian social-democratic settlement of the post-war years. Andrew Gamble, another old friend, as well as a former colleague in Sheffield University's ebullient Politics Department, read the whole of the original manuscript with remarkable speed, and suggested a daunting number of changes, which greatly improved the book. His path-breaking work on Hayek did for the market individualists of the age after Keynes what Skidelsky did for the moral individualists.

I have been strongly influenced by Jared Diamond's account of the catastrophic impact of environmental folly on once-flourishing societies, from the Mayas in Central America to the Easter Islanders in the Pacific, and by Dieter Helm's passionate yet carefully argued call for a world-wide programme of 'de-carbonization'. My critique of the amnesiac culture associated with the masterless capitalism of our day draws heavily on Geoffrey Hodgson's lament for the economic profession's turn away from history. Gertrude Himmelfarb's subtle distinctions between the French, British and American Enlightenments have reinforced my suspicion of the unhistorical rationalism of the French variety.

A number of writers have influenced my treatment of the rise and fall of the public realm – in my view, the central theme of British history since the last quarter of the nineteenth century. The notion of the 'market state', which is fundamental to my interpretation, was invented by the American legal historian and philosopher Philip Bobbitt. The late Harold Perkin, the Marx of the salariat, left an enduring impress on my approach to the complex relationship between the public realm, professionals and the professional ethic. I have found Onora O'Neill's caustic contempt for the humbug that has justified the attrition of professional autonomy since the early 1980s as exhilarating as it is illuminating. As well, I have learned a great deal from her unfashionable insistence that there can be no rights without duties and that focusing on rights without mentioning duties is a dangerous absurdity. I should also acknowledge my debt to Simon Jenkins's mordant account of the 'Tory nationalization of Britain' and of the deliberate erosion of local autonomy which is its hallmark. I owe at least as great a debt to Michael Sandel's warning that democracy cannot survive the indefinite expansion of the empire of money.

My account of the remorseless growth of inequality which has made Britain one of the most dysfunctional societies in the democratic West draws heavily on the work of Richard Wilkinson and Kate Pickett. Nicholas Shaxson's forensically deadly study of tax havens has been a painful but invaluable eye opener. The same is true of Owen Jones's masterly account of the 'demonization' of the victims of growing inequality.

My account of the tribulations of contemporary British democracy draws heavily on Joseph Stiglitz's account of the damage which 'rent-seeking' by the super-rich has done to democracy in the United States and on the astringent publications of Essex University's Democratic Audit. My approach to the complex history of democracy as an ideal owes most to Samuel H. Beer, John Dunn and Quentin Skinner. My search for a new public philosophy has been illuminated by Conor Cruise O'Brien's majestic study of Edmund Burke; by Martha Nussbaum's insistence that we should approach each other as 'souls' rather than as 'useful instruments'; by Rowan Williams's *aperçu* that Christian identity is 'irreducibly political'; by Avishai Margalit's definition of a decent society as one whose institutions do not humiliate its members; and by Amartya Sen's compelling notion of democracy as 'public reasoning'.

Four other debts stand out. The first is to my agent Anthony Goff, whose moral support and entrepreneurial ingenuity have been heartwarming as well as indispensable. The second is to my generous-hearted and eloquent sister, Diana. From her fastness in the hills of west Wales, she has kept me up to the mark in long telephone conversations and multifarious email exchanges. The third is to my indefatigable and inspirational editor, Stuart Proffitt. He believed in me when no one else did; he has been fertile in suggestions, intellectual as well as stylistic; and when necessary he has persuaded me to rein in my tendency to extravagant hyperbole. He once told me that he saw himself as 'the grit in the oyster'. The only possible response is: 'Some grit!'

The fourth of these debts is of a different order. It is to my beloved wife, Judith. She read every page of the manuscript when the work was in progress, in some cases several times. She led me to hone and clarify my arguments, suggested a multitude of new ideas, drew my attention to authorities and literatures I had not previously been aware of, and enriched my understanding of the issues involved. She also sustained me emotionally and kept up my spirits when the going got rough. Without her, this book could never have been written. Her stamp is on every page.

David Marquand, Headington, September 2013

Notes

I. INTRODUCTION

1. Two examples are Andrew Gamble, *The Spectre at the Feast: Capitalist Crisis and the Politics of Recession*, Palgrave Macmillan, Basingstoke, 2009, and Vince Cable, *The Storm: The World Economic Crisis and What It Means*, Atlantic Books, London, 2009.

2. E. P. Thompson, *The Making of the English Working Class*, Penguin Books, Harmondsworth, 1991 (first published by Victor Gollancz, London, 1963).

3. Ibid., pp. 67–8 and 72; and E. P. Thompson, 'The Moral Economy of the English Crowd in the Eighteenth Century', in E. P. Thompson, *Customs in Common*, Penguin Books, London, 1991, p. 229.

4. For Middle Way conservatism see Harold Macmillan, *The Middle Way: A Study of the Problem of Economic and Social Progress in a Free and Democratic Society*, Macmillan, London, 1938.

5. www.thirdworldtraveler.com/Global_Economy/Crisis_Capitalism_Soros .html and http://www.project-syndicate.org/commentary/the-end-of-neo-liberalism.

6. George Orwell, *The Lion and the Unicorn: Socialism and the English Genius*, in George Orwell, *A Patriot After All* (ed. Peter Davison), Secker and Warburg, London, 2000, p. 401.

7. Steve Pincus, *1688: The First Modern Revolution*, Yale University Press, New Haven and London, 2009.

8. Thorstein Veblen, *The Theory of the Leisure Class*, Dover Thrift, New York, 1994, p. 52.

9. Alistair Darling, *Back from the Brink*, Atlantic Books, London, 2011, p. 60.

10. http://online.wsj.com/article/BT-CO-20111212-704707.html. Accessed on 31 December 2011.

11. http//en.wikipedia.org/wiki/Fred_Goodwin (accessed February 2012); Will Hutton, *Them and Us: Changing Britain – Why We Need a Fair Society*, Little, Brown, London, 2010, especially ch. 6; *The Failure of the Royal Bank of Scotland, Financial Services Authority Board Report*, London 2011, *passim*.

12. *FSA Board Report on Failure of RBS*, p. 7.

13. On the other side of the Atlantic, there were fears that Britain's 'amenable and collaborative regulatory environment' was helping London to capture business from New York. Chrystia Freeland, *Plutocrats: The Rise of the New Global Super Rich*, Allen Lane, London, 2012, p. 212.

14. P. J. Cain and A. G. Hopkins, *British Imperialism 1688–2000*, Longmans, London, 2nd edn, 2002, pp. 151 and 164.

15. Quoted in Roy Jenkins, *Churchill*, Macmillan, London, 2001, p. 395.

16. Robert Peston, *Who Runs Britain?*, Hodder and Stoughton, London, 2008, p. 18.

17. Philip Augar, *The Death of Gentlemanly Capitalism: The Rise and Fall of London's Investment Banks*, Penguin Books, London, 2001, p. 114.

18. Bank of England, *Quarterly Bulletin*, Q3, 2011.

19. Gamble, *Spectre at the Feast*, p. 16.

20. John Lanchester, *Whoops!: Why Everyone Owes Everyone and No One Can Pay*, Penguin Books, London, 2010, p. 173.

21. Carmen M. Reinhart and Kenneth S. Rogoff, *This Time is Different: Eight Centuries of Financial Folly*, Princeton University Press, Princeton, NJ, and Oxford, 2009, pp. 344–7.

22. For Will Hutton's attack on the bankers see Robert Skidelsky, *Keynes: The Return of the Master*, Penguin Books, London, 2010, p. 23; for Vince Cable's see *MailOnline*, 9 February 2009.

23. *Financial Times*, 14 February 2011.

24. For Brown's assertions to that effect see http://iandale.blogspot.co.uk/2008/10/gordon-brown-quotes-of-day.html.

25. Credit Action, December 2012, www.creditaction.org.uk/helpful-resources/debt-statistics.html. Accessed 9 December 2012.

26. David Moxon, 'Consumer Culture and the 2011 "Riots"', *Sociological Research online*, www.socresonline.org.uk/16/4/19.html.

2. HEDONISM TRUMPS HONOUR

1. Zygmunt Bauman, *Legislators and Interpreters: On Modernity, Post-Modernity, and Intellectuals*, Polity Press, Cambridge, 1989.

2. A. V. Dicey, *Law and Public Opinion in the England during the Nineteenth Century*, 2nd edn, reprinted Macmillan, London, 1962 (originally published 1905).

3. http://en.wikiquote.org./wiki/William_Harcourt.

4. See, for example, Dicey's reference to John Morley in Dicey, *Law and Opinion in England*, pp. 288–90; J. A. Hobson, *The Crisis of Liberalism: New Issues of Democracy*, Harvester Press, Brighton, 1974; and Sidney Webb, *Socialism in England*, Swan Sonnenschein & Co., London, 1890.

5. Thomas Carlyle, *Shooting Niagara: And After?*, Chapman and Hall, London, 1867.

6. Thomas Carlyle, *Chartism*, Elibron Classics, Boston, Mass., 2005, pp. 39 and 26.

7. Dicey, *Law and Public Opinion in England*, pp. 431–2.

8. F. M. L. Thompson, *The Rise of Respectable Society: A Social History of Victorian Britain, 1830–1900*, Fontana Press, London, 1988, p. 240.

9. John Ruskin, *Unto This Last and Other Writings*, Penguin Books, London, 1997, p. 187.

10. Matthew Arnold, *Culture and Anarchy and Other Writings*, ed. Stefan Collini, Cambridge University Press, Cambridge, reprinted 1995, p. 83.

11. The term is Stefan Collini's. See Stefan Collini, *Public Moralists: Political Thought and Intellectual Life in Britain 1850–1930*, Clarendon Press, Oxford, 1991. However Collini's examples differ from mine.

12. Arnold, *Culture and Anarchy*, p. 109.

13. Quoted in Richard Reeves, *John Stuart Mill: Victorian Firebrand*, Atlantic Books, London, 2007, p. 224.

14. Quoted in Robert Hewison, *Culture and Consensus: England, Art and Politics since 1940*, Methuen, London, 1995, pp. 51–3.

15. R. H. Tawney, *The Attack and Other Papers*, Spokesman, Nottingham, 1981, p. 182.

16. Quoted in John Kent, *William Temple: Church, State and Society in Britain 1880–1950*, Cambridge University Press, Cambridge, 1992, p. 20.

17. A. D. Lindsay, *The Essentials of Democracy*, Oxford University Press, London, 1929, p. 37.

18. Amartya Sen, *The Idea of Justice*, Penguin Books, London, 2010, chs. 15 and 16; and *The Argumentative Indian: Writings on Indian Culture, History and Identity*, Penguin Books, London, 2006, ch. 1.

19. Quoted in David Cannadine, *Class in Britain*, Yale University Press, New Haven, Conn., and London, 1998, p. 121.

20. Quoted in Bernard Crick, *George Orwell: A Life*, Penguin Books, London, 1992, p. 295.

21. George Orwell, *A Patriot After All* (ed. Peter Davison), Secker and Warburg, London, 2000, p. 402.

22. Ibid., pp. 427–8.

23. Quoted in Richard Titmuss, *Problems of Social Policy*, HMSO, London, 1950, ch. XXV, p. 507. www.ibiblio.org/hyperwar/UN/UK/UK-Civil-Social-25.html. Accessed 12 March 2012.

24. I was one of the younger people concerned.

25. Quoted in Robert Watt, 'The Crown and Its Employees', in Maurice Sunkin and Sebastian Payne, *The Nature of the Crown: A Legal and Political Analysis*, Oxford University Press, Oxford, 1999, p. 288.

26. *Report on the Organisation of the Permanent Civil Service together with a Letter from the Rev. B. Jowett*, Her Majesty's Stationery Office, London, 1854, p. 3.

27. Quoted in Robert Skidelsky, *John Maynard Keynes*, vol. 1, *Hopes Betrayed: 1883–1920*, Macmillan, London, 1983, p. 299.

28. See Peter Hennessy, *Whitehall*, Fontana Press, London, 1990, chs. 4 and 5, for a litany of complaints.

29. For Keynes's claim to have revolutionized economic thought (made to Bernard Shaw) see Robert Skidelsky, *John Maynard Keynes*, vol. 2, *The Economist as Saviour*, Macmillan, London, 1992, p. 520.

30. Aneurin Bevan, *In Place of Fear*, E. P. Publishing, Ilkley, 1977, pp. 201–2 (first published 1952).

31. Quoted in Hewison, *Culture and Consensus*, p. 68.

32. A. H. Halsey with Josephine Webb (eds.), *Twentieth-Century British Social Trends*, Macmillan Press, Basingstoke and London, 2000, pp. 63–4.

33. Duncan Campbell-Smith, *Masters of the Post: The Authorized History of the Royal Mail*, Allen Lane, London, 2011, p. 363.

34. Nicole Robertson, *The Co-operative Movement and Communities in Britain 1914–1960: Minding Their Own Business*, Ashgate, Farnham, 2010, p. 24.

35. James Foreman-Peck and Robert Millward, *Public and Private Ownership in British Industry*, Clarendon Press, Oxford, 1994, p. 297.

36. Quoted in Michael Freeden, 'Richard Titmuss and 20th-Century British Welfare Thought: Red Route or Detour?', unpublished. I am grateful to Professor Freeden for drawing this to my attention.

37. Harry Eckstein, quoted in Charles Webster, *The National Health Service: A Political History*, 2nd edn, Oxford University Press, Oxford, 2002, pp. 458 and 390.

38. http://www.thefullwiki.org/Lord_Goddard. Accessed 10 March 2013.

39. Richard Crossman, *The Diaries of a Cabinet Minister*, vol. 1, *Minister of*

Housing 1964–1966, Hamish Hamilton and Jonathan Cape, London, 1975, p. 24.

40. T. H. Marshall, *Citizenship and Social Class and Other Essays*, Cambridge University Press, Cambridge, 1950, p. 56.

41. For 'Keynesian social democracy' see my *The Unprincipled Society: New Demands and Old Politics*, Jonathan Cape, London, 1988. The term was coined by David Heald, *Public Expenditure*, Martin Robertson, Oxford, 1983.

42. For a gripping picture of what it was like to be in the eye of the economic storm see Denis Healey's memoirs: Denis Healey, *The Time of My Life*, Michael Joseph, London, 1989, chs. 18–21.

43. Quoted in Richard Cockett, *Thinking the Unthinkable: Think-Tanks and the Economic Counter-Revolution, 1931–1983*, HarperCollins, London, 1994, p. 187.

44. Germaine Greer, *The Female Eunuch*, Paladin, London, 1971 (first published 1970).

45. E. F. Schumacher, *Small is Beautiful*, Blond and Briggs, London, 1973.

46. Samuel H. Beer, *Britain Against Itself: The Political Contradictions of Collectivism*, Faber and Faber, London, 1982, ch. 4.

47. Keith Joseph, *Reversing the Trend*, Barry Rose, Chichester and London, 1975, p. 57.

48. Keith Joseph, quoted in Cockett, *Thinking the Unthinkable*, p. 237.

49. F. A. Hayek, *The Road to Serfdom*, Routledge Classics, Abingdon and New York, 2001. My quotations from it come from this edition.

50. Andrew Gamble, *Hayek: The Iron Cage of Liberty*, Polity Press, Cambridge, 1996.

51. F. A. Hayek, *Law Legislation and Liberty*, vol. 3, *The Political Order of a Free People*, reprinted Routledge, London, 1998, pp. 164–5.

52. Andrew Gamble, *The Free Economy and the Strong State: The Politics of Thatcherism*, Macmillan, Basingstoke, 1988.

53. Philip Bobbitt, *The Shield of Achilles: War, Peace and the Course of History*, Penguin Books, London, 2003, chs. 10 and 27.

54. Bertrand Russell, *Autobiography*, vol. I, p. 64, quoted in Robert Skidelsky, *John Maynard Keynes*, vol. 1, *Hopes Betrayed: 1883–1920*, Macmillan, London, 1983, pp. 135–6.

55. D. E. Moggridge, *Maynard Keynes: An Economist's Biography*, Routledge, London and New York, 1992, p. 117.

56. John Clay, *R. D. Laing: A Divided Self*, Sceptre, London, 1997, p. 100.

57. R. D. Laing, *The Politics of Experience and The Bird of Paradise*, Penguin Books, London, 1967 (reprinted 1990), pp. 49–57.

58. Ibid., p. 137.

59. Herbert Marcuse, *Eros and Civilization: A Philosophical Inquiry into Freud*, reissued Routledge, Abingdon, 1998, p. 236.

60. Herbert Marcuse, *One-Dimensional Man: Studies in the Ideology of Advanced Industrial Society*, Routledge and Kegan Paul, London, 1964.

61. Ibid., p. 256.

62. Robert Skidelsky, 'Twentieth-Century Britain: A Success Story?' in Jonathan Clark (ed.), *A World by Itself: A History of the British Isles*, William Heinemann, London, 2010, p. 607.

63. Eric Hobsbawm, *Interesting Times: A Twentieth-Century Life*, Allen Lane, London, 2002, p. 250.

3. AMNESIA CONQUERS HISTORY

1. One of my proudest possessions as an eleven-year-old schoolboy in 1945 was just such a globe.

2. For an entertaining account of these differences see F. M. L. Thompson, *The Rise of Respectable Society: A Social History of Respectable Britain, 1830–1900*, Fontana Press, London, *1988*, p. 241.

3. For its creativity see Samuel H. Beer, *To Make a Nation: The Rediscovery of American Federalism*, Belknap Press of Harvard University Press, Cambridge, Mass., and London, 1994, chs. 2 and 3 on John Milton and James Harrington respectively; Quentin Skinner, *Liberty Before Liberalism*, Cambridge University Press, Cambridge, 1998; and Christopher Hill, *The World Turned Upside Down: Radical Ideas during the English Revolution*, Temple Smith, London, 1972.

4. The phrase occurred in the final sentence of Lincoln's First Inaugural as President in 1861. The whole sentence runs: 'The mystic chords of memory, stretching from every battlefield and every patriot grave to every living heart and hearthstone all over this broad land, will yet swell the chorus of the Union, when again touched, as surely they will be, by the better angels of our nature' (www.bartleby.com/124/press31.html).

5. Adam Smith, *An Inquiry into the Nature and Causes of the Wealth of Nations* (ed. Edwin Cannan), University of Chicago Press, Chicago, 1976, vol. II, pp. 302–3.

6. Quoted in Geoffrey M. Hodgson, *How Economics Forgot History: The Problem of Historical Specificity in Social Science*, Routledge, London, 2001, p. 106.

7. Quoted in Roger E. Backhouse and Bradley W. Bateman, *Capitalist Revolutionary: John Maynard Keynes*, Harvard University Press, London and Cambridge, Mass., 2011, p. 68.

8. Edward and Robert Skidelsky describe his judgement as a 'Faustian Bargain'. See their *How Much is Enough? The Love of Money and the Case for the Good Life*, Allen Lane, London, 2012, ch. 2.

9. I am indebted for this information to Judith Marquand, who served in the Government Economic Service from 1965 to 1992.

10. Will Hutton, *Them and Us: Changing Britain – Why We Need a Fair Society*, Little, Brown, London, 2010; Edward and Robert Skidelsky, *How Much is Enough?*

11. Jared Diamond, *Collapse: How Societies Choose to Fail or Succeed*, Penguin Books, London, 2005, pp. 158 and 168.

12. Ibid., p. 109.

13. Dieter Helm, *The Carbon Crunch: How We're Getting Climate Change Wrong – and How to Fix It*, Yale University Press, New Haven, Conn., and London, 2012, pp. 236 and 240.

14. Colin Crouch, *The Strange Non-Death of Neoliberalism*, Polity Press, Cambridge, reprinted 2012; see also A. J. Nicholls, *Freedom With Responsibility: The Social Market Economy*, Clarendon Press, Oxford, 1994.

15. Alfred D. Chandler, *Scale and Scope: The Dynamics of Industrial Capitalism*, The Belknap Press of Harvard University Press, Cambridge, Mass., and London, 1990, p. 594.

16. There is an enormous literature on the Invisible Hand. For an illuminating discussion see Emma Rothschild, *Economic Sentiments: Adam Smith, Condorcet and the Enlightenment*, Harvard University Press, Cambridge, Mass., and London, paperback edition 2002, *passim*.

17. Nicholas Shaxson, *Treasure Islands: Tax Havens and the Men Who Stole the World*, Vintage Books, London, 2012.

18. Karl Polanyi, *The Great Transformation: The Political and Economic Origins of Our Time*, Beacon Press, Boston, Mass., 1957, p. 139.

19. Paul Johnson, *Making the Market: Victorian Origins of Corporate Capitalism*, Cambridge University Press, Cambridge, 2010, *passim*.

20. Smith, *Wealth of Nations*, vol. I, pp. 478–9.

21. Ibid., vol. I, p. 144.

22. Ibid., vol. II, pp. 244–50.

23. High Pay Commission, Final Report, *Cheques With Balances: Why Tackling High Pay is in the National Interest*, 19 January 2012, www.highpaycentre.org. Accessed 27 December 2012. (The firms in the High

Pay Commission's list were Lonmin, BP, Barclays, GKN, Lloyds' Banking Group and Reed Elsevier.)

24. Joseph Stiglitz, *Freefall: Free Markets and the Sinking of the Global Economy*, Penguin Books, London and New York, 2010, p. 248.

25. Gertrude Himmelfarb, *The Roads to Modernity: The British, French and American Enlightenments*, Alfred A. Knopf, New York, 2004, pp. 151 and 152.

26. Quoted in Ernest Gellner, *Plough, Sword and Book: The Structure of Human History*, Collins Harvill, London, 1988, pp. 134–5.

27. Jonathan I. Israel distinguishes between a Scottish Enlightenment, Enlightened Despotism, a German Enlightenment, a Catholic Enlightenment, and an Italian Revolutionary Enlightenment. Jonathan I. Israel, *Democratic Enlightenment: Philosophy, Revolution and Human Rights*, Oxford University Press, Oxford and New York, 2011.

28. Himmelfarb, *Roads to Modernity*, p. 5.

29. Ibid., p. 161.

30. Ibid., pp. 191–226.

31. Alexander Hamilton, James Madison and John Jay (ed. Terence Ball), *The Federalist with Letters of 'Brutus'*, Cambridge Texts in the History of Political Thought, Cambridge University Press, Cambridge, 2007.

32. For a stimulating treatment of these themes, see Francis Fukuyama, *The Origins of Political Order: From Prehuman Times to the French Revolution*, Profile Books, London, 2011, Parts I to III.

33. The phrase is Joseph Stiglitz's. Stiglitz, *Freefall*, p. 249.

34. My quotations from it are taken from *The Communist Manifesto: A Modern Edition*, introduced by Eric Hobsbawm, Verso, London, 1998.

4. THE MARKET STATE INVADES THE PUBLIC REALM

1. *Securing a Sustainable Future for Higher Education: An Independent Review of Higher Education Funding and Student Finance*, 12 October 2010, www.independent.gov.uk/browne-report, pp. 14 and 15.

2. *Securing a Sustainable Future for Higher Education*, p. 47.

3. http://www.harvard.edu/faqs/mission-statement. Accessed 30 March 2013.

4. Iain McLean, *Adam Smith: Radical and Egalitarian, an Interpretation for the Twenty-First Century*, Edinburgh University Press, Edinburgh, 2006, p. 1.

5. For a pellucid and moving account see Tom Bingham, *The Rule of Law*, Allen Lane, London, 2010.

6. R. A. Butler was responsible for the 1944 Education Act providing for free secondary education; Aneurin Bevan for establishing the National Health Service; and David Lloyd George for the 1911 National Insurance Act that paved the way for the post-1945 welfare state.

7. Onora O'Neill, *A Question of Trust: The BBC Reith Lectures 2002*, Cambridge University Press, Cambridge, 2002, p. 32.

8. Arthur M. Schlesinger Jr, *A Thousand Days: John F. Kennedy in the White House*, André Deutsch, London, 1965, p. 4.

9. Michael Dietrich and Jennifer Roberts, 'Beyond the Economics of Professionalism', in Jane Broadbent, Michael Dietrich and Jennifer Roberts, *The End of the Professions? The Restructuring of Professional Work*, Routledge, London, 1997, p. 17.

10. Onora O'Neill, *A Question of Trust*, p. 49.

11. For Roman liberty see Quentin Skinner, *Liberty Before Liberalism*, Cambridge University Press, Cambridge, 1998.

12. Tony Blair's predilection for 'sofa government' is the most egregious recent example. See a devastating critique by the former Cabinet Secretary, Lord Butler, *The Spectator*, 11 December 2004.

13. Bingham, *Rule of Law*, p. 24.

14. Anthony Crosland, *The Future of Socialism*, William Pickering, London, 1994, pp. 62–5.

15. Daniel Bell, *The End of Ideology: On the Exhaustion of Political Ideas in the Fifties*, The Free Press of Glencoe, Illinois, 1960, p. 373.

16. Andrew Shonfield, *Modern Capitalism: The Changing Balance of Public and Private Power*, William Pickering, London, 1994, p. 67.

17. For a characteristic expression see Anthony King (ed.), *Why is Britain Becoming Harder to Govern?*, British Broadcasting Corporation, London, 1976, p. 74.

18. John Campbell, *Margaret Thatcher*, vol. 1, Pimlico, London, 2001, p. 365.

19. For the phrase 'astonishing animosity' and the growing demand for a Scottish Parliament see Kenyon Wright, *The People Say Yes: The Making of Scotland's Parliament*, Argyll Publishing, Argyll, 1997, particularly pp. 140–41.

20. Charles Moore, *Margaret Thatcher: The Authorized Biography*, vol. 1, *Not for Turning*, Allen Lane, London, 2013, p. 528. Chapter 19, in which that quotation appears, is a mine of information on her isolation from the Cabinet mainstream at that time.

21. Simon Jenkins, *Thatcher and Sons: A Revolution in Three Acts*, Allen Lane, London, 2006, p. 149. A full account of the data on which Jenkins based his conclusion can be found in Ivor Crewe, 'Has the Electorate

become Thatcherite?', in Robert Skidelsky (ed.), *Thatcherism*, Chatto and Windus, London, 1988, pp. 25–49.

22. Jenkins, *Thatcher and Sons*. Whether or not the Cameron–Clegg coalition also belongs to the age of Thatcher is still moot.

23. *Woman's Own*, 31 October 1987.

24. Lord Young of Graffham, 'Enterprise Regained', in Paul Heelas and Paul Morris (eds.), *The Values of the Enterprise Culture: The Moral Debate*, Routledge, London and New York, 1992, p. 29.

25. In 1985 a report on 'Faith in the City', issued by a Church of England Commission, insisted that 'a long Christian tradition' rejected 'the amassing of wealth unless it is justly obtained and fairly distributed'. (*Faith in the City: A Call for Action by Church and Nation. The Report of the Archbishop of Canterbury's Commission on Urban Priority Areas*, Church House, London, 1985. One of Thatcher's ministers denounced the report as 'pure Marxist theology'.

26. See Chapter 3 for the details.

27. See Chapter 2 for the concept of the market state.

28. Nigel Lawson, *The View from No. 11: Memoirs of a Tory Radical*, Corgi Books, London, 1993, pp. 64–5.

29. John Kay, 'The Balance Sheet', *Prospect*, 20 July 2002.

30. Joseph E. Stiglitz, *The Price of Inequality*, Allen Lane, London, 2012, pp. 109 and 113.

31. Ian Gilmour, *Dancing with Dogma: Britain under Thatcherism*, Simon and Schuster, London, 1992, p. 105.

32. For the concept of the 'core executive' see Martin J. Smith, *The Core Executive in Britain*, Macmillan Press, Basingstoke and London, 1999.

33. Hugo Young, *One of Us*, Macmillan, London, 1989, p. 232.

34. For a full account see Robert Taylor, *The Trade Union Question in British Politics: Government and Unions since 1945*, Blackwell, Oxford, 1993.

35. Alec Cairncross, *The British Economy since 1945: Economic Policy and Performance, 1945–1995*, Blackwell, Oxford, 1996, p. 231.

36. Andrew Gamble, *The Free Economy and the Strong State: The Politics of Thatcherism*, Macmillan Education, Basingstoke and London, 1988, p. 218.

37. Adam Smith, *An Inquiry into the Nature and Causes of the Wealth of Nations* (ed. Edwin Cannan), University of Chicago Press, Chicago, 1976, vol. I, p. 74.

38. J. M. Keynes, 'The Economic Consequences of Mr Churchill', in *Essays in Persuasion*, Rupert Hart-Davis, London, 1952 (first published 1931), pp. 261–2.

39. The two most egregious examples were Ken Livingstone's Greater London Council and David Blunkett's Sheffield. For the former see Simon Jenkins, *Accountable to None: The Tory Nationalisation of Britain*, Penguin Books, London, 1996, ch. 8; for the latter see Stephen Pollard, *David Blunkett*, Hodder and Stoughton, London, 2005, p. 133.

40. Jenkins, *Accountable to None*, p. 179.

41. Ibid., p. 168.

42. Ibid., p. 163.

43. O'Neill, *A Question of Trust*, pp. 45–54.

44. *Report of the Mid Staffordshire NHS Foundation Trust Public Inquiry*, Stationery Office, London, 2013.

45. Sarah Hale, 'Professor Macmurray and Mr Blair: The Strange Case of the Communitarian Guru That Never Was', *The Political Quarterly*, vol. 73, no. 2, April–June 2002, pp. 191–7.

46. Tony Travers, 'Local Government', in *The Blair Effect: The Blair Government 1997–2000* (ed. Anthony Seldon), Little, Brown, London, 2001, p. 133.

47. David Beetham et al., *Democracy Under Blair: A Democratic Audit of the United Kingdom*, Politico's Publishing, London, 2002, p. 264.

48. www.education.gov.uk/governmentnews/prime-minister-more-new-school-than-ever-before-to-raise-standards-and-increase-choice. Accessed 1 January 2013.

49. Colin Leys and Stewart Player, *The Plot against the* NHS, Merlin Press, Pontypool, 2011.

50. John Curtice and Oliver Heath, 'Does Choice Deliver?', *Political Studies*, vol. 60, no. 3, October 2012, pp. 484–503.

51. For the details see Charles Pattie, Patrick Seyd and Paul Whitely, *Citizenship in Britain: Values, Participation and Democracy*, Cambridge University Press, Cambridge, 2004, *passim*.

52. Michael Sandel, *What Money Can't Buy: The Moral Limits of Markets*, Allen Lane, London, 2012, pp. 202–3.

5. FROM FATE TO CHOICE – AND BACK AGAIN

1. A frequent riposte to criticisms of the monarchy is that the alternative could only be a second-rate political hack. But the post-war German Federal Republic has had at least two immensely distinguished presidents – Theodor Heuss and Richard von Weizsäcker. And the Dutch royal family easily outclasses the British in artistic and intellectual endeavour.

2. Polly Toynbee, 'This fact-free dogma will make more children poor', *Guardian*, 15 June 2012.

3. For a mordant treatment of that theme see Andrew Adonis and Stephen Pollard, *A Class Act: The Myth of Britain's Classless Society*, Hamish Hamilton, London, 1997, especially ch. 5.

4. R. H. Tawney, *Equality*, reprinted as vol. 1 of David Riesman (ed.), *Theories of the Mixed Economy*, William Pickering, London, 1994, ch. 1 and pp. 45–6.

5. Harold Perkin, *The Origins of Modern English Society: 1780–1880*, Routledge & Kegan Paul, London, 1969, p. 52.

6. Ibid., p. 19.

7. Daron Acemoglu and James A. Robinson, *Why Nations Fail: The Origins of Power, Prosperity and Poverty*, Profile Books, London, 2012, pp. 79–83.

8. In fairness I should add that Acemoglu and Robinson don't think so.

9. For a classic account of the social meaning of equality before the law in eighteenth-century Britain see E. P. Thompson, *Whigs and Hunters: The Origins of the Black Acts*, Allen Lane, London, 1975.

10. http://en.wikipedia.org/wiki/Rerum_Novarum. Accessed 18 July 2012.

11. Harold Perkin, *The Third Revolution: Professional Elites in the Modern World*, Routledge, London, 1996, p. 111.

12. John Studzinski, 'Germany is right: there is no right to profit, but the right to work is essential', *Guardian*, 6 February 2010.

13. Sidney Pollard, *The Development of the British Economy*, 3rd edn, Edward Arnold, London, 1983, pp. 192–234.

14. John Hills, *Inequality and the State*, Oxford University Press, Oxford, 2004, p. 27.

15. http://epp.eurostat.ee.europa.eu/tgm/printTable.do?tab=table&plugin=1& language=en. Accessed 3 January 2012.

16. John Hills, *Inequality and the State*, Oxford University Press, Oxford, 2004, p. 27.

17. Chrystia Freeland, *Plutocrats: The Rise of the New Global Super-Rich and the Fall of Everyone Else*, Allen Lane, London, 2012, p. 81.

18. *Racing Away? Income Inequality and the Evolution of High Incomes*, Briefing Note No. 76, Institute for Fiscal Studies, London, 2008.

19. www.rss.org.uk/site/cms/newsarticle.asp?chapter=32&nid=65. Accessed 3 January 2013.

20. www.guardian.co.uk/business/2012/jun/11/executive-pay-soars-survey-shows. Accessed 28 July 2012.

21. Freeland, *Plutocrats*, p. 59.

22. Ibid., *passim*.

23. Hills, *Inequality and the State*, p. 31.

24. John Hills et al., *An Anatomy of Economic Inequality in the United Kingdom*, Report of the National Equality Panel, January 2010, pp. 58–61. http:/eprints.lse.ac.uk/283441/1/CASEreport60.pdf. Accessed 8 July 2012.

25. Tax Justice Network, Wednesday, 27 July 2011, http://taxjustice.blogspot. fr/2011/07/virgin-ente. Accessed 3 August 2012.

26. *Guardian*, 21 July 2012.

27. Nicholas Shaxson, *Treasure Islands: Tax Havens and the Men Who Stole the World*, Vintage Books, London, 2012, p. 15.

28. Ibid., p. 249.

29. Richard Murphy, 'Tax Havens, Secrecy Jurisdictions and the Breakdown of Corporation Tax', *Real World Economics Review*, no. 57.

30. Owen Jones, *Chavs: The Demonization of the Working Class*, Verso, London and New York, 2011, p. 63.

31. Wenchao Jin et al., *Poverty and Inequality in the UK: 2011*, Institute for Fiscal Studies, London, pp. 37–41.

32. www.poverty.org.uk/01/index.shtml.

33. Richard Wilkinson and Kate Pickett, *The Spirit Level: Why More Equal Societies Almost Always Do Better*, Allen Lane, London, 2009.

34. For mental illness, drug abuse, obesity, life expectancy and teenage births see Wilkinson and Pickett, *Spirit Level*, chs. 5–9. For the statistics for youngsters not in employment or education, for the prison population and for cancer death rates see *Social Trends: International Comparisons*, 2011, ISSN 2040–1620.

35. Jones, *Chavs*, pp. 114–15.

36. Quoted in ibid., p. 131.

37. David Selbourne, *The Spirit of the Age: An Account of Our Times*, Sinclair-Stevenson, London, 1993.

38. Avishai Margalit, *The Decent Society* (trans. Naomi Goldblum), Harvard University Press, Cambridge, Mass., and London, 1996.

39. Wilkinson and Pickett, *Spirit Level*, pp. 165–6.

40. Quoted in Stephen Lukes, *Èmile Durkheim: His Life and Works. A Historical and Critical Study*, Penguin Books, Harmondsworth, reprinted 1988, p. 267.

41. Quoted in Geoffrey Hosking, *Trust, Money, Markets and Society*, Seagull Books, London, New York, Calcutta, 2010, p. 4.

42. Ibid., p. 1.

43. Wilkinson and Pickett, *Spirit Level*, pp. 52–6.

44. Simon Baron-Cohen, *Zero Degrees of Empathy: A New Theory of Human Cruelty and Kindness*, Penguin Books, London, 2012, p. 12.

45. Richard Sennett, *Together: The Rituals, Pleasures and Politics of Co-operation*, Allen Lane, London, 2012.

46. Marek Kohn, *Trust: Self-Interest and the Common Good*, Oxford University Press, Oxford, 2009, p. 34.

47. Anna Minton, *Ground Control: Fear and Happiness in the Twenty-First Century City*, Penguin Books, London, 2009.

48. Minton, *Ground Control*, pp. 55–6.

49. Michael Orton and Karen Rowlingson, *Public Attitudes to Economic Inequality*, Joseph Rowntree Foundation, York, 2007.

6. CHARISMATIC POPULISM SMOTHERS DEMOCRATIC DEBATE

1. The phrase is Alan Ryan's. Alan Ryan, *On Politics: A History of Political Thought from Herodotus to the Present*, Allen Lane, London, 2012, p. 11.

2. Thucydides, *The Peloponnesian War* (trans. Rex Warner with an Introduction and Notes by I. M. Finley), Penguin Books, Harmondsworth, reprinted 1975, pp. 145 and 147.

3. Alexis de Tocqueville, *Democracy in America* (ed. Alan Ryan), Everyman's Library, London, 1994, pp. 318–19.

4. See Chapter 4 for O'Neill's insistence on the need for active citizenship.

5. John Dunn, *Setting the People Free: The Story of Democracy*, Atlantic Books, London, 2005, pp. 19–20.

6. Stephen Orgel and Jonathan Goldberg (eds.), *John Milton: A Critical Edition of the Major Works*, Oxford University Press, Oxford and New York, 1991, pp. 264–7.

7. Ibid., p. 266.

8. Samuel H. Beer, *To Make a Nation: The Rediscovery of American Federalism*, The Belknap Press, Harvard University Press, Cambridge, Mass., and London, 1994, p. 69.

9. Orgel and Goldberg, *John Milton*, p. 679.

10. For stimulating reflections on these themes see Tim Soutphommasane, *The Virtuous Citizen: Patriotism in a Multicultural Society*, Cambridge University Press, Cambridge, 2012, ch. 5.

11. Tom Watson and Martin Hickman, *Dial M for Murdoch*, Penguin Books, London, 2012, pp. 281–7.

12. Ibid., p. 7.

13. John Lloyd, *What the Media are Doing to Our Politics*, Constable, London, 2004, p. 17.

14. Onora O'Neill, *A Question of Trust: The BBC Reith Lectures 2002*, Cambridge University Press, Cambridge, 2002, pp. 90–91.

15. Pomerania, Silesia and East Prussia (all parts of present-day Poland) were ruled by the Hohenzollerns; Galicia, much of which is now in Poland – including Cracow, the ancient capital of the Polish kings – was ruled by the Hapsburgs.

16. Colin Crouch, *The Strange Non-Death of Neoliberalism*, Polity Press, Cambridge, reprinted 2012, p. 131.

17. Joseph E. Stiglitz, *The Price of Inequality*, Allen Lane, London, 2012, p. 28.

18. Ibid., p. 95.

19. http://news.uk.msn.com/us-elections-2-12/race-for-the-white-house-blogspot. aspx? Accessed 10 January 2013.

20. www.oecd.org/els/socialpoliciesanddata/41525323.

21. www.guardian.co.uk/2012/feb/24/why-super-rich-love-uk. Accessed 22 September 2012.

22. David Beetham, *Unelected Oligarchy: Corporate and Financial Dominance in Britain's Democracy*, www.democraticaudit.com. My account of 'revolving doors' is based on this.

23. Mara Faccio, 'Politically Connected Firms', *The American Economic Review*, March 2006, pp. 369–86.

24. *Guardian*, 10 July 2012, www.guardian.co.uk/business/2012/jul/10/city-lobbying-lords-financial-industry. Accessed 22 September 2012.

25. See Beetham, *Unelected Oligarchy*, and Colin Leys, *The Dissolution of the Mandarins: The Sell-Off of the British State*, Open Democracy, 15 June 2012, www.opendemocracy.net/print/66495, accessed 10 September 2012.

26. *Guardian*, 14 October 2012.

27. Beetham, *Unelected Oligarchy*, p. 18.

28. Ibid., p. 11.

29. Richard Rose, *The Prime Minister in a Shrinking World*, Polity Press, Cambridge, Cambridge, 2001, p. 219.

30. Max Weber (ed. Talcott Parsons), *The Theory of Social and Economic Organization*, Free Press, New York, 1964, pp. 358–63.

31. For which see Chapter 2.

32. Lord Hailsham's warning that the British conception of absolute parliamentary sovereignty, which provides no real check on the power of a government with a Commons majority, was leading to an 'elective dictatorship' is as pertinent today as it was when he gave it nearly forty years ago. See Lord Hailsham, *The Dilemma of Democracy*, Collins, London, 1978.

7. WHO DO WE THINK WE ARE?

1. A good example is Keith Joseph, *Reversing the Trend: A Critical Reappraisal of Conservative Economic and Social Policies*, Rose, Chichester, 1975.

2. Mary Douglas, the doyenne of British cultural anthropologists before her death in 2007, held that cultures embrace four ways of life – the 'hierarchical', the 'sectarian' or 'egalitarian', the 'individualistic' and the 'fatalist'. 'Fatalists' opt out, but 'hierarchists', 'sectarians' and 'individualists' struggle endlessly over which way of life is to prevail. These struggles drive cultural change in complex and unpredictable ways. See Michael Thomas, Richard Ellis and Aaron Wildavsky, *Cultural Theory*, Westview Press, Boulder, Colo., 1990.

3. Alasdair MacIntyre, *Whose Justice? Which Rationality?*, Duckworth, London, 1988, pp. 350–66.

4. George Orwell, 'England Your England', in George Orwell, *A Patriot after All, 1940–1941* (ed. Peter Davison), Secker and Warburg, London, 2000, p. 393.

5. The term is Zygmunt Bauman's, *Collateral Damage: Social Inequalities in a Global Age*, Polity Press, Cambridge, 2011.

6. Peter Jenkins, *Mrs Thatcher's Revolution: The Ending of the Socialist Era*, Jonathan Cape, London, 1987, p. 66.

7. Shirley Letwin, *The Anatomy of Thatcherism*, Fontana, London, 1992, ch. 2.

8. Samuel Smiles, *Self-Help with illustrations of character and conduct*, Ticknor and Fields, Boston, Mass., 1861, pp. 15–17. http://books.google.co.uk/books?id=P5EWAAAAYAAJ&pr. Accessed 19 October 2012.

9. Quoted in David Kynaston, *The City of London*, vol. 4, *A Club No More*, Chatto and Windus, London, 2001, p. 720.

10. The phrase was Tony Blair's. John Rentoul, *Tony Blair, Prime Minister*, Little, Brown, London, 2001, p. 553.

11. The term is Susan Strange's. Susan Strange, *Casino Capitalism*, Basil Blackwell, Oxford, 1986.

12. www.number-10.gov.uk/output/Page6129.asp.

13. John Campbell, *Margaret Thatcher*, vol. 2, Pimlico, London, 2004, p. 182.

14. Amartya Sen, *The Idea of Justice*, Penguin Books, London, 2010, p. 245.

15. I should declare an interest. I am a Compass member.

16. Rowan Williams, *Faith in the Public Square*, Bloomsbury, London, 2012, p. 198.

17. Polly Higgins, *Eradicating Ecocide: Laws and Governance to Prevent the Destruction of Our Planet*, Shepheard-Walwyn, London, 2010, p. 135.

18. Quoted in David Bromwich (ed.), *On Empire, Liberty and Reform: Speeches and Letters, Edmund Burke*, Yale University Press, New Haven, Conn., and London, 2000, p. 5.

19. Quoted in Conor Cruise O'Brien, *The Great Melody: A Thematic Biography and Commented Anthology of Edmund Burke*, Minerva, London, 1993, p. 480.

20. Conor Cruise O'Brien, *Edmund Burke*, Vintage, London, 2002, p. 3.

21. *Edmund Burke's Speech on Conciliation with America* (ed. Albert S. Cook), Longman's English Classics, London, 1921, Classic Reprint Series, pp. 21–5.

22. O'Brien, *Great Melody*, p. 322.

23. Ibid., pp. 389–90.

24. Edmund Burke, *Reflections on the Revolution in France* (ed. J. C. D. Clark), Stanford University Press, Stanford, Calif., 2001, pp. 260–61.

25. For which see Chapter 6.

26. John Stuart Mill, *On Liberty; with The Subjection of Women; and Chapters on Socialism* (ed. Stefan Collini), Cambridge University Press, Cambridge, 1989, p. 20.

27. See Chapter 2 for these.

28. Mill, *On Liberty*, pp. 59–60.

29. Ibid., p. 76.

30. Ibid., p. 115.

31. Geraint L. Williams (ed.), *John Stuart Mill on Politics and Society*, Fontana Press, London, 1985, p. 173.

32. Ibid., p. 205.

33. Quoted in ibid., pp. 205–6.

34. John Stuart Mill, *Principles of Political Economy*, George Routledge and Sons, London, 1903, pp. 607–8.

35. Ross Terrill, *R. H. Tawney and His Times: Socialism as Fellowship* (Harvard University Press, Cambridge, Mass., 1973, pp. 79 and 119.

36. R. H. Tawney, *The Acquisitive Society*, G. Bell and Sons, London, reprinted 1922, p. 48.

37. Ibid., pp. 32–3.

38. Ibid., p. 38.

39. Ibid., p. 39.

40. Ibid., p. 241.

41. R. H. Tawney, *The Attack and Other Papers*, Spokesman, Nottingham, 1981, p. 165.

42. Quoted in Terrill, *Tawney*, p. 173.

43. *The New Statesman and Nation*, 22 June 1935.

44. Malise Ruthven, *Islam in the World*, Penguin Books, Harmondsworth, 1984, p. 139.

45. Williams, *Faith in the Public Square*, p. 29.

46. Martha C. Nussbaum, *Not for Profit: Why Democracy Needs the Humanities*, Princeton University Press, Princeton, NJ, and Oxford, 2010, pp. 6–7.

47. Avishai Margalit, *The Decent Society* (trans. Naomi Goldblum), Harvard University Press, Cambridge, Mass., and London, 1996, p. 9.

48. For which see Chapter 3 of this book.

49. Thomas Paine, *Rights of Man, Common Sense and Other Political Writings* (ed. Mark Philp), Oxford University Press, Oxford, 1995, p. 96.

50. See the last chapter for Beetham's description.

51. Only then did all adult women get votes.

52. Sen, *The Idea of Justice*, p. 354. My other quotations from Sen all come from pp. 330–34.

53. For an illuminating discussion see Vernon Bogdanor, *The New British Constitution*, Hart Publishing, Oxford and Portland, Ore., 2009, pp. 304–10.

Index

ABN AMRO 8–9
Aborigines 83
abortion 39
Abramovich, Roman 14
academic duties 101
academies 118, 120
accountability 33, 116, 163, 164,
    170, 216
Acemoglu, Daron 128, 166
Acheson, Dean 30
Adam Smith Institute 46
Adonis, Andrew, Baron 120
AEU (Amalgamated
    Engineering Union) 37
Afghanistan war 66
Agricultural Labourers'
    Union 23
alcoholism 175
Alfa Sea yachts 126
alienation 55
altruism 87
Amalgamated Engineering
    Union (AEU) 37
Amazon deforestation 2
American Enlightenment 84
Amery, Leo 154
amnesia *see* social amnesia
anomie 144
Antarctic ice caps 73

anti-Catholic discrimination 44
anti-Semitism 33, 38, 162
anti-terror laws 66
Apostles (Cambridge Conversazione
    Society) 51, 52
Applegarth 12
Apprentice, The 58
Aquinas, St Thomas 71, 184
Arab–Israeli war 44
Arabs, Israeli 211, 212
Arcadia Group 169
Arch, Joseph, Agricultural
    Labourers' Union 23
Archer, James 190
Aristotle 97, 154, 184, 200, 217
    epigraph 91
Armstrong, Sir Robert 32
army 104, 148
Army Bureau of Current Affairs
    (ABCA) 29
Arnold, Matthew 22, 24, 25, 41
Arnold, Thomas 24
Arrow, Kenneth 68
arson 15–16
Ashcroft, Michael, Baron 169
Ashoka, Emperor 217
Ashworth, Tony 148
Asquith Government 160
asymmetrical information 101

Athens, birth of democracy 153–4
Augar, Philip 12
Augustine of Canterbury 62, 184
austerity 15
Australia 147, 171
Austria 147, 171
authority, kinds of 176
Avaaz 218

Babbs, David 193
Baldwin, Stanley 160
Baldwins 37
Balls, Ed 10
Bancroft, Ian Powell, Baron
    31–2, 111
Bank of England 10
banking
    American investment banks
        11–12, 82
    bailouts 13
    bankers' bonuses 16
    British bank loans 13
    casino 190
    credit crunch 20, 64, 86
    and financial skulduggery 16
    German banks 11–12
    Good Banking Forum 194
    interbank lending 16
    investment bankers 10, 69, 86
    Italian bankers 163
    Japanese banks 11–12
    nationalization 64
    Northern Rock collapse 12–13,
        64, 82
    RBS and the banking crisis 8–9,
        11, 64
    regulation 2, 9–10, 11, 166
    subsidiaries in 'secrecy
        jurisdictions' 138
Barclay brothers 137

Barclays 16, 78–9, 193
Baring, Edward (Ned), 1st Baron
    Revelstoke 129
Baron-Cohen, Simon 147
Barratts 15
barristers 100
Bartlett, Vernon 160
Bauman, Zygmunt 21
BB Magic Gold watches 126
BBC 30, 37, 108
    ITMA 37
    Third programme 37
Beaverbrook, Max Aitken,
    1st Baron 160
Beer, Samuel H. 158
    'romantic revolt' 45, 56
Beetham, David 175, 216
Belgian Congo genocide 2
Belgium 140
Bell, Brian 135
Bell, Daniel 105
Benn, Tony 106
Bentham, Jeremy 86
Bentley, Derek 39
Berezovsky, Boris 14
Berlin, Isaiah 37
Berners Lee, Sir Tim 80, 101
Bernstein, Eduard 213
Bevan, Aneurin 34, 35, 62,
    98, 159
    NHS 1946 Act 38
Beveridge, William 30–31, 34, 42,
    61–2
Beveridge Report 30–31, 105, 143
Bevin, Ernest 34, 61, 62, 132
Bible, King James 61, 65
'Big Bang' (financial) 11, 134, 168
Big Society 119–20
Big Switch initiative 193–4
binge-drinking 144–5

Bingham, Thomas, Baron Bingham
    of Cornhill 103–4
Birmingham 104
Blacks, American 211–12
Blair, Cherie 161
Blair, Tony 10, 117, 118, 154, 178,
    185, 190, 191
  call for a society of respect
    191, 192
  and the 'forces of conservatism'
    179
  and the Iraq War 180
  and J. P. Morgan 172
  and Murdoch 161–2, 165
Blair governments 118, 168,
    174–5
  'sofa government' 179–80
Blake, William 205
Blitz 36
Bloomsbury Group 52
Blue Labour 61
Bobbitt, Philip 51, 108
Bolton 104
bond markets 76
Bondfield, Margaret 39
bonds of sympathy 97, 109, 122
Bonham-Carter, Helena 162
Bonhoeffer, Dietrich 208
Boots 16
bourgeoisie 88–9
BP 78–9, 109, 189
Bradford 104
Branson, Sir Richard 58, 137, 161
Bridges, Edward (later Lord) 30
Britain
  amnesia see social amnesia
  banking see banking
  British Enlightenment 84–5
  Cameron's promise to fix 'broken
    Britain' 191

'Condition of England
    Question' 24–5, 27, 187
  Conservative–Lib Dem
    Coalition Government see
    Coalition Government,
    Conservative–Lib Dem
  Conservative Party see
    Conservative Party
  devolution 117, 219
  as a dysfunctional society 140
  economy see economy; moral
    economy; political economy
  elites see elites
  and the empire 60–61, 63
  and the EU 64
  feminization of public
    culture 186
  financial sector see financial
    sector, Britain
  GDP 12, 13, 15
  'Glorious Revolution' 4, 103–4
  identity question and crisis 65,
    184, 219–20
  inequality see inequality
  insular self-sufficiency myth 64
  Labour Party see Labour Party;
    New Labour
  Mammon worship see
    Mammon worship
  Office for Budget
    Responsibility 15
  opportunities and steps for a
    national conversion and new
    public philosophy 192–220
  politically connected firms and
    corporate power 171–2
  post-financial crisis 15–17
  public realm see public realm
  public spending see public
    spending

Britain – *cont.*
  railway boom 6
  recession 15
  recognizing the British trap
    182–92
  Reform Acts *see* Reform Acts
  society and social structures at
    mid-twentieth century 36–40
  South Sea Bubble 5–6
  sterling 70
  technological and economic
    changes 20
  transformation into
    post-industrial society 20
  transition from individualism to
    collectivism 21–2, 104
  as a union state 60–64
  veto on proposed EU fiscal
    agreement 16
  as a 'young country' (Blair/New
    Labour rhetoric) 66, 185
British Airports 109
British American Tobacco 78–9
British army 104, 148
British Broadcasting Corporation
  see BBC
British Coal 109
British Empire 60–61, 63
British Gas 109
British Medical Bulletin 143–4
British non-doms 169
British Petroleum 78–9, 109, 189
British Rail 109
British Steel 109
British Telecom 109
Brittain, Vera 39
Brooks, Charles (Charlie) 161
Brooks, Rebekah 161
Brown, Gordon 10, 14
Brown Government 168, 174

Browne, John, Baron Browne
  of Madingley 92, 174
Browne review 92–6, 210
Bryant, Chris 161
BSkyB 162
BT 109
Buchan, James 5
Buddhism 217
Bullock, Alan 132
Bunyan, John: *Pilgrim's Progress* 6
Burke, Edmund 68, 85, 159, 185,
    196–9, 204
  social contract critique
    198–9, 213
Bush, George W. 154
businesses *see* firms
Butler, R. A. 41, 98

Cabinet 36
Cable, Vince 13
Caesar, Julius 163
Callaghan, Jim (Leonard James,
    Baron) 44
Callaghan Government 44
Calvinism 210
Cambridge Conversazione Society
    (the Apostles) 51, 52
Cameron, David 13, 16, 119–20, 191
  and the Leveson Inquiry 161
  and Murdoch 162
Camilla, Duchess of Cornwall 125
Campbell, Alastair 118, 161
Canada 140, 147, 171
Canary Wharf 149
cancer 140
cannabis 53
Capita 173
capital gains tax 169
  American 166
capital punishment 38–9

capitalism 6–7, 23, 25
  and choice *see* choice
  collateral damage 87, 187;
    see also inequality
  Crosland on transformation
    of 105
  decent/good 71, 214, 215–16
  and democracy 163–81
  environmental cost 87; *see also*
    environmental damage
  and freedom 75, 183; *see also*
    freedom
  and humiliation 214
  and the individual 165, 178, 183,
    190; *see also* individualism
  and inequality *see* inequality
  and Marxism 88–90, 106
  and materialism 27
  Orwell on 28
  and property rights *see* property
    rights
  stakeholder 132, 215
  success of post-war
    capitalism 106
  and the super-rich 134–7, 166–7,
    189, 190
  tamed/taming of 42–3, 81, 90,
    105, 106, 165, 215
  untamed 69, 71, 72, 75, 81, 87,
    90, 139–41, 144, 175, 178,
    183, 187, 188, 191, 213,
    214–15
  'vigorous virtues' and British
    moral vision underpinning
    188–92
  see also laissez-faire economics
car industry 64
'carbon crunch' 74
Carlyle, Thomas 4, 22–3,
    24, 25, 88

'Condition of England
    Question' 24–5, 27, 187
  epigraph, *Past and Present* 1
cartels 80
Casburn, April 161
Catherine, Duchess of Cambridge
    125
caveat emptor (buyer beware)
    principle 101–2
Cayman Islands 137, 138
Cecil, Lady Gwendoline 52
celebrity 58
censorship 157, 201
Center for Responsive
    Politics, US 167
centralism 108
  centralized control of
    polytechnics 115
  effects in London 115
  and war on local democracy
    113–15, 118–19
  and war on professionalism
    115–17
Centre for Policy Studies 46
CERN 80, 101
Chandler, Alfred 78
charismatic populism 175–81, 216
Charles, Prince of Wales 125
Charles II 159
Chartist movement 206
Chicagoan economics/neoliberalism
    74–83, 165, 189–90, 192, 220
child labour 2
Chile 164
China 164, 177
chivalry, orders of 126
choice 122–3, 183, 190, 191–2
  effects on others 192
  and fate 126, 150–51
  fetish of free choice 134, 150–51

choice – *cont.*
  marketization and the
    rhetoric of 122
  and morality 192
  trinity of Choice, Freedom
    and the Individual 183,
    190–93, 199
  Virginia School of public-choice
    theorists 46
Christian Democrats 24
Christianity
  adaptation and survival of 186
  Christian church *see* church
  Christian ethics 205
  Eucharist 97
  and intolerant tolerance
    207–11
  martyrdom and openness 208–9
  Protestant *see* Protestantism
church 36–7
  Anglican *see* Church of England
  initiatives 105
  Roman *see* Roman Catholicism
Church of England 62, 64,
  108, 210
Churchill, Winston 11, 159,
  168, 214
  wartime coalition under 28, 61,
    105, 133
Churchill Insurance Group 8
Cicero 159
Citizens UK 193, 218
Citizens United v. *Federal Election
  Commission* 167
citizenship
  and democracy 123
  and Mill 203
  and public trust 103; *see also*
    trust
  and social rights *see* social rights

  Tawney's vision of democratic
    citizenship 206
  widening of circle of political
    citizenship 104
Citrine, Walter 34
civic activism 104
civic duty 34, 104, 122, 216
civic enterprise 104
civic pride 104
civil aviation, nationalization 38
civil rights 42, 44, 98, 212, 218
  pension rights 136
civil service 30, 31–2, 36, 58,
  111–12
  civil servants as market agents
    111–12, 173
  Northcote–Trevelyan Report/
    reforms 32, 99, 104, 118
  and revolving doors to private
    sector 172, 174
  Top 200 group 174
  Whitehall culture and 'grovel
    count' 111, 134
Clarkson, Jeremy 162
class
  class-war proletarianism 106
  divide 61
  middle classes 133, 200
  and shame 144
  and shoppers 149
  structures 20
  Victorian middle-class
    pieties 200
  working classes *see* working-class
    elite; working classes
clerisy 21–9, 32, 33–4, 36, 39, 61,
  71, 98
  and its fall 21–9
climate change 72, 73–4, 193
Close Protection UK 125

clothing
  expensive 126
  rationing 42
Co-operative Energy 193–4
Co-operative Movement/
  co-operatives 23, 38, 62,
  105, 193
coal
  nationalization 36
  privatization 109
Coalition Government,
  Conservative–Lib Dem 15,
  120–22, 174, 191
  demonstrations against spending
  cuts 193
Cobden, Richard 75
cod liver oil 133
Cole, G. D. H. 26, 27
collateral damage 187
collectivism 21–2, 47–8, 104
  and Thatcherism 108, 188
  transition from individualism
  to 21–2, 104
Comet 15
command economy 28
Commission on Wealth Creation
  and Social Cohesion
  (Dahrendorf) 132, 215
Commons, House of see House of
  Commons
Commons, John Rogers 67
Commons Culture, Media and Sport
  Select Committee 161
Communism 6–7, 43, 177, 185
  collapse, and former Soviet
  satellites 163–4
  Communist Party of
  Great Britain 35–6
  Marxist see Marxism
  Orwell on 28

Communist Manifesto 88–90,
  106, 190
Communist Party of Great Britain
  (CPGB) 35–6
companies see firms
Compass 194
complacency 103–6
computerized tills 20
Connery, Sean 137
Conservative Party
  1951 membership 37
  championing of local
  authorities 114
  donators 170–71
  Eden's 107
  governments in the 1950s and
  early 1960s 133
  Heath Government 43–4, 46
  Lib Dem coalition see
  Coalition Government,
  Conservative–Lib Dem
  Major Government 107–8, 109,
  117, 118
  and the right's ideology 106–8
  Scottish Conservatives
  107, 210
  Thatcher Government see
  Thatcher governments/
  Thatcherism
  working-class Toryism 61
conservative tradition 195–9
consultancies 174
Contagious Diseases Act 200
Cook, James 73
corporations see firms
Corrupt and Illegal Practices
  Prevention Act (1883) 99
Corruption Perceptions Index 164
Corus 64–5
Coulson, Andy 161

council house sales 114
Courtaulds 37, 63
CPGB (Communist Party of
    Great Britain) 35–6
Cranmer, Thomas 209
Crassus, Marcus 163
credit 14, 15, 20
    crunch 20, 64, 86
credit rating agencies 76
Credit Suisse 190
Cripps, Stafford 35
Croesus, King 1
Crosland, Anthony 71, 105
Crossman, Richard 40
Crouch, Colin 166
cultural determinism 185
cultural hegemony 108–9, 114–15
cultural presentism 66–72, 185
Culture, Media and Sport Select
    Committee 161
Cunningham, William 67–8
Czech Republic 164

Dahrendorf, Ralf, Baron 132
Dahrendorf Commission 132, 215
Daily Herald 160
Daily Mail 162
Daily Mirror 29
Daley, Janet 141
Dannatt, Richard, Baron 173
Dante Alighieri 5–6
Darling, Alistair 9
Davos 136
Dawkins, Richard 207
de Gaulle, Charles 177
de Tocqueville, Alexis see
    Tocqueville, Alexis de
death instinct (Thanatos) 54, 55
debt
    national see national debt

private 14, 15, 20, 190
    see also credit
decarbonization 74
decent capitalism 71, 214, 215–16
decent democracy 216–17
decent elites 216
decent society 143, 211–12,
    214, 216
defence, national 80, 99
deforestation 72
    Amazonian 2
Delingpole, James 141, 143
Deloitte 138
democracy 29, 153–7
    and accountability 163, 164,
        170, 216
    American 119, 154–5, 166–7
    Athens and the birth of 153–4
    Bevan on democratic
        socialism 35
    and capitalism 163–81
    and censorship 157, 201
    and citizenship 123
    decent 216–17
    democratic dialogue see public
        debate and reasoning
    democratic suffrage see suffrage
    dependence on public reasoning
        95, 96, 155, 176, 217–19
    dialogue as a norm of 156–9
    Dunn on 156
    enemies of 157–81
    following collapse of Soviet
        Union 164
    and hubristic media 159–63
    Keynesian social democracy
        41–3, 44, 45, 54, 106, 130
    and lobbying 165–7
    and Mill 155
    and Milton 157–9, 201

New Labour and local democracy
118–19
norms of 156–9, 161, 163, 165,
176, 181, 183
oligarchic substance beneath
democratic forms 170–72, 183
Open Democracy 100
Pericles on 153–4
and Protestant dissent 157
and rationality 95; *see also*
public debate and reasoning
republican liberty and democratic
self-government 103, 119,
156–9
and revolving doors between
public service posts and
private sector 172–5
Royal Commission on
industrial 132
Tawney and the culture
of 204–7, 217; *see also*
Tawney, R. H.
and de Tocqueville 119, 154–5
UK democratic audit, Essex
University 118–19, 170–71
war on local democracy 113–15,
118–19
Democratic Audit 118–19, 170–71
demonstrations 91–2
Denning, Lord (Alfred 'Tom') 29
deregulation 11
derivatives 12n
determinism, cultural 185
Deutsche Bank 11–12
devaluation 70
dialogue, democratic *see* public
debate and reasoning
Diamond, Bob 135
Dicey, A. V. 21–2, 23, 104
Dickens, Charles 17, 22, 200

A Christmas Carol, Scrooge 1
Hard Times 129
Little Dorrit, Mr Merdle 7
Dietrich, Michael 101
discrimination, anti-Catholic 44
Disraeli, Benjamin 159
distributive justice 48–9
distrust 145–7, 150
divorce 37, 57
dock strike, London (1889) 23
doctors 110, 115, 145
dollar 70
Donne, John 97, 108
epigraph 91
Dorling, Danny 135
Dostoevsky, Fyodor 5
Dowler, Milly 161, 162
Dresdner Bank 11–12
drug abuse 140, 144–5
drug trade 191
Druids 186
Dubai 137–8
Duggan, Mark 15
Dunn, John 156
Durkheim, Émile 144
duties
academic 101
civic 34, 104, 122, 216
and rights 98, 205
Dyson, James 145

East India Company 85, 196,
198, 200
Easter Island 72–3
ecocide 194–5, 215
economic agents 2, 49, 77
see also market agents
economics
and the abandonment of history
67–72

economics – *cont.*
assumption of rationality
5, 77, 83
Cambridge, as part of Moral
Sciences Tripos 67
Chicagoan (neoliberalism)
74–83, 165, 189–90, 192, 220
devaluation 70
economic behaviour 2, 5, 20, 79,
82–3, 85, 111
economic individualism 110–11;
see also individualism
economic planning 47
economic risk 47, 69
emulation of science 68–9
exchange rate 70
German historical school of 67–8
Gini coefficient 133–4, 147
Homo sapiens vs *Homo
economicus* 86–7
interest rates 70
juggernaut theory 113, 171
Keynesian *see* Keynesianism
laissez-faire *see* laissez-faire
economics
link between economic and social
life (Tawney) 205
and morality 24–5, 68–9, 71–2;
see also moral economy
and offshore finance 137–8
purpose of economic activity 24
religion and economism
210, 214
responses to 2008–9 economic
crisis 70–72, 86–7
and social amnesia 67–72, 74–83
state-led economic development
43, 70, 80
students 69
US academic 67

economy
command economy 28
French *économie concertée* 43
German 'social-market economy'
43, 75–6, 131–2
growth 43, 70, 71, 78, 139, 167,
183, 214, 215
inflation *see* inflation
and the Keynesian state 33
Keynesian theory 33, 113
market economies *see* market
economies
mixed 105, 130
moral *see* moral economy
political *see* political economy
recession 15
responses to 2008–9 economic
crisis 70–72, 86–7
transformation through
privatization 109
Eden, Anthony 107
education
academies 118, 120
action zones 118
Browne review 92–6, 210
centralized control of
polytechnics 115
and the global race for the
top 93–5
governmental control of school
curricula 116
Gove's marketization 120–21
higher 92–6; *see also* universities
and the market fundamentalist
moral economy 92–6
mutual, and the open society 181
and New Labour 118, 120
OFSTED 118
and the public realm 92, 93–6
reconstruction attempts 65

rights to 98
schools *see* schools
student fees 91–2, 93
students *see* students
teachers 54, 102, 115, 116, 145
teaching history 65
Education Act (1944) 41
Education Reform Act (1988) 115
Edward VIII 36
elections 44, 99, 104, 165, 218
  campaign spending and funding
    170, 171
  electoral promises 43
  see also suffrage
electricity
  nationalization 38
  privatization 109
Eliot, George 22
Eliot, T. S. 26, 33
elites
  anti-elitism 216
  and the building of the
    public realm 216
  clerisy 21–9, 32, 33–4, 36, 39,
    61, 71, 98, 201
  corporate 88, 170–75, 184
  decent 216
  hedonism and the humbling
    of 57–8
  and the individualists 57–8,
    65, 183
  male preponderance 39
  power elite 175, 177, 216
  professional service 21, 29–34,
    36, 39, 61
  revolt against 45
  and the taming of capitalism
    175, 215
  and tradition 61–2
  working-class 21, 34–6, 39, 216

Elizabeth II
  coronation 36
  diamond jubilee 124–5, 127
empathy 147–50, 220
employment
  contracts 111, 117
  electoral promises of full 43
  employer–employee relations *see*
    industrial relations
  loss of jobs for life 57–8
  manufacturing employment
    decline 112
  pay *see* wages
  rights 98, 131, 132
  working conditions 98
  see also unemployment
Enfield, Harry 190
Engels, Friedrich 88–90, 190,
  214–15
Enlightenments 84–5
enterprise culture 108, 139, 177
Entertainments National Service
  Association (ENSA) 29
environmental damage 2, 72–4, 87
  'ecocide' 194–5, 215
  see also climate change; Green
    movement
environmental sustainability 17,
  195, 213–14
equality 29, 133
  German egalitarian economy 132
  legal 4
  of pay 98
  of rights 42
  slow growth before the law 129
  see also inequality
equity 104
  ethic of 103
  private *see* private equity
Eradiciting Ecocide 195

Erhard, Ludwig 131
Ernst and Young 138
Eros 53, 54, 55
Essex University, UK democratic
    audit 118–19, 170–71
ethics *see* morality and ethics
ethnicity *see* race and ethnicity
Eucharist 97
European Central Bank 76
European Commission 76
European Convention on Human
    Rights 97
European Court of Justice 16
European Union
    Britain's attitude to 184
    and Britain's union state 64
    and Chicagoan economics 76
    Citizens' Initiative for
        ecocide law 195
    directive to combat human
        trafficking 193
    proposed fiscal agreement 16
Euroscepticism 64
Eurostat 134
Evans, Harold 162
exchange rate 70
executive pay 82, 135–6
externalities 83

Fabian socialism 26
Faccio, Mara 171
Facebook 100
Faith in the City 210
family 36, 37, 62, 64, 213
    as breeding ground of
        schizophrenia (Laing) 53–4, 55
    and Smith 97
    strain put on traditional
        family 57
Fascism 47

fate 126, 150–51
Federal Communications
    Commission 166
Federal Reserve 166
feminization 186
financial regulation/regulators 2,
    9–10, 11, 69, 71–2, 166, 169
financial sector, Britain 16–17, 168
    banking *see* banking
    the City 10–12, 16, 134, 137,
        138, 168
    financial services 10, 11, 12, 19,
        167, 172, 215
Financial Services Authority (FSA)
    9–10, 11
firms
    corporate elites 88, 170–75, 184
    corporate power 79, 171–2
    and markets 78–9
    organizational capability 78
    politically connected 171–2
    and revolving doors between
        public service posts and private
        sector 172–5
    tax avoidance 137–8, 190, 193
First Active 8
First World War 27, 148
'Flaming Ferraris' 190
flummery and flunkyism, culture of
    125, 127, 207
Flynn, Paul 172–3
food rationing 42
Foot, Michael 29
foreign trade manipulation 80
Forster, E. M. 52
Fox, Charles James 159
Fox, Henry 128
France
    British comparison of mental
        illness 140

économie concertée 43
falling inequality 168
French Enlightenment 84
French Revolution 154
trente glorieuses 43, 54
franchise *see* suffrage
Francis Report 116
Franks, Oliver (later Lord) 30
freedom 17, 29, 75, 190, 191
 American 119
 bearing the burdens of 181
 and Burke 198
 and capitalism 75, 183
 to dissent 218
 free choice *see* choice
 and the goods of the public
  realm 103
 and the Great Society (Hayek) 49
 liberalism *see* liberalism
 Mill's *On Liberty* 200–201,
  202–3
 Milton's vision of 157–8
 and morality 192
 neoliberalism/Chicagoan
  economics 74–83, 165,
  189–90, 192, 220
 republican liberty 103, 119,
  156–9
 and security (Popper) 19, 75
 of speech 218
 trinity of Choice, Freedom
  and the Individual 183,
  190–93, 199
Freeland, Chrystia 135
French Enlightenment 84
French Revolution 154
Freud, Sigmund 1
Friedman, Milton 46
friendly societies 105
Friends of the Earth 194

FSA (Financial Services Authority)
 9–10, 11
Fukuyama, Francis 165

Gaitskell, Hugh 204
Gamble, Andrew 50
gang warfare 144–5
Gardiner, A. G. 160
gas-guzzling 191
gas, nationalization 38
Gas and General Workers' Union
 63
Gaskell, Mrs (Elizabeth) 22
GDP, British 12, 13, 15
GEC 37
Geithner, Timothy 166
General and Municipal Workers'
 Union (GMWU) 37
George I 64
George III and the 'King's Friends'
 196
George VI 36
Germany
 Christian Democratic Party 43
 corporate power 171
 First World War 148
 historical school of economics
  67–8
 militarism 47
 Mittelstand 131–2
 Nazi *see* Nazism
 'Ordo-liberals' of West Germany
  75–6
 public trust 147
 'social-market economy' 43,
  75–6, 131–2
Gibbon, Edward 4, 184
 *The Decline and Fall of the
  Roman Empire* 85
Gibraltar 137

Gini coefficient 133–4, 147
Gladstone, William 52, 104, 159, 177, 192, 196, 199
GlaxoSmithKline 78–9, 189
global race 93–5
global warming 73–4
globalization 20, 167–8
'Glorious Revolution' 4
GMWU (General and Municipal Workers' Union) 37
Goddard, Rayner, Baron 39
gold standard 70
golden calf worship 1, 6
Goldman Sachs 11–12
Gollancz, Victor 29
Good Banking Forum 194
'Good Society' 194
Goodwin, Frederick, 'Fred the Shred' 8, 9
Gove, Michael 120–21, 162
Graham, Sir John 11–12
Grant, Albert, 'Baron Grant' (born Abraham Gottheimer) 6
Great Depression 70, 177
Great Society (Hayek) 49
Great War see First World War
Greater London Council 115
greed 17
Green, Sir Philip 58, 169
Green movement 44, 187, 194–5, 213–14
Green Party 194
Greenlanders, Norse 73, 83, 85
Greenpeace 194
Greenspan, Alan 166
Greer, Germaine: The Female Eunuch 44
Guardian 161, 172
Guernsey 137, 138
Guild Socialism (Cole) 26

Habitat 15
Haji-Ioannou, Stelios 137
Haley, Sir William 30
Hammond, Eric 112
Handley, Tommy 37
Harcourt, William 22
Hardie, Keir 192
Harland and Wolff 37, 64
Harris, Ralph 46
Harry, Prince 125, 161
Harvard College 95–6
Hastings, Warren 196, 198
Hatry, Clarence 6
Hayek, Friedrich A. 45, 46–51, 106–7, 165, 188
  The Constitution of Liberty 48, 107
  Law, Legislation and Liberty 48
  The Road to Serfdom 46–7, 48
Healey, Denis 32
Health and Safety Executive 100
health care
  doctors 110, 115, 145
  marketization 115, 116, 121–2, 183
  nationalization of hospitals 114
  NHS see National Health Service
  rights to 98
Heath, Edward 44
Heath Government 43–4, 46
Hebrew prophets 184
hedge fund managers 10, 20, 69, 86
hedonism 2, 57
  culture of hedonistic individualism 45–57, 216, 219; see also individualism
  and ever-rising living standards 14, 43, 70, 71
  and the humbling of the elites 57–8

trumping honour 19–58
  see also Mammon worship
hegemony, cultural 108–9, 114–15
Helm, Dieter 74
Henry, G. A. 60
Henry VIII 62
Hewitt, Patricia 172
Hickman, Martin 161
Higgins, Polly 194–5, 215
High Pay Commission 82, 194
Hills, John 136
Himmelfarb, Gertrude 84
history
  abandonment of 60–72, 165, 185
  and amnesia 60–72; see also
    social amnesia
  elites steeped in see elites
  teaching of 65
Hitchens, Christopher 207
Hitler, Adolf 36, 70, 176–7, 180
Hobbes, Thomas 86, 108, 154
Hobsbawm, Eric 57
Holbach, Paul-Henri Thiry,
    Baron d' 84
homosexuality 39
honour, and hedonism 19–58
honours 58
  list 126
Horner, Arthur 34, 35–6, 62
hospitals
  Francis Report 116
  nationalization 114
House of Commons 46, 64, 118,
    129, 196, 197–8
  committee power 170
  Culture, Media and Sport Select
    Committee 161
House of Lords 126, 172
house owners 14
house prices 15, 20

household incomes 28, 42, 133
housing
  council house sales 114
  Right to Buy legislation 114
  see also property rights
Howe, Geoffrey 169
Hoyle, Fred 37
HSBC 16, 78–9, 131
hubris 43–5
  of the media 159–63
Hudson, George 6
human rights 97, 193
  see also social rights
Hume, David 4
humiliation 142–3, 211–12
  avoidance in a decent society 211
  German 177
  governmental 44
  and inequality 87, 142–4,
    211–12, 216
  of medical examinations 200
  and poverty 142–4, 212
  and untamed capitalism 214
  and the welfare state 143
Hundred Years War 163
Hungary 164
Hutton, Will 13, 72

ice caps 73
ICI 37
ideology 86, 105, 106, 127,
    129–30
  anti-market 115
  Catholic 186
  Communist 165
  of marketization 110–23,
    218, 219
  and the moral economy 3
  of property rights 126–32
  of the right 106–8

ideology – *cont.*
  Soviet 165
  of untamed capitalism 141, 188
IMF 76
income tax 11, 133, 169
incomes
  CEOs' 135–6
  household 28, 42, 133
  and the increase of poverty 138
  from property 133
  salary incomes 133; *see also*
    wages
  and the super-rich 134–7, 166–7
Independent 170–71
India 197–8, 217
  East India Company 85, 196,
    198, 200
individualism 104, 183, 191–2,
    219–20
  and Burke 198
  capitalism and the individual
    165, 178, 183, 190; *see also*
    capitalism
  and centralism 108
  and Christianity 210
  and cultural revolution and
    abandonment of history 65
  culture of hedonistic
    individualism 45–57, 216, 219
  economic 110–11
  and the elites 57–8, 65, 183
  and intolerant tolerance 208, 210
  libertarian 56–7
  market 45–51, 56–7, 65,
    165, 210
  Mill and individuality 201–3
  moral 45–6, 51–7, 65, 201–2
  populism and hyper-individualism
    178–9
  and the public realm 98, 104

rational economic (Stiglitz)
    110–11
  and rights discourse 98
  and social ethics 192
  vs stewardship 199, 213–14
  and Thatcherism 108, 111–12
  and transition to collectivism
    21–2, 104
  trinity of Choice, Freedom and
    the Individual 183, 190–93,
    198–9
industrial relations 21–2, 144
  co-determination 131–2
  of the German *Mittelstand*
    131–2
  law 44
  militancy 44
  and property rights 130–31
  trade disputes 112
industrialism
  Industrial Revolution 189
  and Tawney 205–6, 214
inequality 2, 87, 160, 165
  American 139–40, 166–7
  British following of America
    167–9
  and distrust 145–7
  gap between the rich and others
    86, 135, 150
  and the Gini coefficient 133–4
  and humiliation 87, 142–4,
    211–12, 216
  pillars of 126–32
  and poverty 138–9, 140–43, 160,
    168, 183, 184
  'religion of inequality' 127, 133,
    134, 218
  social ills of 138–45; *see also*
    humiliation; poverty
  sting of 138–40

and the super-rich 134–7, 166–7;
  see also wealth: the super-rich
as a swelling boil 137–8
and unconditional property rights
  126–32
inflation
  stagflation 44, 45, 51, 71,
    106, 177
  of wages 43
information access 218
Institute for Fiscal Studies (IFS) 135
Institute of Economic Affairs 46
insurance companies 10
interest rates 70
International Monetary Fund 76
international trade 94
internet gambling 191
Inuit people 73, 85
Iran 154, 217
  ayatollahs 154, 155–6
Iraq war 66, 91, 180
Ireland 137–8, 147, 171
  Irish Catholics 197, 212
Islam and Muslims 6, 97, 184, 208,
    209–10, 214
  British population proportion of
    Muslims 63
Isle of Man 137, 138
Israel
  Arab–Israeli war 44
  Israeli Arabs 211, 212
Israelites 1, 6
  Hebrew prophets 184
  see also Judaism and the Jews
IT revolution 20
Italy 171, 175, 186

J. P. Morgan 172
Japan 140, 171, 217
Jenkins, Arthur 24

Jenkins, Simon 107
Jersey 137, 138
Jesus Christ 209, 214
Jews see Judaism and the Jews
Joseph, Sir Keith 46
Jowell, Tessa 162
Judaism and the Jews 97, 208,
    209–10
  Israelites see Israelites
  Russian Jews 212
judges 100
judiciary 36, 58
juggernaut theory of wages 113, 171
junk food 145
justice 80, 99
  capital punishment 38–9
  distributive 48–9
  social 48–9, 57

Kant, Immanuel 211
Kay, John 109
Kennedy, John F. 98
Keynes, John Maynard 32–3, 42, 43,
    51, 68, 75, 112, 113, 132, 192
  epigraph 19
Keynesianism
  distinction between risk and
    uncertainty 69
  economic management 44, 105
  and economic recovery 71
  economic theory 33, 113
  social democracy 41–3, 44, 45,
    54, 106, 130
King, Mackenzie 60–61
Kipling, Rudyard 60, 66
Kiszely, Sir John 173
Knights of Labor 23
Koestler, Arthur 29, 160
Kohn, Marek 148–9
KPMG 138

labour market 112
labour movement 61
Labour Party 28, 37, 132
  and Bevan 35
  Blue Labour 61
  Callaghan Government 44
  and Compass 194
  Labour Opposition 15
  New Labour see New Labour
  post-war Labour Government
    38, 100, 105, 114
  spending 170
  statist tendencies 114
  trade union funding 171
  Wilson Government 43
Laing, R. D. 46, 53–4, 55
laissez-faire economics 3, 4, 23,
    26, 41, 69, 79, 108, 144,
    203, 214
  see also capitalism
Lanchester, John 169
language of the marketplace 110
Lansley, Andrew 121–2, 175
Laski, Harold 26, 27
Latimer, Hugh 209
Law, Andrew Bonar 160
Lawrence, Sir Timothy 173
Lawson, Nigel 169
Leach, Edmund 46, 54
Leeds 104, 149
leisure class, theory of (Veblen) 5
Leo XIII, De Rerum Novarum
    23–4, 130
Letwin, Shirley 188, 192
  'vigorous virtues' 188–92
Levellers 98
Leveson Inquiry 161
Levy, Michael, Baron 58, 170
Leys, Colin 121
Liberal Democrats 193, 199

coalition with Tories see Coalition
    Government, Conservative–
    Lib Dem
Liberal Party
  Liberal Government (1905–14)
    105
  'Yellow Book' 132
liberalism 75
  Coalition Government's
    diminished version of
    191–2
  and Mill 199–204; see also Mill,
    John Stuart
  New Liberals 75
  'Ordo-liberals' of West Germany
    75–6
  see also neoliberalism/Chicagoan
    economics
libertarian individualism 56–7
liberty see freedom
Liberty (National Council for Civil
    Liberties) 193
libido 55
Libor 16
life expectancy 140
Lilley, Peter 141, 143
Lincoln, Abraham 63, 154
Lindsay, A. D. 26–7, 158
linguistic revolution, and
    marketization 110
Litvinenko, Alexander,
    murder 14
Liverpool 104, 149
living standards 14, 43, 70, 71
Living Wage campaign 193
Lloyd George, David 75, 98, 132,
    159, 177, 199
Lloyd George Government 160
Lloyds TSB 64
lobbying 165–7

local authorities 108, 114, 120–21
  schools opting out of local-
    authority control 115
local councils 118
local government 113–14, 203
  Council of Europe's Charter of
    Local Self-Government 119
localism 113–14
  war on local democracy 113–15,
    118–19
Locke, John 86, 127
London
  Canary Wharf 149
  and centralism 115
  the City 10–12, 16, 134, 137,
    138, 168
  derivatives market 12
  dock strike (1889) 23
  Docklands 115, 149
  Mayor 117
  Metal Market 12
  Milton on 157–8
  mixed races 63
  Occupy London protests
    187, 193
  and Russian oligarchs 14
  student protests 91–2
  and the super-rich 169
  urban redevelopment 149
  Victory Parade (1946) 60
London Citizens 193
London School of Economics (LSE)
  46, 135
London Transport 115
looting 15–16
Lopokova, Lydia 33
Lords, House of 126, 172
LSE (London School of Economics)
  46, 135
Lugard, Frederick, 1st Baron 40

Luhmann, Niklas 146
Luther, Martin 6, 71, 186

MacDonald, Ramsay 180
MacIntyre, Alasdair 186
Macmillan, Harold 133,
  168, 180
Macmurray, John 117
Mafia 100
magnates, landed 128
Magnificat 209
Major, John 178
Major Government 107–8, 109,
  117, 118
Mammon worship 2
  anathemas against 6–7
  in Britain 3–10, 15–16, 20, 70
  as fosterer of wrong values 192
  Keynesian view of 68
  as worship of a false god 187
  as wrong 192
  see also hedonism
Manchester 104, 149
Mandela, Nelson 217, 219
Mandelson, Peter, Baron 1,
  92, 162
Manning, Henry Edward, Cardinal
  22, 23
  De Rerum Novarum 23–4, 130
Marcuse, Herbert 46, 54
  Eros and Civilization 54
  One-Dimensional Man 54
Margalit, Avishai 143, 211–
  12, 214
market agents 82–3, 97, 173
  civil servants as 111–12, 173
market economies 33, 50, 77–8,
  130, 164
  German 'social-market economy'
    43, 75–6, 131–2

market economies – *cont.*
  market fundamentalist moral
    economy 3, 92–6, 187
  rise and growth of the market
    order (Hayek) 49–50
market forces 47, 74, 93, 166–7,
  175
market individualism 45–51, 56–7,
  65, 165, 210
market socialism 23, 75
market state 51, 219
  agents *see* market agents
  invasion of public realm 91–123;
    see also marketization
  and the Thatcher governments
    108–9, 111–12
marketization 109, 110–23, 134,
  169, 173–4, 175, 183, 184,
  216, 218, 219
  and accelerating attrition of the
    public realm 119–23
  Gove's marketization of education
    120–21
  of health care 115, 116, 121–2,
    183
  and linguistic revolution 110
  and the political return to
    patronage 117–19
  and public trust 103
  and the rhetoric of choice 122
  and Thatcherism 111–13
  and war on local democracy
    113–15, 118–19
  and war on professionalism
    115–17
markets 48, 77–8
  anti-market ideology 115
  bond markets 76
  'great engine of the market' 190
  labour market 112

market norms 109, 110
mortgage market 82
NHS 'internal' market 116
reflexive market behaviour 82–3
states and the market order
  79–81
Victorian narrowing of the
  market 104
marriage 36, 37, 57, 62, 64
Mars UK 175
Marshall, Alfred 68
Marshall, T. H. 42
Marshall Aid 30
martyrs 208–9
Marx, Karl 5, 87–90, 105, 106,
  190, 214–15
Marxism 62, 87–90, 106, 142
  Communist Manifesto 88–90,
    106, 190
materialism 25, 27, 210
Mathewson, George 8
Matthew the evangelist 6
Maxwell, Robert 6
Maya civilization 72
McCann family 161
McCarthy, Joe 177
McDonald's 175
media
  corrosive populism of 190
  and democracy 159–63
  hubristic 159–63
  Leveson Inquiry 161
  Murdoch empire 161–2, 165
  phone-hacking scandal 161, 162
  press lords of the early twentieth
    century 160
  race for the bottom 218
Members of Parliament
  connections with private-sector
    corporations 171–5

expenses claims 103
with revolving doors to private
    sector 172–5
mental illness 140
mercantilism 94
Merrill Lynch 11–12
Metal Market, London 12
Methodist values 190
Metropolitan counties 115
Metropolitan Police 161
Mid Staffordshire Foundation Trust
    Hospital 116
Midas, King 1
middle classes 133, 200
Miliband, David 162
Miliband, Ralph 162
milk 133
Mill, James 23, 86
Mill, John Stuart 22, 23, 25, 75, 105,
    126, 130, 159, 199–204, 217
  and democracy 155
  On Liberty 200–201, 202–3
  Principles of Political Economy
    200, 203
  'The Spirit of the Age' 203
  System of Logic 200
Milton, John 157–9, 189
  Areopagitica 157–8, 201
  Paradise Lost 6
  Samson Agonistes 158–9
miners 44
Minton, Anna 149–50
Mittal, Aditya 136
Mittal, Lakshmi 169
Mittelstand 131–2
mixed economy 105, 130
modernity 17
Molière: L'Avare 1
monarchy 36, 58, 62, 64, 104, 126
  House of Windsor 62

Milton and the return of the
    monarchy 159
monetarism 46
money
  and the economy see economics;
    economy; moral economy;
    political economy
  fascination about 1–2, 5
  'filthy lucre' 1
  finance and the state 10–14
  fungibility of 4, 165
  laundering 16
  Mill and 'private
    money-getting' 203
  moral neutrality of 2
  mystery of 4, 5
  and power 1, 5, 10–11, 163
  sterling 70
  and the 'theory of the leisure
    class' (Veblen) 5
  worship see Mammon worship
  as a yardstick of social
    achievement 58
  see also wealth
Montfort, Simon de 62
Moore, G. E. 51–2
moral economy 2–3, 19–20
  and the British trap 182–220
  challenge of change in 74–5,
    193–220
  crisis 184
  and higher education 92–6
  market fundamentalist 3,
    92–6, 187
  multiple moral economies 3
  and a national conversion and
    new public philosophy
    192–220
  solidaristic 25, 106, 123,
    130, 160

moral economy – *cont.*

moral individualism 45–6, 51–7,
65, 201–2

morality and ethics

battle over social ethics 192

and choice 192; *see also* choice

Christian ethics 205

and economics 24–5, 68–9, 71–2;
see also moral economy

ethic of equity 103

ethic of service 102, 103

ethic of stewardship 199,
213–14, 220

and freedom 192

and individualism 192; *see also*
individualism

moral corruption 17

moral sentiments (Smith) 59, 67,
97; *see also* Smith, Adam: *The
Theory of Moral Sentiments*

moral signs 24, 99

professional ethic of the public
realm 101–2, 115

and the public interest 34, 38, 42

and wealth 24

work ethic 24

Morgan Stanley 11–12, 173

Morley, John 52, 196

Morrell, Lady Ottoline 26

Morris, William 182, 192, 205

Morris Motors 37

Morrison, Herbert 38, 64

mortgages 12, 14

mortgage market 82

mortgage salesmen 100

Moses 6

Mosley, Oswald 163

Moxon, David 16

municipalization of public utilities
104

Murdoch, Rupert 161–2, 165, 170

Murdoch empire 161–2, 165, 191

Murphy, Richard 138

Muslims *see* Islam and Muslims

nabobs 163

Napoleon I 154

National Coal Board 36

national debt 10

cancellation in developing
countries 193

debt crisis 13

national defence 80, 99

National Guilds 26

National Health Service (NHS)
35, 38

1946 Act 38

founding principles 215

Francis Report 116

'internal' market 116

Lansley's revolution 121–2

repeated reconstruction
attempts 66

White Paper 121–2

National Insurance Act (1911) 38

National Parks 100

national planning 106

National Reform League 142

National Union of General and
Municipal Workers 63

National Union of Mineworkers
(NUM) 36, 37

nationalism 44

nationalization 48, 64, 106, 130

coal 36

by post-war Labour Government
38, 114

Nature 94–5

NatWest 8

Nazism 47, 70, 208

neoliberalism/Chicagoan economics 74–83, 165, 189–90, 192, 220
nepotism 104
  see also patronage
Netherlands 140, 147, 171
  tulip bubble 5
New Deal, US 42–3, 70
New Labour 1, 13–14, 66, 107–8, 120, 138, 168, 174
  Blair governments 118–19, 168, 174–5
  Brown Government 168, 174
  Thatcher–Major legacy 117–19
New Liberals 75
New Zealand 140, 147
Newcastle 104, 149
News Chronicle 160
News International 161
News of the World 161
NHS *see* National Health Service
Nokia Vertu mobile phones 125
Nomura 11–12
Norse Greenlanders 73, 83, 85
North Atlantic Alliance 30
North Government 196
North Sea oil 139
Northcliffe, Alfred Harmsworth, 1st Viscount 160
Northcote–Trevelyan Report/ reforms 32, 99, 104, 118
Northern Ireland 44, 60, 64, 212
Northern Rock 2, 12–13, 64, 82, 100
nuclear energy 109
NUM (National Union of Mineworkers) 36, 37
Nussbaum, Martha 210–11, 213

obesity 140, 175
O'Brien, Conor Cruise 197

occupational structures 20
Occupy movement 218
  Occupy London protest 187, 193
offshore finance 137–8
OFSTED 118
oil prices 44
'Old Corruption' 104, 163
oligarchy 170–72, 183
one-dimensional man/society (Marcuse) 54–5
O'Neill, Onora 98, 102, 116, 122, 155, 162
Open Democracy 100, 218
open society 50, 181
  Popper (epigraph) 19
Open University 95
'Ordo-liberals', West Germany 75–6
Orwell, George 4, 27–9, 34, 64, 159, 186
over-the-counter (OTC) derivatives 12n

Paine, Thomas 206, 215
Palliser, Sir Michael 31–2
Palmerston, Henry Temple, 3rd Viscount 62
Pandora LovePod rings 125–6
Paris 115
Parliament 36, 62
  authority and independence of 104
  House of Commons 46, 64, 118, 129, 196, 197–8
  House of Lords 126, 172
  MPs *see* Members of Parliament
  Scottish 63, 107, 117
parliamentary expenses 103
patronage 32, 104, 117–19

Paul, Swraj, Baron 169
Peasants' Revolt 91
Peel, Sir Robert 100, 159
Pennine Way 99, 100
pension funds 6, 10
pension rights 136
People's Temple 176
Pepsico 175
performance-related pay 111
Perham, Dame Margery 40
Pericles 153–4
Perkin, Harold 127–8
philanthropists 105
Philip, Prince, Duke of Edinburgh
    125
phone-hacking scandal 161, 162
picketing 112
Pickett, Kate 139–40, 143–4,
    146–7
Pincus, Steve 4
Pirie, Madsen 46
Pitt, Brad 161
Pitt, William the Elder, 1st
    Earl of Chatham 159
Pitt, William the Younger 159
Plaid Cymru 63
Plato 154, 200
Player, Stewart 121
Pliatzky, Sir Leo 31–2
Poland 164
Polanyi, Karl 79, 108
police 15, 16, 99, 100
    appraisal systems 117
    and marketization 117
    Metropolitan 161
    and the phone-hacking
        scandal 161
political economy 2, 11
    and the financial sector see
        financial sector, Britain

laissez-faire 3, 4, 23, 26, 41, 69,
    79, 108, 144, 203, 214
    and privatization see
        privatization
    and tax breaks 166, 168, 169
political institutions, 'extractive'
    and 'inclusive' 128
political parties
    funding 170–71, 175
    spending 170
    see also specific parties
political rights 42, 193
poll tax 180
polytechnics 115
pop musicians 100
Popper, Karl 75
    epigraph 19
populism
    charismatic 175–81, 216
    and hyper-individualism 178–9
    of the mass media 190
    and oligarchic substance 170
    populist age 178–81
    populist style 175–8, 218
post-Christian society 57, 63
Post Office 37–8
Pound, Stephen 141
poverty 23, 68, 150, 160, 212
    gap between rich and poor
        135, 150
    and humiliation 142–4, 212
    and inequality 138–9, 140–43,
        160, 168, 183, 184
Powell, Enoch 46
Powell, Jonathan 118, 173
power elite 175, 177, 216
power of money 1, 5, 10–11, 163
Prescott, John, Baron 125, 161
presentism 66–72, 185
press see media

pressure groups 193–4, 218
Priestley, J. B. 29
Prime Minister's Questions 170
Prior, Jim (James Michael, Baron
    Prior) 107
private debt 14, 15, 20, 190
private equity
    firms 10, 20, 174
    fund managers 100
Private Finance Initiative 66
private sector
    corporations *see* firms
    managerialism 119
    revolving doors between public
        service posts and 172–5
privatization 64, 109, 134,
    168, 169
    and Thatcher 107
    of utilities 107
professionalism 101–2
    consumers of professional
        services 101–2
    growth in professional
        occupations 105
    marketizers' war on 115–17
    O'Neill on 102, 116
    professional army officer
        corps 104
    professional ethic of the public
        realm 101–2, 115
    professional service elite 21,
        29–34, 36, 39, 47, 61
    professional state bureaucracy
        104; *see also* civil service
    and qualifying bodies 105
Profumo Affair 29
proletarianism, class-war 106
property rights 23, 75, 105, 114
    conditional 131
    and nationalization 37–8, 130

and property divorced from
    function 205
    and Tawney 205
    unconditional 126–32, 215
prostitution 191
protest movements 44, 56, 91–2,
    157, 187, 193
    riots 15–16
Protestantism
    Calvinist 210
    Protestant dissent 157
public-choice theorists, Virginia
    School 46
public administration 32, 99
    professional state
        bureaucracy 104
    see also civil service
public authorities 104, 109
public debate and reasoning 27, 66,
    72, 95, 96, 100, 118, 155, 176,
    217–19
    vs charismatic populism 176–81,
        216
    in a common language 219–20
    democratic debate vs charismatic
        populism 175–81, 216
    dialogue as a norm of democracy
        156–9
    Mill and discussion 203
    philosophy of dialogue 212
    and religious belief 210
    towards a national conversion
        and new public philosophy
        192–220
public goods/interest 29, 80, 97,
    99–100, 104–5, 181
    as greater than the sum of private
        interests 97, 173, 216
    higher education and 92, 93–6
    and liberty 103

public goods/interest – *cont.*
  and morality 34, 38, 42, 173
  private–public revolvers and the
    public interest 173–4
public realm 25, 96–8, 118, 129
  attrition of 92–123, 183; *see also*
    marketization
  and Big Society 119–20
  boundaries 99–101
  coal nationalization and
    growth of 36
  effect of privatization 109
  elites and the building of 216
  ethos 97
  feminization of Britain's public
    culture 186
  goods of *see* public goods/interest
  and higher education 93–6
  and individualism 98, 104; *see*
    also individualism
  market state's invasion of *see*
    marketization
  people belonging to 100–101
  professional ethic 101–2, 115
  public interest *see* public goods/
    interest
  rebuilding of 220
  and the regulators 109
  and revolving doors between
    public service posts and private
    sector 172–5
  and soporific complacency 103–6
  spending *see* public spending
  and Thatcherism 106–9
  and trust 101–3, 146–7, 179
  utilities *see* public utilities
public spending 13, 71, 133
  on consultancies, committees of
    inquiry and task forces 174–5
  cuts 71

  demonstrations against Coalition
    cuts 193
public spirit 34, 87
public utilities
  municipalization 104
  nationalization 114
  privatization 107
public works 70, 71, 80, 99
Purnell, James 162
Putin, Vladimir 155–6
PWC 138

quangos 115, 116, 149
quants (quantitative analysts) 69

race and ethnicity
  mixed race in Britain 63
  racism 33, 38, 162, 216
railways
  boom 6
  nationalization 38
Rainborough, Thomas 98
rates capping 114–15
rationality
  assumption in economics 5, 77,
    83
  as a contestable concept 84–5
  and democracy 95; *see also*
    public debate and reasoning
  a priori rationalism 85
  public reasoning *see* public debate
    and reasoning
  rational economic individualism
    (Stiglitz) 110–11
RBS *see* Royal Bank of Scotland
reason *see* rationality
reasoning, public *see* public debate
    and reasoning
recession 15
redistribution, state 48–9

Reform Acts 104
    1867 Act 22, 142, 200
Reinhart, Carmen M. 13
Reith, John, 1st Baron 30, 33–4
relativism 57
religion 17, 57, 87, 187
    Buddhist deliberation 217
    Christian *see* Christianity
    and debate 210
    and economism 210, 214
    and intolerant tolerance 207–11
    Jewish *see* Judaism and the Jews
    Muslim *see* Islam and Muslims
    'religion of inequality' 127, 133,
        134, 218
rent-seeking 166–7, 169, 183, 184,
    216
repression 54, 55
republicanism 62, 159
    republican liberty 103, 119,
        156–9
respect, society of 191, 192
responsibility deal groups 175
revolving doors, between public
        service posts and the private
        sector 172–5
Reynolds News 160
Ricardo, David 101
Rich List, *Sunday Times* 58,
        169, 171
Richard Thomas (steel) 37
Ridley, Nicholas 209
Right to Buy legislation 114
Rights, Bill of (1689) 103–4
riots 15–16
risk, economic 47, 69
Roberts, Jennifer 101
Robinson, James A. 128, 166
Rochdale Pioneers 62
Rogoff, Kenneth S. 13

Roll, Eric (later Lord) 31
Roman Catholicism
    adaptation and survival of 186
    anti-Catholic discrimination 44
    Catholic social teaching 131
    ideology 186
    Irish Catholics 197
    and market individualism 210
    Northern Ireland Catholic
        minority 44, 212
romantic revolt (Beer) 45, 56
Rome Statute 195
Roosevelt, Franklin D. 70
Rose, Richard 175–6
Rosebury, Archibald Primrose, 5th
        Earl of 11–12
Rothermere, Harold Harmsworth,
        1st Viscount 160
Rothermere, Jonathan Harmsworth,
        4th Viscount 169
Rothschild, Lionel de 129
Rothschild, Nathaniel Philip ('Nat')
        137
Roubini, Nouriel 13
Royal Bank of Scotland (RBS) 8–9,
        11, 12, 16, 64
Ruddock, Paul 58
Ruskin, John 22, 24, 99, 205
Ruskin College, Oxford 24
Ruskin School of Drawing and Fine
        Art 24
Russell, Bertrand 26, 27, 37, 51
Russia 10, 76, 154, 155, 164, 171,
        175
    Russian Jews 212

Salford 149
Salisbury, Robert Gascoyne-Cecil,
        3rd Marquess 52, 62
Samuelson, Paul 68

Sandel, Michael 122–3
Sargent, Sir Orme 62
Scandinavia 147, 164, 171
Scardino, Dame Marjorie 136
schizophrenia 53–4, 55
Schonfield, Andrew 106
schools
  free school meals 133
  Gove and free schools 120
  governmental control of
    curricula 116
  marketization 120–21, 183
  opting out of local-authority
    control 115
  see also education
Schumacher, E. F.: Small is Beautiful
  44–5
Scotland 44, 65
  devolution 117, 219
  and the EU 64
  Scottish Conservatives 107, 210
  Scottish Parliament 63, 107, 117
  Secession referendum 63
  and Thatcher 117
Sebald, W. G.: Austerlitz 59–60
Second World War 4, 29, 80,
  133, 217
  and the Arnoldian state 41–2
  Blitz 36
  and Horner 35–6
  wartime coalition 28, 61,
    105, 133
  wartime sharing 41
Securities and Exchange
  Commission, US 166
Selbourne, David 141–2
Seldon, Arthur 46
self-harm 144–5
self-help 38, 189
self-respect 191, 211

Sen, Amartya 27, 68, 95, 100, 155,
  192, 217–18
Sennett, Richard 147
service 30, 31, 96, 104
  ethic of 102, 103
  professional service elite 21,
    29–34, 36, 39, 47, 61
sex and sexuality 55
  homosexuality 39
  unprotected sex 145
sexism 216
Shakespeare, William
  Merchant of Venice, Shylock 1
  Troilus and Cressida, Ulysses
    126–7
shame 144, 162; see also
  humiliation
Sharp, Dame Evelyn 40
Shaw, George Bernard 25, 26
Shaxson, Nicholas 78, 137
Sheffield 104
Shelley, Percy Bysshe:
  'Ozymandias' 72
Shils, Edward 36
Shotoku, Prince 217
Sicilian Mafia 100
Sidgwick, Henry 67
Sierra Leone 164
Singapore 137–8
Skidelsky, Edward 72
Skidelsky, Robert 55–6, 72
slave trade 2
Smiles, Samuel 189
Smith, Adam 4, 67, 78, 80, 94, 97,
  99, 109, 112–13, 185
  epigraph 59
  The Theory of Moral Sentiments
    59, 67, 85, 97, 98
  The Wealth of Nations 67, 97
smoking 144–5

Smuts, Jan 60–61
Soar, Sir Trevor 173
social amnesia 59–90, 208
  and the abandonment of history
    60–72
  and economics 67–72, 74–83
  and environmental folly 72–4
  and *Homo sapiens* vs *Homo*
    economicus 86–7
  and Marxism 87–90
  and neoliberalism/Chicagoan
    economics 74–83
  and unrooted rationality 84–6
social contract
  Burke's critique 198–9, 213
  theorists 86
social democracy, Keynesian 41–3,
  44, 45, 54, 106, 130
social engineering 43, 185
social justice 57
  and state redistribution 48–9
social rights
  and citizenship 42
  civil rights *see* civil rights
  and duties 98, 205
  franchise *see* suffrage
  individualism and rights
    discourse 98
  political rights 42, 193
  workers' rights 98, 131, 132
  see also human rights
social structures 36–8, 41
Social Trends 138–9
socialism
  and the battle between head and
    heart 49
  Bevan on democratic
    socialism 35
  Fabian 26
  Guild Socialism (Cole) 26

Keynesian *see* social democracy,
  Keynesian
  market 23, 75
  Orwell on 28
  post-war 48
  state-directed war socialism 28
  statist 106, 114
  and Tawney 204–7; *see also*
    Tawney, R. H.
  Thatcher's hatred of 108
  'war socialism' 28–9, 133
society of respect 192
soil erosion 72
Soros, George 3, 87
Sorrell, Sir Martin 136
South Africa 164
South Sea Bubble 5–6
South Sea Company 5–6
Soviet Union 6–7, 26, 165, 185
  former Soviet satellites 163–4
  see also Russia
Spain 140, 147
Spencer, Herbert 75
spontaneity 45, 47–8
  spontaneous orders (Hayek)
    48, 77
stagflation 44, 45, 51, 71, 106, 177
stakeholder capitalism 132, 215
Stalin, Joseph 36
Standard Chartered Bank 16
Starbucks 193
state
  Arnoldian 41–2
  British, in Second World War 80
  centralism 108
  and economic development 43,
    70, 80
  intervention 48–9, 74, 75, 79, 80,
    86, 151
  investment 215

state – *cont.*
  Keynesian state and the
    economy 33
  Labour's statist tendencies 114
  and the market order 79–81
  market state *see* market state
  and patronage 32, 104, 117–19
  in a planned economy 47
  post-war settlement 42
  redistribution 48–9
  regulatory 104
  statist socialism 106, 114
  Victorian reconstruction 104
state-facilitated cartels 80
steel industry 64–5
sterling 70
stewardship ethic 199,
  213–14, 220
Stiglitz, Joseph 3, 83, 110–11, 166
stock market, American 2
Strachey, (Giles) Lytton: *Eminent
  Victorians* 52
students
  fees 91–2, 93
  foreign 94–5
  population expansion 95
  protests 56, 91–2
  rebellions 56
Studzinski, John 131–2
suffrage 25, 142, 192, 216
  American voter registration
    rules 167
Sugar, Sir Alan 58
Sumerians 72
Sun 58
Sunday Times
  Rich List 58, 169, 171
  sting 173
surtax 133
Susa 217

sustainability, environmental 17,
  195, 213–14
Switzerland 147
sympathy, bonds of 97, 109, 122

task forces 174–5
Tawney, R. H. 26, 27, 127, 133,
  214, 218
  The Acquisitive Society 204, 205–6
  and the culture of democracy
    204–7, 217
  epigraph 152, 153
tax 11, 16, 133
  American 166
  avoidance 137–8, 190, 193
  breaks 166, 168, 169
  capital gains *see* capital gains tax
  exiles 137
  on financial services 215
  havens 78, 137–8, 215
  poll tax 180
  reforms under New Labour 138
Tea Operatives' and General
    Labourers' Union 62–3
teachers 54, 102, 115, 116, 145
Temple, William 26, 214
Tennessee Valley Authority 70
TGWU (Transport and
    General Workers' Union) 34,
    37, 62–3
Thanatos 54, 55
Thatcher, Margaret 31, 106–7,
    111–13, 168, 177–8, 188, 191
  and Bancroft 32
  and the civil service 31, 32, 111
  conviction politics 179–80
  and the poll tax 180
  and the pursuit of changing
    souls 111
  and Scotland 117

Victorian values 191, 192
and the 'vigorous virtues'
189–90, 191
Thatcher governments/Thatcherism
106–9, 111–13, 117, 138
'Big Bang' 11, 134, 168
New Labour and the Thatcher–
Major legacy 117–19
and the trade unions 107,
108, 112
think tanks 46
38 Degrees 193–4, 218
Thomas Aquinas 71, 184
Thompson, E. P. 3
Thompson, F. M. L. 23
Thorne, Will 63
Tillet, Ben 62–3
Times, The 29
Titmuss, Richard 38
Tocqueville, Alexis de 119, 154–5,
159
Democracy in America 119, 203
and Mill 203
tolerance 55, 159
intolerant 207–11
tombstone biographers 52
Tony Blair Associates 172
Top 200 group 174
Tories see Conservative Party
'tough love' 143
town halls 104
trade disputes 112
trade unions 37, 62–3, 64, 105,
106, 112–13, 130, 142, 193
and Bevin 34, 62
funding of Labour Party 171
and Horner 36
and marketization 112
and the miners' strike 44
and New Labour 118

and Thatcherism 107, 108, 112
see also specific unions
Trades Union Congress (TUC) 24,
34, 39, 62
traditions
adaptation and survival of 186
and collectivism 47–8
and cultural determinism 185
and cultural presentism 185
of elites see elites
of localism 113–14
of mutualism and self-help 38
overturning of 46, 47–8, 88,
114–15, 185
of protest 91–2; see also protest
movements
Protestant 157
religious 17, 157, 187
Transport and General Workers'
Union (TGWU) 34, 37, 62–3
Trollope, Anthony 17
The Way We Live Now,
Melmotte 1, 7
Trump, Donald 193
trust
betrayal of 102
and empathy 147–50
inequality and distrust 145–7
in the marketplace 103
in the polity 103
and professional ethic 101–2
and the public realm 101–3,
146–7, 179
TUC (Trades Union Congress) 24,
34, 39, 62
tulip bubble, Netherlands 5
Turing, Alan 39

UBS 16
UK Uncut 193

Ukraine 164
Ulster Loyalists 106
unemployment 15, 42, 71, 87
  and Chicagoan economics 77
  stagflation 44, 45, 51, 71,
    106, 177
United Kingdom *see* Britain
United Nations, Universal Declaration
  of Human Rights 97
United States of America
  academic economics 67
  American Blacks 211–12
  American Enlightenment 84
  American freedom 119
  democracy 119, 154–5, 166–7
  dollar 70
  founding fathers of American
    republic 180, 216
  inequality 139–40, 166–7
  investment banks 11–12, 82
  lobbying 166–7
  Marshall Aid 30
  mental illness 140
  New Deal 42–3, 70
  politically connected firms 171–2
  public trust 147
  rent-seeking 184
  Virginia School of public-choice
    theorists 46
  voter registration rules 167
universities 92–6, 108, 183
  academic duties 101
  academic economics 67
  academic salaries 101
  American 140
  funding 116–17
Universities Funding Council 117
University Grants Committee
  116–17
Unlock Democracy 193

Urban Development Corporations
  149
urban redevelopment 149–50
Uslaner, Eric 147
utilitarianism 2, 86, 192
  vs approaching others as 'souls'
    210–11, 213
utility privatization 107
utopias
  Hayek 46–51
  laissez-faire 79

Van Reenen, John 135
Vaughan, Dame Janet 40
Veblen, Thorstein 5, 67
Versailles settlement 177
Vespasian, Emperor 2
Victorian values 191, 192
Victorians 52, 104
  clerisy 21, 22–5, 201; *see also*
    clerisy
  middle-class pieties 200
Vietnam War protests 44
'vigorous virtues' (Letwin) 188–92
violence 16
Virgin Group 78–9, 137
Virginia School of public-choice
  theorists 46
Vodafone 78–9, 193
Voser, Peter 136
voter registration rules, US 167
voting rights *see* suffrage

wages
  academic salaries 101
  bargainers 43
  controls 43, 44
  equality 98
  High Pay Commission 82, 194
  inflation 43

juggernaut theory of 113, 171
Living Wage campaign 193
performance-related pay 111
salary incomes 133
top executive pay 82, 135–6
see also incomes
Wales 44, 63, 65
 devolution 117, 219
 and the EU 64
 Plaid Cymru 63
 Welsh Assembly 63, 117
Walzer, Michael 5, 163
wartime sharing 41
Washington Consensus 76
 see also Chicagoan economics/
 neoliberalism
water authorities 109
Watson, Sam 34
Watson, Tom 161
WEA (Workers' Educational
 Association) 204
wealth
 Dahrendorf Commission on
 Wealth Creation and Social
 Cohesion 132, 215
 extractors 128–9
 gap between the rich and others
 86, 135, 150
 of landed magnates in the
 eighteenth century 128–9, 136
 Mammon worship *see* Mammon
 worship
 marketable 136–7
 and morality 24
 Ruskin on 24
 the super-rich 134–7, 166–7,
 169, 189, 190
 and unconditional property rights
 128–9
 see also money

Webb, Beatrice 26
Webb, Sidney 26
Weber, Max 176
welfare state 54, 105
 benefit reforms under New
 Labour 138
 and humiliation 143
 redistributive 48–9
welfare systems 42
Wertheimer, Egon 180
Whitehall culture and 'grovel count'
 111, 134
Who Wants to be a Millionaire? 58
Wilkinson, Richard 139–40, 143–4,
 146–7
William, Prince 125, 161
William the Conqueror 62
William of Orange 64
Williams, Raymond 196
Williams, Rowan 194, 209
Wilson Government 43
Windsor, House of 62
Wine and Spirit Trade Association
 175
winter of discontent 44
Witty, Sir Andrew 136
Wolfe, Humbert, epigraph 152,
 159–60
Wolfe, Tom 16
Women's Institutes 193
women's liberation 44
Woodcock, George 24
woodlands 193
Woolf, Virginia 39, 52
Woolworths 15
Wootton, Barbara 39–40
work *see* employment
work ethic 24
Workers' Educational Association
 (WEA) 204

working-class elite 34–6, 39, 216
  and its fall 21, 34–6
working classes 61, 133
  Chartist movement 206
  as force for repression 55
  and National Insurance 38
  and shame 144
working conditions 98
World Development Movement
  194
World Trade Organization 76
World Wars see First World War;
  Second World War

World Wide Web 80, 101
World Wildlife Fund 194
Wyndham, John, later Lord
  Egremont 180

Yeats, William Butler 63
Young, David 108
Young, Hugo 107
Young, Michael 36
youth unemployment 15

Zimbabwe 164
Zionists 185